D1242032

HOUSING
AND
COMMUNITY DEVELOPMENT
IN NEW YORK CITY

SUNY series in Urban Public Policy
James Bohland and Patricia Edwards, editors

HOUSING
AND
COMMUNITY DEVELOPMENT
IN NEW YORK CITY

Facing the Future

EDITED BY

Michael H. Schill

STATE UNIVERSITY OF NEW YORK PRESS

Published by
State University of New York Press, Albany

© 1999 State University of New York

All rights reserved

Printed in the United States of America

No part of this book may be used or reproduced in any manner whatsoever
without written permission. No part of this book may be stored in a retrieval
system or transmitted in any form or by any means including electronic,
electrostatic, magnetic tape, mechanical, photocopying, recording, or
otherwise without the prior permission in writing of the publisher.

For information, address State University of New York Press,
State University Plaza, Albany, N.Y. 12246

Production by Marilyn P. Semerad
Marketing by Dana E. Yanulavich

Library of Congress Cataloging-in-Publication Data

Housing and community development in New York City : facing the future
   / edited by Michael H. Schill.
      p.   cm. — (SUNY series in urban public policy)
   Includes bibliographical references and index.
   ISBN 0-7914-4039-7. — ISBN 0-7914-4040-0 (pbk.)
      1. Housing policy—New York (State)—New York.   2. Housing
   development—New York (State)—New York.   I. Schill, Michael H.
   II. Series: SUNY series on urban public policy.
   HD7304.N5H544   1999
   363.5'09747'1—dc 21   98-29902
                                                               CIP

10 9 8 7 6 5 4 3 2 1

CONTENTS

LIST OF ILLUSTRATIONS

LIST OF TABLES

PREFACE

Like many good things, the genesis of *Housing and Community Development in New York City: Facing the Future* involved food. One day in the summer of 1995, I was having lunch with my colleague Frank Upham and his college roommate, Bob Rosenbloom, a vice president for Corporate Social Responsibility at Chase Manhattan Bank. The subject turned to housing policy, an area we cared about deeply and one that was undergoing tremendous change, particularly in light of the recent election of Republican majorities in the House and Senate. During our conversation, we talked about how important it would be for thoughtful research to be done and disseminated regarding how New York City might adapt to the changes that were sure to come from federal and State budgetary cutbacks and the advent of welfare reform.

Several months later, we acted on this idea by planning a conference entitled "New Directions for New York City: Housing and Community Development in a Changing Fiscal Environment." Chase Manhattan Bank, a leader in community lending in New York City under the leadership of Carol Parry, committed to co-sponsoring the event. Funding responsibilities were shared with the Surdna Foundation, a foundation run by Ed Skloot, a longtime supporter of housing and community development initiatives, and the New York University School of Law Center for Real Estate and Urban Policy.

Leading experts in New York City housing were asked to write papers that would form the basis for the conference that was held at New York University School of Law on March 28, 1996. In selecting topics and authors, care was taken to ensure coverage of as many of the pressing housing issues facing New York as possible and to gather together people who had a diversity of perspectives and experience. Thus, some of the papers were written by tenant advocates and others were written by people whose sympathies lean more toward landlords. Several of the authors had actual experience running housing programs or agencies while others had spent most of their careers in academia.

The conference, at which HUD Secretary Andrew Cuomo gave the keynote address, drew a standing-room-only crowd. Each of the papers was substantially revised over the next two years to take into account the release of new data and changes in housing policy emanating from Washington, Albany, and New York. Although every possible effort has been made to ensure that the information about housing programs is as current as possible, the pace of legislative change has been so quick that, no doubt, some of the programmatic information is already out of date. Nevertheless, care was taken in preparing the chapters to focus on general themes that would outlast any particular policy or program.

MICHAEL H. SCHILL

ACKNOWLEDGMENTS

This book could not have been prepared without the tireless efforts of many people. In particular, I would like to thank each of the authors who, without ever complaining, repeatedly revised their chapters to take into account changes in housing policy since 1996. I would also like to thank those who made the conference at which these chapters were first presented possible: Carol Parry and Bob Rosenbloom of Chase Manhattan Bank, Ed Skloot and Lisa Yates of the Surdna Foundation, and Bobbie Glover at NYU. Special thanks are also owed to more than twenty commentators who gave generously of their time and expertise. I would also like to express my gratitude to Colleen Duncan and Carrie Ortiz, who assisted me in preparing the chapters for publication, and Clay Morgan, Zina Lawrence and Marilyn Semerad at State University of New York Press, who shepherded the book to publication.

Finally, I would like to reserve special thanks for John Sexton, Dean of the New York University School of Law, who attracted me to NYU and who has supported me both personally and as Director of the Center for Real Estate and Urban Policy. He is the guy who makes dreams come true.

INTRODUCTION: HOUSING POLICY IN THE NEW FISCAL ENVIRONMENT

As the 1990s draw to a close, American housing policy is at a crossroads. A combination of factors promise to shift the locus of policy creation and innovation from the White House and Congress to state legislatures and city halls. Pressures to cut the federal budget will continue to squeeze housing resources flowing from our nation's capital. Politicians of both parties will argue, sometimes justifiably, that federal housing programs have done more harm than good. Just as devolution has affected many aspects of social policy, so housing policy will devolve to cities, large and small, throughout the nation.

As cities become ever more important actors in the creation and implementation of housing policy, mayors and social policy analysts will need to look for examples of successful municipal programs and policies. It is virtually certain that New York City will be one of the first cities these people will look to. In many ways, housing policy will have come full circle in the twentieth century. During the second half of the nineteenth century and the first half of the twentieth, New York City was the unquestioned pioneer in the development of policies to assist low- and moderate-income families in obtaining decent, safe, and sanitary housing. The nation's first local tenement house law was enacted in New York in 1867 (Friedman 1968; Pluntz 1990). In 1934, the city built low-income housing developments three years before Congress passed the Housing Act of 1937, which created the public housing program (Marcuse 1995). The nation's first law outlawing discrimination by private landlords was passed by the New York City Council in 1957 (Schill 1996). The city and state Mitchell-Lama Program, enacted in 1955, was used by the federal government ten years later as a model for the development of hundreds of thousands of units of subsidized apartments.

After several decades in which Congress took the initiative in creating scores of new categorical programs with acronyms such as Section 202, Section 8, Section 221(d)(3), Section 236, HOME, and a veritable legion of HOPEs, the spotlight will now once again shine on local governments. However, many local governments will be ill-prepared to shoulder the responsibilities formerly carried out by the federal government. Over the past decade, New York City has taken upon itself the creation of an elaborate set of housing programs and policies. Perhaps one of the most oft-cited statistics in housing bears repeating in this context: During the 1980s, the city of New York spent more of its own revenues on housing than the next fifty largest cities combined (Berenyi 1989). Certainly, the city's experience has not been entirely successful. Nevertheless, New York's experiment with housing policy, both its successes *and* its failures, bear careful scrutiny, particularly in the coming era of devolution.

NEW YORK CITY AND THE ISSUE OF EXCEPTIONALISM

One question for policymakers and housing policy analysts is whether New York City's experience is relevant to their own municipalities. It is commonplace to hear references to New York as the exception among American cities. Indeed, New York is clearly not the average American city. It is, by far, the largest city in the United States. In 1994, its population exceeded 7.3 million; the next largest city, Los Angeles, was less than half as large. Furthermore, unlike most older cities in the Northeast and Midwest, New York's population is stable and growing, creating increased demand for housing. Fueled by a burst of immigration since the mid-1980s, the Census Bureau estimates that the population of New York grew by 262,000 from 1980 to 1994. In all likelihood these numbers substantially underestimate the city's true population because of their failure to adequately account for racial and ethnic minorities and illegal immigrants. The population dynamics of New York stand in sharp contrast to cities such as Philadelphia and Chicago, which each experienced a substantial decline in population during the same period.

New York City's housing stock is also unusual. As the author and Benjamin P. Scafidi describe in chapter 1, most housing is occupied by renters. Over 70 percent of all housing in New York is renter occupied compared to only 59 percent and 38 percent in Chicago and Philadelphia, respectively. Furthermore, the density of housing in New York City is substantially different from other cities. Most rental units are in large, multifamily buildings; in other large cities, they are predominantly in smaller buildings. New York's housing market is also much more heavily regulated than housing in most American cities. As Peter D. Salins describes in chapter 2, over half of all rental units are subject to rent regulation. Compared to other cities, New York also has a much larger number of publicly owned housing units. In 1996, the New York City Housing Authority (NYCHA) owned over 172,000 units of public housing, constituting 8.5 percent of New York's rental housing stock. The city also owns and manages an additional 25,000 units of tax foreclosed housing.

Despite these differences in population and housing markets, New York City experiences many of the same problems as other large American cities. As in most American cities, the overwhelming majority of the housing stock is structurally sound, although pockets of substandard housing exist in certain neighborhoods. The major housing problem that affects city residents is one of affordability. Despite the existence of rent regulation and a large stock of public housing, approximately one out of every four tenants pays over half of his or her income for rent. These crushingly high rent-to-income burdens are caused both by a combination of rising rents and stagnating tenant incomes. Indeed, although New York, as well as most American cities, has enjoyed economic growth after the recessionary years of the late 1980s and early 1990s, its poverty and unemployment rates have remained persistently high.

Like the rest of the nation, the spatial distribution of poverty in New York is uneven. Poverty has grown more concentrated in certain neighborhoods, typically those occupied by racial and ethnic minorities. Indeed, in 1990, 13 percent of the population lived in census tracts where over 40 percent of the population earned incomes below the federally prescribed poverty rate as compared to 14 percent in Chicago and 12 percent in Philadelphia (Kasarda 1993). In addition to experiencing the same concentrations of poverty as many other older American cities, New York also experiences roughly similar levels of racial segregation. According to Yinger (1995), 78 percent of the black population would have to move in order to be evenly distributed throughout the New York metropolitan area compared to 82 percent in Philadelphia and 87 percent in Chicago.

HOUSING POLICY AND PROGRAMS IN NEW YORK CITY

Although New York's size, density, and demographics may increase the intensity of its housing problems, it is clear that the city experiences many of the same housing and housing-related problems as other large American cities. In part because of this, and in part because of its history of social welfare activism, New York City has enacted policies and programs that can serve as guideposts to the rest of the nation in the coming era of devolution. In a time when public housing has become synonymous with urban squalor, crime, and welfare dependency, NYCHA maintains a reputation as one of the finest housing authorities in the nation. In chapter 5, Phillip Thompson describes how NYCHA developed this reputation. One of the reasons why public housing in New York has not fared as badly as public housing in other large American cities is that it has, at least until recent years, attracted and admitted tenants with a broad range of incomes.

New York City has also created the most extensive set of programs in the nation to care for its relatively large population of homeless individuals and families. In chapter 8, Dennis P. Culhane, Stephen Metraux, and Susan M. Wachter recount the city's response to the problem of homelessness. As the magnitude of the homelessness problem emerged in the 1980s, New York, prodded by its judiciary, guaranteed shelter to all who needed it. This unprecedented housing entitlement required the city to establish a set of options ranging from shelters and SROs for single men and women, transitional and permanent housing for families, and supportive care facilities for persons with mental or physical disabilities.

As Kathryn Wylde describes in chapter 3, the city also pioneered the creation of public-private partnerships to carry out a variety of housing and community development projects. These partnerships have combined the efforts of banks, community development corporations, and a variety of intermediaries with the city. By using public resources to leverage private financing and investment, entire neighborhoods have been rebuilt. The housing constructed by these public-private partnerships has been occupied by a broad range of people, including families who were formerly homeless, low- and moderate-income families, and middle-income households. Similarly, in chapter 4, Frank P. Braconi describes the city's innovative efforts to redevelop and privatize city-owned properties in partnership with nonprofit organizations, cooperative corporations, and profit-motivated entrepreneurs.

Not all of the authors of chapters in this book view New York City's interventions in the housing market as benign. For example, Salins argues in chapter 2 that despite revitalizing sections of East New York, the South Bronx, and Harlem, many of the development programs lauded by Wylde have actually destabilized privately owned housing. According to Salins, housing built or renovated with city capital subsidies unfairly competes with "low-end" private apartments for "the limited number of responsible, working, moderate income families willing to live in these neighborhoods." In the end this competition could lead to the future abandonment of housing by private landlords.

New York City's regulatory policies also create difficulties for private sector landlords. Over the past decade, New York City has experienced a rate of new housing construction that is extremely low, both in comparison to historical standards and to rates of new construction in other large American cities. In addition to the aforementioned competition from government, Salins argues that rent regulation bears substantial responsibility for this lack of new housing. In addition to reducing profits and increasing the risk of development, rent regulation establishes the wrong price signals for potential builders of housing. Many middle-income households that would otherwise demand market rate housing are presently living in apartments with artificially low rents. This removes a market incentive for new construction as well as tightening the market for existing housing. In addition to rent regulations, Salins argues that city and state environmental review procedures effectively squelch private development.

According to Braconi and Salins, the city's fiscal policies also make it difficult to operate and maintain affordable housing. In particular, both criticize the city's system of property taxation. Under local law, most residential buildings with four or more units are assessed at a higher proportion of their value than single-family homes. The comparatively higher operating expenses attributable to the property tax system either lead landlords to raise rents in parts of the city where the market will permit such increases or disinvest in their properties in areas where it will not.

In chapter 7, Paula Galowitz critically examines one particularly dysfunctional actor in the city's housing establishment—the Housing Court. The Housing Court was created in 1972 as a low-cost and accessible way for tenants to enforce their rights to decent and habitable housing. Over the years, however, housing maintenance and code enforcement litigation has taken a back seat to landlord actions to evict tenants. Housing Court does not work particularly well for either side in landlord/tenant disputes. Landlords criticize seemingly endless delays in litigation and the allegedly protenant bias of Housing Court judges; tenant advocates complain about the absence of legal counsel for tenants facing eviction and the lack of attention judges are able to give to individual cases due to enormous caseloads.

HOUSING AND COMMUNITY DEVELOPMENT POLICY IN NEW YORK CITY: FACING THE FUTURE

Future changes in federal and state housing policy present enormous challenges for New York City as well as other large American cities. As Schwartz and Vidal describe in the concluding chapter of this book, Congress and the New York State Legislature have already passed or are considering legislation that will make it more difficult for New York City to maintain its commitment to housing and community development. Some of these changes will directly affect housing built under various federal programs. For example, as Victor Bach describes in chapter 6, New York City's vast stock of HUD-assisted housing is at risk as Congress seeks ways to cut the projected growth in spending that would be required to maintain housing built with federally insured mortgages and rent subsidies. Even if Congress were to successfully restructure the nation's portfolio of privately owned, subsidized housing, landlords in some of the city's stronger rental markets might nonetheless choose to exercise their rights to end their participation in the programs, thereby reducing the city's stock of affordable housing. Budgetary cutbacks by Congress, together with widespread public disillusionment, also will have a tremendous impact on New York City's public housing.

Landlords and tenants alike, both in privately and publicly owned housing, will face tremendous challenges as the recently enacted welfare reform legislation is implemented. Although some provisions have already taken effect, the major impact will occur within five years as households have their public assistance benefits taken away from them. In the absence of the city unexpectedly generating a large number of low-skilled jobs or a migration of low-income households from New York to other parts of the nation, the rent-paying ability of these households will decline. This will have an immediate impact on all sectors of the housing market.

The public-private partnerships portrayed by Wylde are all based on the ability of tenants to pay some rent. This housing stock is frequently not deeply subsidized and will come under tremendous pressure as tenant income declines. Even programs such as public housing that receive operating subsidies from the federal government will be strained as their rental revenues decline. One response, described by Thompson in chapter 5, is for NYCHA to seek to admit moderate-income tenants in place of very low-income households, a policy that Congress has facilitated. Although creating a mixture of incomes might have salutory effects for public housing developments and their current residents (Schill 1993), such a change in admissions policy would, no doubt, cause hardship among the city's poor. With fewer apartments available in the subsidized sector and with declining incomes, these households could swell the city's homeless population.

Declining tenant incomes will also harm private, unsubsidized landlords. According to Braconi, in many parts of the city the rents that landlords can charge tenants barely cover operating costs. If tenant incomes were to decline these landlords might disinvest in their properties and become delinquent in paying their property taxes and mortgages. In the absence of additional rent subsidies or municipal action to reduce the tax burden on these landlords, the city could be faced with a new wave of housing abandonment. Furthermore, properties once owned by the city and disposed of through its privatization programs could well be in danger of insolvency since many were not underwritten with sufficient reserves to weather a reduction in rent revenue.

There is little doubt that the twenty-first century will bring a range of challenges for housing policymakers, providers, and tenants in New York City, as well as in the rest of the nation. In some respects, devolution and deregulation will create opportunities for creation of just the type of flexible and creative initiatives at which New York City has excelled for years. However, adapting to an era of devolution without resources, particularly for a city with New York's demographic pressures and heritage of government activism, may be the toughest challenge it has yet had to face.

Housing and Community Development in New York City: Facing the Future consists of nine chapters. In chapter 1, the author and Benjamin P. Scafidi examine the forces affecting both the supply and demand for housing in New York City. We then describe the complicated structure of housing tenure in New York and examine the magnitude and spatial distribution of three types of housing problems: poor housing quality, unaffordable housing, and racial and ethnic discrimination. In chapter 2, Peter D. Salins, Provost of the State University of New York, examines the shortage of housing in New York City with particular emphasis on how the city's regulatory environment deters new housing construction. He finds a number of culprits, including rent control and rent stabilization, the city's zoning laws, building codes, and environmental rules.

The next four chapters examine several ways government has intervened in New York City's housing market to either promote the construction of new housing or rehabilitate and stabilize existing buildings. In chapter 3, Kathryn Wylde, up until recently the president of the New York City Housing Partnership, describes how New York City used public resources, including land, money, and tax credits, to leverage housing development through partnerships with financial institutions, community development corporations, and a variety of intermediaries. From her first-hand experience as one of the city's leading housing practitioners, Wylde describes how consistent, replicable models of production were created and examines some of the potential and pitfalls of public-private partnerships. Frank P. Braconi, Executive Director of

Citizens Housing and Planning Council, a venerable institution in New York dedicated to promoting debate and research on development and planning issues, begins chapter 4 by describing the crisis of abandonment that plagued New York City throughout the 1970s and mid-1980s. Braconi describes some of the reasons private landlords failed to pay property taxes and, in some instances, "milked" their buildings. Braconi also recounts an amazing chapter in New York's history in which the city itself, inadvertently and reluctantly, became the second largest landlord in New York. Braconi describes how New York utilized public-private partnerships to divest itself of many of its properties in conjunction with its $5 billion capital program.

New York City has also been an eager participant in federal housing programs. In chapter 5, Phillip Thompson, a politics professor at Barnard College and former NYCHA acting general manager, places public housing in New York City in a national context. NYCHA has long maintained a reputation as one of the finest public housing authorities in the nation. Thompson's critical examination of public housing in the city suggests that this reputation may be at jeopardy unless NYCHA improves its administration and adopts policies that successfully navigate between its historic mission in helping the poor and its desire to maintain a mixture of incomes in its developments. New York City also is home to a multitude of projects built with federal mortgage and rent subsidies, but owned and operated by private landlords. In chapter 6, Victor Bach, head of housing policy research at the Community Service Society, another venerable institution in New York dedicated to advocating on behalf of the city's disenfranchised population, examines the problems currently facing the stock of HUD-assisted housing. At present, the future of this housing is jeopardized by a number of different factors. Many developments have reached the end of their initial contract periods and Congress, as part of its budget-cutting efforts, is seeking to reduce costs by restructuring finances. If the federal government does not offer developers sufficient incentives to maintain their buildings as subsidized housing, some units could be lost as owners convert units to free-market rentals while others could be lost as a result of disinvestment.

In chapter 7, Paula Galowitz, a clinical law professor at New York University, critically examines the New York City Housing Court, an institution whose impact is pervasive among landlords and tenants alike. Galowitz, a former chair of the Association of the Bar of the City of New York's Committee on the Housing Court and an attorney who has represented tenants before that tribunal, describes how the court has failed to achieve its intended objective of preserving affordable housing. The

Housing Court's effectiveness has been severely undermined as a result of a number of institutional problems, such as enormous judicial caseloads, a lack of counsel for parties, and a shortage of income among low-income tenants.

Dennis P. Culhane, Stephen Metraux and Susan M. Wachter, professors at the University of Pennsylvania, examine the persistent problem of homelessness in chapter 8. After a description of the emergence of homelessness as a recognized public policy problem in the late 1970s and 1980s, the authors describe the litigation that spurred New York's unprecedented creation of a network of shelters and transitional and permanent housing earmarked for homeless adults and families. They then present the results of research that indicate that the magnitude of the homelessness problem in New York is higher than commonly thought. Their research also suggests that homeless persons and families can be separated into three groups, each of which might require different combinations of housing and social service interventions.

In the concluding chapter, Alex F. Schwartz, a professor at the New School for Social Research, and Avis C. Vidal, a Principal Research Associate at the Urban Institute, describe the future prospects for housing policy in New York City. They analyze how federal and State cutbacks in housing program budgets are likely to impact New York's stock of affordable housing. They further speculate on how emerging changes in social welfare programs are likely to affect landlords and tenants in the City. Schwartz and Vidal conclude their chapter by suggesting ways in which the city of New York can assist housing providers in weathering a future, which is certain to present major challenges.

REFERENCES

Berenyi, Eileen B. 1989. *Locally Funded Housing Programs in the United States: A Survey of the Fifty-one Most Populated Cities*. New York: New School for Social Research.

Friedman, Lawrence M. 1968. *Government and Slum Housing: A Century of Frustration*. Chicago: Rand McNally & Co.

Kasarda, John D. 1993. "Inner-City Poverty and Economic Access." In *Rediscovering Urban America: Perspectives on the 1980s*, ed. Jack Sommers and Donald A. Hicks, 4-1–4-60. Washington, D.C.: U.S. Department of Housing and Urban Development.

Marcuse, Peter. 1995. "Interpreting 'Public Housing' History." *Journal of Architectural and Planning Research* 12, 3:240–58.

Plunz, Richard. 1990. *A History of Housing in New York City: Dwelling Type and Social Change in the American Metropolis*. New York: Columbia University Press.

Schill, Michael H. 1996. "Local Enforcement of Laws Prohibiting Discrimination in Housing: The New York City Experience." *Fordham Urban Law Journal* 23, 4:991–1030.

———. 1993. "Distressed Public Housing: Where Do We Go from Here?" *University of Chicago Law Review* 60, 2:497–554.

Yinger, John. 1995. *Closed Doors, Opportunities Lost: The Continuing Costs of Housing Discrimination*. New York: Russell Sage Foundation.

CHAPTER 1

HOUSING CONDITIONS AND PROBLEMS IN NEW YORK CITY

Michael H. Schill and Benjamin P. Scafidi

New York City's housing market has been in a state of perpetual crisis, real or perceived, for much of the twentieth century. Following World War II, the New York State Legislature justified the continuation of rent regulation by declaring that the city faced a housing emergency. This declaration of emergency remains in place more than a half-century later. Despite the construction of over 1.07 million units of housing since the war (NYC Department of City Planning 1992b; Kober 1996), the rental vacancy rate in 1996 was only 4 percent. Low vacancy rates impede mobility and contribute to housing prices that are beyond the reach of many New Yorkers. Despite enormous improvements in the quality of New York City housing over the past three decades, a substantial proportion of low- and moderate-income residents still live in substandard housing or pay rents that are beyond their means. An additional segment of the population have no homes at all.

The recent release of data from the 1996 Housing and Vacancy Survey (HVS) makes an analysis of the New York City housing market both timely and indispensable to the development of public policy. The HVS is a survey of over 17,000 housing units periodically conducted by the United States Bureau of the Census.[1] The HVS provides a wealth of current information on the socioeconomic, racial, and housing characteristics of New Yorkers. One limitation of the 1996 HVS, however, is that the survey includes income and rent estimates that are somewhat inconsistent with prior years. Because a relatively large proportion of households fail to report their incomes and rents, in 1996, for the first time, the HVS imputed incomes and rents for nonrespondent households.[2] All references to income and rent in the text and tables of this chapter utilize the estimates derived by the Census Bureau, except when we compare incomes, rents, and rent burdens in 1996 to prior years. For these longitudinal comparisons, we utilize only the data obtained from people who disclosed this information to the Census Bureau enumerators. A second limitation of the HVS is inherent in that it is a survey based upon a sample of housing units. Therefore the data presented in this paper are subject to sampling and rounding errors, and small numbers and proportions, in particular, should be interpreted with caution.

In this chapter, we use the HVS, as well as other sources of data, to provide an overview of New York City's housing market and to examine several housing-related problems. We begin by describing some of the forces that influence the supply and demand for housing in New York City. The second part of the chapter describes the housing stock of New York and examines recent trends. We then turn to a description and analysis of several housing-related problems that affect a substantial segment of the city's population, including unaffordability, substandard housing quality, homelessness, and racial discrimination. As part of this analysis, we estimate that 735,819 New Yorkers have "severe" housing problems. An imbalance between tenants' incomes and apartment rents accounts for the overwhelming majority of severe housing problems in New York City. Estimates of this imbalance are derived and presented. We conclude the chapter by speculating on what the future might hold with respect to housing conditions and problems.

Factors Influencing the Supply and Demand of Housing in New York City

New York City's housing market is shaped by the interplay of numerous complicated and interrelated forces. Many demographic, economic, and social factors influence both the demand for housing in the city and the amount that is supplied. Further complicating a description of the housing market is the fact that in a city as large and diverse as New York, speaking of a single housing market is an oversimplification. Instead, New York City is a collection of housing submarkets, differentiated by space, tenure, regulatory status, and occupancy. Although a detailed analysis of the determinants of supply and demand is beyond the scope of this chapter, in this part we will selectively describe some of the factors that influence supply and demand for housing in New York City.

The Demand for Housing

One of the most important determinants of housing demand is the growth or decline of the city's population. According to data from the decennial census, after sharp declines from 1960 to 1980, the population of New York City grew by 3.5 percent during the 1980s. Since 1990, the population of New York has either increased modestly or remained constant, depending upon the source of estimates. The most current estimate of the city's population can be obtained from the HVS. According to the HVS, the city's population increased from 7.14 million in 1991 to 7.23 million in 1996. During the first half of the 1990s, the population of the Bronx and Brooklyn declined by 0.8 percent and 3.2 percent, respectively. However, the number of people increased in Manhattan (7.1 percent), Queens (2.5 percent), and Staten Island (5.5 percent).

For each dwelling unit surveyed in the HVS, the Census Bureau identifies its sub-borough area, a geographic unit that closely resembles a community district. In the first half of the 1990s, thirty of the city's sub-borough areas gained population while twenty-five experienced population losses. The majority of the shrinking sub-borough areas were located in Brooklyn and the South Bronx.

The impact of population growth or decline on the demand for housing is mediated by changes in the number of households.[3] Between 1991 and 1996, the number of households in New York City remained constant at approximately 2.78 million. Gains in the Bronx, Queens, and Staten Island offset losses of households in Brooklyn and Manhattan. Although the aggregate number of households held constant, the city's total population increased slightly. This discrepancy can be explained by an increase in the size of the average New York City household. After steady declines from 1960 to 1980, the average household size increased slightly from 2.57 to 2.60 during the early 1990s (U.S. Department of Commerce 1960, 1970, 1980, 1990). It is likely that this increase in average household size was caused, in part, by increasing levels of immigration. From 1991 to 1996, the city's immigrant population increased in both absolute and relative terms. The number of immigrant households increased by 115,390, and their proportion of the total number of households rose from 40.0 percent to 44.3 percent.[4] On average, households composed of recent immigrants have larger household sizes (2.85 persons) compared to their native-born counterparts (2.27 persons).

Demand for housing is also affected by the financial resources available to New York City households. From 1990 to 1992, median household income (in real terms) decreased by more than 11 percent (Blackburn 1995). Between 1992 and 1995, however, median household income increased by 0.5 percent (in real terms). As Table 1.1 indicates, the median household income of New Yorkers in 1995 was $29,500.[5] Median household incomes were highest in Staten Island ($42,800) and lowest in the Bronx ($20,000).

TABLE 1.1
Household Characteristics by Borough

	City	Bronx	Brooklyn	Manhattan	Queens	Staten Island
Median Income ($)	$29,500	$20,000	$24,000	$35,000	$34,800	$42,800
Median Age	45	44	45	43	46	47
% Householders ≥ 65	20.6	19.5	21.4	17.7	22.4	24.6
% Receiving Public Assistance	19.2	33.6	23.0	15.9	11.1	8.3
% Receiving AFDC	6.8	13.8	7.9	6.0	3.4	1.2
% below Poverty Level	20.6	32.3	25.3	18.9	12.2	10.5
Mean Household Size	2.44	2.60	2.59	1.91	2.64	2.73
Mean Years of Tenure	11.55	10.98	11.53	10.96	12.20	12.94

Source: 1996 Housing and Vacancy Survey Data File.

A substantial portion of New York City residents, however, live in poverty. In 1996, approximately one-fifth of all households in the city had incomes below the federally prescribed poverty threshold. Importantly, poverty is not spread evenly through the city. In absolute terms, Brooklyn was home to the largest number of poor households in 1995 (209,080 persons). The Bronx, however, had the highest rate of household poverty (32.3 percent), with the lowest incidence in Staten Island (10.5 percent).

The Supply of Housing

The supply of housing is influenced by a wide variety of factors that resist easy quantification. The quantity of housing provided in a market is likely to be affected by the availability of substitutes, the prices of land, construction (labor and materials), and the cost of capital (Pozdena 1988, 47).

Construction costs in New York are extremely high. Among construction workers, the average hourly earnings in New York City in 1995 were $25.56, roughly two-thirds higher than similar costs throughout the nation (U.S. Department of Labor). One index, which measures the construction cost per square foot of various types of buildings, estimates that in 1996 the cost of constructing an eight- to twenty-four-story apartment building in New York City was $125 (excluding sitework, land costs, development costs, and specialty finishes) compared to a nationwide average cost of $92.80 (R. S. Means Co. 1997). This figure represents an increase of more than one-third since 1990. According to the index, apartment construction costs are higher than any other form of construction with the exception of hospitals and churches.

Furthermore, construction costs for apartment buildings in New York City were the highest in the nation followed by parts of Alaska ($122 per square foot) and Berkeley, California ($121 per square foot).

The cost of capital for constructing residential buildings is typically pegged to the prime rate, ranging from two to five points over prime. The prime rate rises and falls with general economic conditions. From a recent peak of close to 11 percent in 1989, the prime rate hovered at 6 percent in the early 1990s until rising again in 1994. For much of 1997 and 1998, the prime rate was 8.5 percent. Similarly, since 1989, home loan mortgage rates have fluctuated; in April 1998, the average interest rate for a thirty-year conventional home mortgage loan in New York City was 7.3 percent.

An important additional consideration for providers of housing is the comparable return offered by alternative investments. From February 1996 to February 1997, the average yield on thirty-year treasury bills increased by one-half point to 6.7 percent (Market Source 1997, 2). As measured by the Standard & Poor index, however, stocks increased in value by over 26 percent between May 1996 and May 1997. Capitalization rates for office properties in midtown increased from 7.5 percent in 1985 to 8.7 percent in the second quarter of 1995, reflecting the increased risk caused by the overbuilding of the 1980s. By the fourth quarter of 1996, however, capitalization rates had declined to 8.0 percent. In the downtown Manhattan market, capitalization rates shot up from 7.9 percent in 1985 to 9.2 percent in 1996 (National Real Estate Index 1995).

The supply of housing can also be affected by government. Permitting housing to be built in areas heretofore reserved for other uses or relaxing restrictions on the number of units that can be constructed can promote new construction. In addition, actions to remove impediments to converting existing nonresidential buildings to housing can augment supply. Several commentators have criticized New York City's zoning ordinance for inhibiting the development of housing by placing large parcels of developable land in manufacturing zones, despite the fact that manufacturing employment has declined significantly and by making it difficult to convert nonresidential buildings to residential uses (Real Estate Board of New York 1992, Salins and Mildner 1992).

In recent years, the City of New York has modestly sought to ease land use restrictions. As part of its effort to revitalize the downtown central business district, conversions of now obsolete office buildings are being facilitated by reductions in minimum apartment sizes, greater flexibility for mixed uses, and reductions in parking requirements. Between January 1996 and January 1998, an estimated 2,400 new units of housing had been or were being converted (Hamilton, Rabinovitz &

Alschuler 1998). Rezoning of former industrial or manufacturing properties to residential uses has also taken place on Sixth Avenue and in Tribeca in Manhattan, Hunters Point in Queens, and Charleston in Staten Island.

Government can also directly increase the supply of housing by subsidizing the development of new or renovated units. In 1986, Mayor Ed Koch announced the beginning of an ambitious program to spend $4.2 billion from the city's capital budget over ten years to increase housing production in the city. This program, the largest of its kind by far among American cities,[6] utilized a variety of approaches ranging from construction by the city itself to the transfer of land and resources to community development corporations and business-sponsored intermediaries (Wylde, chapter 3 in this volume). Although spending under the program has been reduced as a result of the city's fiscal difficulties, over 50,000 housing units have been constructed or substantially renovated under the capital program (Finder 1995, Schwartz and Vidal, chapter 9 in this volume).

New York City also affects the supply of housing in the city through its tax policies. High tax rates increase operating costs and therefore either raise the cost of housing to city residents, or, alternatively, decrease the amount of housing that is supplied. Real property tax burdens are a function of both assessed valuation and the rate of tax applied to that valuation. Under New York law, multifamily rental housing, cooperatives, and condominiums are treated less favorably than single-family homes by being assessed at higher proportions of market value. For example, in 1997, single-family homes were assessed at a maximum of 12 percent of full value and multifamily buildings with more than three apartments at a maximum rate of 34 percent (New York City 1997). Tax rates, which, of course, also affect tax burdens, rose modestly in the 1990s. For single-family homes, the tax rate in 1997 was 10.785 per $100 of assessed value, up from 9.45 in 1990; for multifamily dwellings the rate increased from 9.23 to 11.056.

Tax policy may also promote the construction of housing by, in effect, selectively reducing tax burdens and providing incentives to build. New York City operates several tax abatement or exemption programs to spur construction or renovation of housing (Hevesi 1997; Salins, chapter 2 in this volume). For example, under the 421-a program, tax exemptions are available to developers of new residential buildings throughout the city. In much of Manhattan south of 96th Street these incentives are only available to developers who reserve one-fifth of their units for low- and moderate-income families. As of 1997, the city had granted benefits under this program to spur the construction of 115,000 units of housing. Frequently, these property tax exemptions are paired with tax exempt financing and federal low-income housing tax credits to make development feasible.

Outcomes of Supply and Demand

The interaction of demand and supply determines housing prices, vacancy rates, and housing density. New York City is among the most densely settled cities in the United States. This intense usage of land contributes to land values that are extremely high when compared to other parts of the nation. Estimating changes in land values for the city is extremely difficult because of the small number of annual raw land transactions and the importance of locational influences. Nevertheless, a land value index computed for commercial land in Manhattan suggests that the recession that hit New York in the early 1990s substantially reduced the price of land. According to this index, after hitting a high in 1990 of over $120 per square foot of buildable area, land prices declined to about one-third that level in 1993 (Austrian, Roth & Partners 1995, 1). The city's economic resurgence in the late 1990s, however, has once again caused land values to rise.

High land values (with respect to other parts of the United States) contribute to the relatively high price of housing in New York City compared to the nation as a whole. In 1995, the median housing cost for renters in New York City area was $632 compared to $515 for all American central cities. Similarly, the vacancy rate for rental housing in the New York metropolitan area was 5.2 percent, compared to a national average of 7.2 percent (U.S. Department of Commerce 1995a, 1995b).[7]

HOUSING IN NEW YORK CITY

Describing New York City's housing stock and housing market is an exceedingly complicated undertaking. In most American cities, the housing stock is typically divided into two main tenures: homeownership and renting. Within each of these two groups there is some variation, but for the most part, each tenure is relatively homogenous. Renters typically occupy apartments in multifamily dwellings; homeowners occupy single-family detached or semidetached buildings. In New York City, however, there is considerable differentiation both among and within the two major tenure groups. A majority of rental units are subject to rent regulation; a smaller yet still substantial proportion of the housing stock is publicly owned. Even the owner-occupied stock is unusual, with its substantial stock of condominium and cooperative apartments. Differences in housing conditions, occupancy characteristics, and market dynamics exist not only among these different subtenures, but also across the city's varied geography.

In this part, we begin with a brief description of the city's aggregate housing stock. We then describe each housing subtenure and housing and household characteristics within that subtenure. Particular attention is given to the occupant and building characteristics as well as to differences that exist among the city's five boroughs. Discussion of housing-related problems, such as substandard physical condition, unaffordability, homelessness, and racial disparities in housing outcomes, are deferred to the next part of the chapter. Unless otherwise stated, all data in this part of the chapter are obtained from the 1996 HVS.

The Aggregate Housing Stock

According to Table 1.2, 2.89 million occupied dwelling units or units vacant and available for occupancy exist in New York City. This number represents a net increase of 154,396 units over the preceding fifteen years.

The recession that hit New York in the early 1990s and subsequent cutbacks in public sector capital spending on housing have significantly slowed additions to New York City's housing stock. The annual number of new completions shrank from a fifteen-year high of 14,685 in 1989

TABLE 1.2
New York City Housing Relative to the United States

	New York City	United States
Units Available for Sale or Rent	2,885,186	104,767,000
Owner Occupied	834,184	66,024,432
% Owner Occupied[1]	30.0	65.4
Total Owner Units	857,765	67,098,000
Vacant and Available for Sale	23,581	1,073,568
% Vacant and Available for Sale[2]	2.8	1.6
Renter Occupied	1,946,165	34,956,832
% Renter Occupied[1]	70.0	34.6
Total Rental Units	2,027,421	37,669,000
Vacant and Available for Rent	81,256	2,712,168
% Vacant and Available for Rent[3]	4.0	7.2

Source: 1996 Housing and Vacancy Survey Data File, 1996 U.S. Housing Vacancy.
1. As a proportion of all occupied units.
2. As a proportion of owner housing only.
3. As a proportion of rental housing only.

to only 5,510 in 1993. By 1995, the number of new completions rebounded slightly to 7,426, and in 1997 the city issued building permits for 8,987 new units of housing (New York City Department of City Planning 1998). Despite this increase in housing production, the city still loses more housing than it gains. According to the 1996 Housing and Vacancy Survey, from 1993 to 1996, the city lost an average of 12,000 housing units per year to demolition, condemnation, disinvestment and merger with other units (U.S. Department of Commerce 1998).

Owner Occupancy

Unlike most other American cities, New York City is overwhelmingly a city of renters. According to the 1993 American Housing Survey, 49.1 percent of all households in central cities owned the homes in which they lived. In New York, however, as shown in Table 1.2, only 30 percent of all housing units were owner occupied in 1996. Furthermore, rates of owner occupancy vary dramatically by borough and even within boroughs. In Staten Island, more than three out of every five households own their own homes compared to one in five in the Bronx.

As indicated in Table 1.3, of the 834,184 housing units occupied by owners, 543,304, or approximately two-thirds, were in one- or two-family homes characterized by the HVS as "conventional" homeowner units. In most other American cities, the next largest category of owner units would be condominium apartments, a form of tenure in which the owner holds individual title to his or her own apartment but typically

TABLE 1.3
Housing Characteristics of Owners by Subtenure

	All Owner Units	Conventional	Co-ops/Condos	Mitchell-Lama
Occupied Housing Units	834,184	543,304	240,245	50,634
Vacant and Available	23,581	12,014	9,441	2,127
Owner Vacancy Rate	2.8%	2.2%	3.8%	4.0%
Median Value	$175,000	$190,000	$100,000	$10,000
Crowded Households	6,376	2,199	3,965	212
% Crowded Households	0.8	0.4	1.7	0.4
% Built before 1930	32.1	38.8	23.8	0.0
Mean # of Maintenance Deficiencies	0.51	0.48	0.58	0.63
% with Boarded-Up Buildings Nearby	6.6	7.9	3.8	5.8

Source: 1996 Housing and Vacancy Survey.

shares ownership of common spaces and the land underlying the apartment. In New York City, however, the number of occupied condominium units (44,099) is dwarfed by the number of occupied cooperative apartments (196,146). Unlike the conventional single-family or condominium owner, a cooperative apartment "owner" does not own his or her apartment, but instead owns shares in the corporation with title to the unit. The individual owner is legally a tenant of the cooperative corporation. In New York City, an additional 50,634 cooperative owners live in Mitchell-Lama buildings. These buildings were built with state mortgage interest subsidies and have income limitations designed to ensure occupancy by middle-income households. The composition of owner units varies across the city's five boroughs. Over three-quarters of all homeowners occupy conventional one- or two-family homes in Brooklyn, Queens, and Staten Island compared to three-fifths in the Bronx and only one in twenty-five in Manhattan.

As indicated in Table 1.4, the values of owner-occupied housing and homes available for sale vary substantially among the city's five boroughs. The highest median value for single-family homes is in Manhattan ($1,027,569), with the Bronx having the lowest value ($180,000). Home values in the other three boroughs are much closer to the Bronx

TABLE 1.4
Housing Characteristics by Borough

	City	Bronx	Brooklyn	Manhattan	Queens	Staten Island
Occupied Housing Units	2,780,349	411,775	813,544	703,943	713,978	137,109
Vacant and Available	104,837	22,401	30,145	26,653	21,206	4,432
Overall Vacancy Rate	3.63%	5.16%	3.57%	3.65%	2.88%	3.13%
Rental Vacancy Rate	4.01%	5.43%	4.20%	3.47%	3.28%	4.17%
Owner Vacancy Rate	2.75%	4.10%	1.85%	4.36%	2.34%	2.53%
Median Contract Rent	$595	$508	$550	$650	$647	$600
Median Rent/Income	28%	31%	29%	26%	26%	23%
Median House Value[1]	$190,000	$180,000	$200,000	$1,027,569	$190,000	$185,000
Median Co-op/Condo Value	$100,000	$60,000	$65,000	$190,000	$70,000	$118,000
Crowded Households	73,923	13,007	20,544	22,094	16,647	1,630
% Crowded Households	2.7	3.2	2.5	3.1	2.3	1.2
% Built before 1930	41.6	47.5	49.0	54.1	24.4	6.3
Mean # of Maintenance Deficiencies	1.17	1.57	1.13	1.35	0.73	0.56
% with Boarded-Up Buildings Nearby	10.0	9.3	14.8	11.5	4.0	6.9

Source: 1996 Housing and Vacancy Survey Data File.
1. Excludes Mitchel-Lama cooperatives.

than to the unusually expensive Manhattan. Cooperative and condominium values follow similar geographic patterns.

Tables 1.5 and 1.9 demonstrate that the median income of homeowners ($48,562), unsurprisingly, is greater than that of tenants ($23,704). Similarly, the median age of homeowners (52 years) is higher than the average for all renters (42 years). Conventional homeowners and Mitchell-Lama owners are older, on average, than owners of condominiums or cooperatives.

The proportion of owner-occupied housing units rose by about two percentage points from 1981 to 1996. This increase is largely attributable to the wave of condominium and cooperative conversions that swept New York in the 1980s. In addition, the city and the New York City Housing Partnership have combined forces to build over 13,000 one- or two-family homes over the past decade. In 1996, the vacancy rate for owner housing was 2.75 percent. Manhattan had the highest vacancy rate; Brooklyn and Queens the lowest.

Rental Dwellings

New York City's rental housing stock is divided into a bewildering array of subtenures that can usefully be categorized according to the type of regulatory regime they operate under. The subtenures include housing subject to rent regulation, housing owned by the government either under the public housing program or as a result of tax foreclosure, and housing available in the private rental sector at market rents.

A Description of Six Subtenures.   In 1942, President Franklin D. Roosevelt signed into law the Emergency Price Control Act, which froze rents in most counties of the state (New York State Division of Housing

TABLE 1.5
Occupant Characteristics of Owners by Subtenure

	All Owner Units	Conventional	Co-ops/Condos	Mitchell-Lama
Median Income	$48,562	$47,000	$57,600	$33,000
Median Age	52	55	47	54
% Householders ≥ 65	28.5	30.9	22.3	31.2
% Receiving Public Assistance	5.9	5.7	5.9	9.1
% Receiving AFDC	0.5	0.4	0.8	0.9
% below Poverty Level	7.5	7.7	6.5	9.3
Mean Household Size	2.61	2.95	1.94	2.06
Mean Years of Tenure	16.01	18.54	10.70	14.14

Source: 1996 Housing and Vacancy Survey Data File.

and Community Renewal 1993). With the end of the war and the normalization of the nation's economy, the federal law was allowed to lapse in 1947. In 1951, however, the New York State Legislature enacted a comprehensive rent control ordinance that permitted the city to extend rent control on apartments built before 1947 while providing for decontrol of apartments in one- or two-family homes and certain high-rent "luxury" apartments. Today, after further decontrol and the enactment of rent stabilization, rent controlled units predominantly consist of (1) units in buildings with three or more apartments that were constructed prior to February 1, 1947 and where the tenant moved in before July 1, 1971, (2) units in buildings with one or two apartments that were constructed before February 1, 1947 and where the current tenant moved in before April 1953, and (3) apartments constructed under certain tax abatement and subsidy programs that have a tenant who moved in before 1976. Over the fifteen-year period between 1981 and 1996, the number of rent controlled units in New York City declined from 285,555 to only 70,572 apartments, or 3.4 percent of the rental stock.

In 1969, the New York State Legislature enacted the Rent Stabilization Law, which provided that all units in buildings with six or more apartments built between 1947 and 1969 would be subject to rent stabilization, a less stringent form of rent regulation than rent control. Under rent stabilization, landlords are entitled to periodic rent increases as operating costs rise and sizable vacancy bonuses when units turn over. Later statutes brought within rent stabilization apartments in buildings with six or more units that were constructed between 1969 and 1974 as well as formerly rent controlled units that are decontrolled. By 1996, the number of rent stabilized apartments in New York City had reached 1,052,300, or just over one-half of all rental units in the city.

Rent regulation also applies to an additional 131,576 apartments in the city that do not formally fall within the purview of rent control or rent stabilization. These units are typically those subsidized by the federal government under the Section 8 construction and rehabilitation programs, apartments built under State-financed limited-profit programs, and units subject to oversight by the New York City Loft Board. A large number of the units in this subtenure are likely owned or managed by nonprofit organizations. In addition to large citywide nonprofit organizations such as Phipps Houses and the Settlement Housing Fund, approximately 225 community-based nonprofit groups own and manage over 50,000 housing units in the city (see Wylde, chapter 3 in this volume).

Two sizable subtenures in New York are distinguished not so much by the form of rent regulation they operate under, but instead by who owns the housing. Since 1937, NYCHA has constructed or otherwise acquired 172,096 units of public housing. The construction of this housing was largely funded by the federal government, which continues to provide substantial operating subsidies and modernization grants. In return for this support, NYCHA limits the incomes of successful public housing applicants to 80 percent of the metropolitan area's median income and charges tenants no more than 30 percent of their incomes for rent. New York City's public housing stock is, by far, the largest of any city in the nation. Public housing constitutes 8.5 percent of all rental housing in the city.

In 1996, New York City itself owned approximately 25,211 units of housing that were either occupied or available for rent. The city took title to this housing as a result of the failure of former owners to pay real property taxes for at least one year. The legal action through which the city obtained title, an *in rem* proceeding, gives the housing its common name—*in rem* housing. The city's stock of *in rem* housing has declined in recent years as a result of a variety of initiatives to transfer ownership to tenants, community groups, and private entrepreneurs (see Braconi, chapter 4 in this volume). In addition, since 1994, the city has, for the most part, stopped taking title to *in rem* housing.

The final subtenure of rental housing is unregulated private market housing. All housing that was built in New York City since 1974 without governmental subsidies or tax abatements is free of rent regulation. In addition, most rental units in buildings with less than three apartments and those in buildings with fewer than six apartments that were built after 1947 are part of the unregulated sector. Finally, units that were deregulated over the years, such as those with "luxury" rents or those with a change of tenancy in a building that underwent conversion to condominiums or cooperatives, are part of the unregulated sector. In most cities, unregulated private market units would constitute the overwhelming majority of the rental housing stock. In New York City, however, the unregulated sector consists of 575,666 units, comprising only 28.4 percent of all rental housing.

Significant variation exists among the city's five boroughs with respect to the prevalence of subtenures. Partly due to its older housing stock and denser building patterns, Manhattan has the greatest proportion of rent regulated housing. In 1996, four-fifths of Manhattan's rental housing stock was subject to rent regulation compared to a citywide average of 62.2 percent. Brooklyn, Queens, and Staten Island had the lowest proportions of rent regulated housing—54.3 percent, 51.1 percent, and 22.2 percent, respectively. The Bronx had the city's highest proportions of public housing and *in rem* housing; Queens had the city's lowest shares of housing in these two categories.

Vacancy Rates.   As shown in Table 1.6, the overall vacancy rate for rental housing in New York City in 1996 was 4.01 percent. This rate, while below the 5 percent threshold set forth in state statutes to signal a housing "emergency," nevertheless is substantially higher than the 2.10 percent level of 1981 as well as the 3.44 percent vacancy rate of 1993. Of the city's fifty-five sub-borough areas, thirty-one experienced increases in vacancy rates between 1993 and 1996. Seventeen sub-borough areas, predominantly in the South Bronx, Central Brooklyn, and Manhattan north of 96th Street, had 1996 vacancy rates in excess of 5 percent. The highest vacancy rate existed in the city's stock of *in rem* housing, with almost 9 percent of the stock available for rent. Rent stabilized housing had a vacancy rate of 3.57 percent, whereas unregulated rental housing had a significantly higher 5.29 percent rate of availability. Surprisingly, the number of vacant public housing units increased by over 350 percent between 1993 and 1996, which translated into a 1996 vacancy rate of 3.75 percent.

TABLE 1.6
Vacant Units and Vacancy Rates by Subtenure, 1993 and 1996

Subtenure	Vacant Units Available for Rent		Net Vacancy Rate (Percent)	
	1993	1996	1993	1996
Rent Controlled	0	0	0.00%	0.00%
	0.0%	0.0%		
Rent Stabilized	34,071	37,549	3.36%	3.57%
	48.4%	46.2%		
Other Regulated	2,900	4,575	2.09%	3.48%
	4.1%	5.6%		
Unregulated	29,465	30,468	5.07%	5.29%
	41.9%	37.5%		
Public Housing	1,801	6,450	1.03%	3.75%
	2.6%	7.9%		
In Rem Housing	2,108	2,214	5.79%	8.78%
	3.0%	2.7%		
All Rental Units	70,345	81,256	3.44%	4.01%
	100.0%	100.0%		
Conventional owner	6,590	12,014	1.21%	2.16%
	32.1%	50.9%		
Co-ops/Condos	11,604	9,441	4.86%	3.78%
	56.5%	40.0%		
Mitchell-Lama	2,328	2,127	5.30%	4.03%
	11.3%	9.0%		
All Owner Units	20,522	23,582	2.48%	2.75%
	100.0%	100.0%		

Source: 1993 and 1996 Housing and Vacancy Survey Data Files.

Rental vacancy rates in the Bronx, as depicted in Table 1.7, increased from 3.99 percent in 1993 to 5.43 percent in 1996, giving that borough the highest rental vacancy rate in the city. Rental vacancy rates were below 5 percent in each of the city's other four boroughs. The tightest market was in Queens, with a 3.28 percent vacancy rate. In absolute terms, the boroughs of Brooklyn and Manhattan had the most rental units available for rent—25,937 and 20,185, respectively. The median asking rent for vacant apartments, however, was $619, slightly above the median rent for all apartments in the city.

Characteristics of the Rental Housing Stock. As might be expected, the age of New York City's housing stock varies with its subtenure. As shown in Table 1.8, just over three-quarters of all rent controlled units were built before 1930, compared to only 53.3 percent of rent stabilized housing. *In rem* housing has the highest proportion of pre-1930 dwelling units (85.5 percent) and public housing, of course, the lowest. Almost one-half of unregulated dwelling units were built before 1930. The age of the city's housing stock also varies by borough. Unsurprisingly, Manhattan has the greatest proportion of pre-1930 housing (58.9 percent), with Queens and Staten Island having only 24.3 percent and 6.1 percent, respectively.

As might be expected, Table 1.8 shows that median contract rents were highest for unregulated apartments ($680) and lowest for public and *in rem* housing ($225 and $250, respectively). As expected, median rents for rent controlled apartments ($428) were substantially lower than rents for rent stabilized dwellings ($600). Among the city's boroughs, Manhattan, despite its relatively high proportions of rent regulated, public, and *in rem* housing units, had the highest median rents. The median rent in Queens was a close second, followed, in order, by Staten Island, Brooklyn, and the Bronx. When only rents in the unregulated

TABLE 1.7
Vacant Units Available for Rent by Borough, 1993 and 1996

Subtenure	Vacant Units Available for Rent		Net Vacancy Rate (Percent)	
	1993	1996	1993	1996
Bronx	13,620	18,825	3.99	5.43
Brooklyn	20,015	25,937	3.25	4.20
Manhattan	21,213	20,185	3.52	3.47
Queens	13,304	14,020	3.07	3.28
Staten Island	2,193	2,289	4.14	4.17
Total	70,345	81,256	3.44	4.01

Source: U.S. Bureau of the Census, 1993 and 1996 New York City Housing and Vacancy Survey Data Files.

TABLE 1.8
Housing Characteristics of Renters by Subtenure

	All Rental Units	Controlled	Stabilized	Other Regulated	Other Unregulated	Public Housing	In Rem
Occupied Units	1,946,165	70,572	1,014,751	127,000	545,198	165,646	22,997
Vacant and Available	81,256	NA	37,549	4,576	30,468	6,450	2,214
Rental Vacancy Rate	4.01	NA	3.57	3.48	5.29	3.75	8.78
Median Contract Rent	$595	$428	$600	$530	$680	$225	$250
Median Rent/Income	28%	30%	28%	33%	26%	28%	30%
Crowded Households	67,547	0	48,959	944	15,129	1,606	909
% Crowded Households	3.5	0.0	4.8	0.7	2.8	1.0	4.0
% Built before 1930	45.7	75.9	53.3	22.4	45.3	0.0	85.5
Mean # of Maintenance Deficiencies	1.37	1.41	1.55	1.19	0.89	1.71	3.18
% of Boarded-Up Buildings Nearby	11.4	14.6	10.3	11.0	11.6	11.3	49.4

Source: 1996 Housing and Vacancy Survey Data File.

market are considered, however, Manhattan's median contract rent of $1,175 is considerably higher than the average Queens rent of $700.

Characteristics of Tenants. Median household income, as shown in Table 1.9, roughly tracks the average rents of housing in the various subtenures. The lowest annual incomes are earned, on average, by public housing tenants ($9,000) and residents of *in rem* housing ($8,400). Rent controlled tenants earn one and a half the incomes of public housing residents ($13,428), but much less than rent stabilized tenants ($25,350) or occupants of unregulated housing ($30,000). In terms of geographic variation, the median incomes of tenants in Manhattan were the highest ($30,000), followed by those in Queens ($28,500), Staten Island ($28,000), Brooklyn ($20,000), and the Bronx ($16,224).

The poverty rate among renter households in New York City is 26.3 percent. As might be expected, the highest rates of poverty are experienced by residents of public (55.3 percent) and *in rem* (57.8 percent) housing. The proportion of households in poverty in rent controlled

TABLE 1.9
Occupant Characteristics of Renters by Subtenure

	All Rental Units	Controlled	Stabilized	Other Regulated	Unregulated	Public Housing	In Rem
Median Income ($)	23,704	13,428	25,350	13,500	30,000	9,000	8,400
Median Age	42	70	41	50	38	50	45
% Householders ≥ 65	17.2	61.7	14.9	31.4	10.6	24.2	14.4
% Receiving Public Assistance	23.1	12.6	21.0	29.5	16.4	52.9	56.6
% Receiving AFDC	9.5	2.5	8.8	10.1	6.4	22.8	27.6
% below Poverty Level	26.3	26.6	23.6	37.5	18.4	55.3	57.8
Mean Household Size	2.37	1.65	2.25	2.16	2.66	2.55	2.75
Mean Years of Tenure	9.64	35.59	8.69	10.79	6.16	14.72	11.37

Source: 1996 Housing and Vacancy Survey Data File.

dwellings (26.6 percent) is greater than for rent stabilization (23.6 percent) and also greater than for the private unregulated sector (18.4 percent).

The proportion of households receiving public assistance likewise varies among the subtenures, although not necessarily in lockstep with median income. Fifty-seven percent of all residents of *in rem* housing receive public assistance, as do 52.9 percent of public housing tenants. Interestingly, the proportion of households receiving assistance is lowest for rent controlled dwellings. Only 12.6 percent of rent controlled tenants receive public assistance, compared to 16.4 percent of households in the unregulated rental market and 21.0 percent in rent stabilized apartments.

The surprisingly low proportion of households receiving public assistance in rent controlled apartments may be partly explained by age differences among the various subtenures. The median age of householders in rent controlled housing (70 years) is thirty-two years higher than the average for tenants of unregulated housing and twenty-nine years more than tenants in rent stabilized dwellings. Median ages for public and *in rem* housing tenants are 50 and 45 respectively.

Households of different racial and ethnic backgrounds are not distributed evenly throughout the rental sector. As Table 1.10 indicates, although they constitute only 39.9 percent of all renters, white households occupy 66 percent of the city's rent controlled apartments. White households are also overrepresented in rent stabilized apartments, although the magnitude of the discrepancy is much smaller than for rent control. Black households, while underrepresented in rent regulated housing, are overrepresented in public and *in rem* housing. Although

TABLE 1.10
Race and Immigrant Status of Renters by Subtenure

Householder	All Rental Units	Rent Controlled	Rent Stabilized	Other Regulated	Unregulated	Public Housing	In Rem Housing
White	776,520	46,578	440,402	38,481	237,706	12,589	1,288
	39.9%	66.0%	43.4%	30.3%	43.6%	7.6%	5.6%
Black	500,164	9,527	203,965	52,832	132,483	88,124	13,059
	25.7%	13.5%	20.1%	41.6%	24.3%	53.2%	56.8%
Non-Puerto	272,463	7,269	171,493	11,049	65,424	14,577	3,265
Rican Hispanic	14.0%	10.3%	16.9%	8.7%	12.0%	8.8%	14.2%
Puerto Rican	253,001	5,575	123,800	19,050	52,884	46,216	5,334
	13.0%	7.9%	12.2%	15.0%	9.7%	27.9%	23.2%
Asian	132,339	1,270	70,018	4,953	53,429	2,485	23
	6.8%	1.8%	6.9%	3.9%	9.8%	1.5%	0.1%
Other	11,677	353	5,074	635	3,271	1,491	69
	0.6%	0.5%	0.5%	0.5%	0.6%	0.9%	0.3%
Total[1]	1,946,165	70,572	1,014,751	127,001	545,198	165,647	22,992
	100.0%	100.0%	100.0%	100.0%	100.0%	100.0%	100.0%
Immigrants[2]	933,292	24,912	535,789	48,514	258,969	56,486	8,622
	47.7%	35.3%	52.8%	38.2%	47.5%	34.1%	37.5%

Source: 1996 Housing and Vacancy Survey Data File.
1. Universe: All occupied units.
2. A household is defined to be an immigrant household if the householder was foreign born and both of his or her parents were foreign born. For purposes of this analysis a person born in Puerto Rico is considered foreign born.

they constitute only 25.7 percent of the city's renter households, black households comprise over half of the households living in public and *in rem* housing. Similar patterns are exhibited by Puerto Rican households.

SEVERE HOUSING PROBLEMS IN NEW YORK CITY

Under New York State law, since 1950, housing conditions in New York City have constituted an emergency. In this section, we describe and attempt to quantify, where possible, several housing-related problems. These problems include unaffordable housing and substandard housing conditions. Issues having to do with racial and ethnic disparities in housing outcomes and discrimination are reserved for the final section of this chapter.

Micro-data recently made available from the 1996 Housing and Vacancy Survey make it possible to estimate the number of households in New York City who experience one or more "severe" housing problems as well as to examine the households' characteristics, subtenures, and locations.[8] For the purpose of this analysis, a severe housing problem is defined as any one of the following:

- For tenants, contract rents that exceed 50 percent of their incomes.
- For owners, housing expenses (including mortgage payments) that exceed 60 percent of their incomes.
- For owners or renters, living in buildings that are dilapidated.
- For owners or renters, living in units that have five or more housing maintenance deficiencies.

Severe Housing Quality Problems

A severe housing quality problem is defined to include those households living in a dilapidated building *or* in a dwelling unit with five or more specified maintenance deficiencies. The Census Bureau characterizes a building as dilapidated if it fails to provide safe and adequate shelter to the occupants. A structure is rated dilapidated if it shows one or more critical defects or a combination of intermediate defects or inadequate original construction (U.S. Department of Commerce 1994). The judgment as to whether a building is dilapidated is made by a Census Bureau employee based on his or her observation of a building. Unlike the dilapidation indicator, maintenance deficiencies are based on the responses of dwelling unit occupants themselves. Each occupant is asked whether any of the following maintenance deficiencies exist in his or her unit: (1) heating equipment breakdowns, (2) insufficient heat, (3) rodent infestation, (4) cracks and holes in the walls, ceilings, or floors, (5) broken plaster or peeling paint larger than 8.5 by 11 inches, (6) toilet breakdowns, and (7) water leaks (U.S. Census Bureau 1994).

In 1996, an estimated 147,507 households, or 5.3 percent of all households in New York, experienced one or more severe housing quality problems. Consistent with the experience of other American cities, the proportion of the city's housing stock that has severe housing quality problems has declined substantially over the past twenty-five years. Nevertheless, the proportion of households experiencing severe housing quality problems in 1996 increased from 4.4 percent in 1993. As reported in Table 1.11, in 1996, approximately 1 percent of the households in New York (30,164) lived in dilapidated buildings. The number of households living in dwelling units that had five or more maintenance deficiencies (123,773) was more than four times the number in dilapidated buildings.

TABLE 1.11
Severe Housing Problems in New York City: Boroughs and Subtenures

	Unit Has Five or More Maintenance Deficiencies	Unit Is in Dilapidated Building	Renter Pays More Than 50% of Income for Rent	Owner Pays More Than 60% of Income for Housing	Occupant Has Affordability or Housing Quality Problem
Number of Households	123,773	30,164	525,736	67,916	735,819
	4.5%	1.1%	18.9%	2.4%	26.5%
Borough					
Bronx	32,633	6,148	109,281	5,179	141,531
	7.9%	1.5%	26.5%	1.3%	34.4%
Brooklyn	35,895	7,937	180,403	25,644	245,975
	4.4%	1.0%	22.2%	3.2%	30.2%
Manhattan	43,506	11,191	136,818	7,675	186,939
	6.2%	1.6%	19.4%	1.1%	26.6%
Queens	11,826	3,341	88,955	26,002	137,976
	1.7%	0.5%	12.5%	3.6%	19.3%
Staten Island	1,131	1,538	10,287	3,958	18,898
	0.8%	1.1%	7.5%	2.9%	13.8%
Tenure/Subtenure					
Rent Controlled	4,264	747	17,527	NA	20,582
	6.0%	1.1%	24.8%		29.2%
Rent Stabilized	76,714	14,338	290,026	NA	346,132
	7.5%	1.4%	28.6%		34.1%
Other Rent Regulation	5,048	563	47,188	NA	49,281
	4.0%	0.4%	37.2%		38.8%
Unregulated Rental	16,721	6,172	134,200	NA	140,874
	3.1%	1.1%	24.6%		25.8%
Public Housing	11,496	187	28,685	NA	38,410
	6.9%	0.1%	17.3%		23.2%
In Rem Housing	6,048	3,786	8,113	NA	13,527
	26.3%	16.5%	35.3%		58.6%
Conventional Owner	1,836	3,407	NA	64,963	70,787
	0.3%	0.6%		12.0%	13.0%
Co-ops/Condos	1,266	829	NA	21,199	22,189
	0.5%	0.3%		8.8%	9.2%
Mitchell-Lama Housing	379	141	NA	6,351	6,504
	0.7%	0.3%		12.5%	12.8%
Rental Buildings with More Than 100 Units	3.8%	0.2%	24.7%	NA	26.1%
Frequency in Units Where Rent < $500	8.5%	2.1%	25.5%	NA	33.0%

Source: 1996 Housing and Vacancy Survey Data Files.

The geographic pattern of dilapidation and maintenance deficiencies varied a bit. The largest number of dilapidated buildings were located in the borough of Manhattan followed by Brooklyn and the Bronx. With respect to dwelling units with five or more maintenance deficiencies, Manhattan again had the most units with this problem, with Brooklyn and the Bronx close behind. As a proportion of all buildings or dwelling units in a borough, Manhattan led the way in dilapidation (1.6 percent), and the Bronx had the highest rate of maintenance deficiencies (7.9 percent). Queens and Staten Island have far fewer dwelling units that experience severe quality problems than the city's other three boroughs.

In absolute terms, the largest numbers of severe quality problems are located in Central Harlem, East Harlem, Washington Heights and the Lower East Side in Manhattan, Crown Heights in Brooklyn, and Kingsbridge Heights in the Bronx. As a proportion of total housing units, Figure 1.1 shows that the highest rates of severe housing quality problems tend to cluster in these same neighborhoods as well as several neighborhoods in the South Bronx and North Crown Heights in Brooklyn.

The largest proportion of severe housing quality problems were found in the rent stabilized sector. Approximately one-half of all units in dilapidated buildings and 62 percent of units with five or more maintenance deficiencies were rent stabilized. These proportions are not quite as surprising as they appear considering that rent stabilized apartments are the largest of the city's subtenures, constituting more than one-third of all its housing and just over half of all rental housing.

The highest incidence of severe housing quality problems in each subtenure is unquestionably found in the city's *in rem* housing stock. As Table 1.11 shows, 16.5 percent of all *in rem* units were in dilapidated buildings, almost twelve times the rate of dilapidation in the second highest ranking subtenure, rent stabilized housing. With respect to maintenance deficiencies, 26.3 percent of *in rem* housing units had severe problems compared to the next highest rate of 7.5 percent for rent stabilized housing. In the rental sector, the lowest rates of dilapidation and maintenance deficiencies existed in public housing and unregulated units, respectively. When all housing subtenures are analyzed, the owner-occupied housing subtenures exhibited the lowest rates of severe housing quality problems.

In terms of building characteristics, severe housing quality problems are less likely to occur in large buildings, perhaps because of the higher volume of rents commanded by these buildings, their locations, or different styles of management. The dilapidation rate for buildings with one hundred or more units is less than one-fifth the rate for all buildings; similarly the rate of maintenance deficiencies is much smaller than the citywide average. Unsurprisingly, the prevalence of severe housing quality problems is greater in low-rent dwellings. Com-

FIGURE 1.1
Proportion of Households with Severe Quality Problems, New York City by Sub-Borough Area

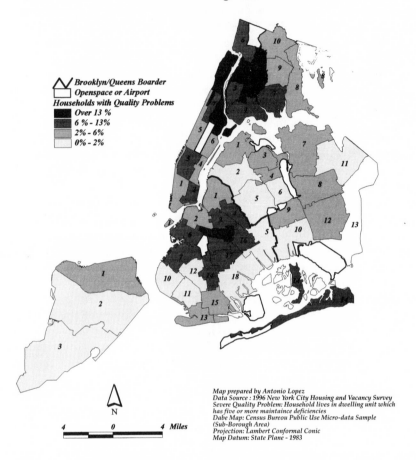

Map prepared by Antonio Lopez
Data Source : 1996 New York City Housing and Vacancy Survey
Severe Quality Problem: Household lives in dwelling unit which
has five or more maintaince deficiencies
Dabe Map: Census Bureau Public Use Micro-data Sample
(Sub-Borough Area)
Projection: Lambert Conformal Conic
Map Datum: State Plane - 1983

pared to the citywide averages, the rate of dilapidation is almost double for apartments that rent for less than $500, and maintenance deficiencies are almost 1.9 times as likely to occur.

The profile of people living in dwellings with severe housing quality problems is not surprising. As Table 1.12 demonstrates, over one-third of all households in the City of New York have "very low incomes," defined by HUD to be incomes less than half of the median income for the metropolitan area.[9] However, over half of all households

TABLE 1.12
Severe Housing Problems in New York City: Household Characteristics

Characteristic	Single Persons with Children	Elderly Household	Household Income below 50% of Median	Householder Not in Labor Force	Household Receives Public Assistance	Household Receives Housing Subsidy	Immigrants
All Households	8.5%	23.6%	37.4%	38.1%	19.2%	10.9%	44.3%
Households Living in Units with Five or More Maintenance Deficiencies	21.9%	14.2%	61.6%	45.6%	46.1%	31.4%	47.4%
Households Living in Dilapidated Buildings	13.3%	17.5%	52.4%	35.1%	32.7%	19.8%	51.5%
Renters Paying More Than 50% of Income for Rent	22.0%	27.8%	94.5%	67.0%	50.0%	32.1%	52.9%
Owners Paying More Than 60% of Income for Housing	5.8%	46.1%	69.0%	56.0%	6.1%	NA	51.9%
Households with Affordability or Housing Quality Problem	21.1%	27.6%	85.6%	61.3%	42.1%	30.2%	52.3%

Note: Cells indicate what proportion of households experiencing a given severe housing problem (row) are composed of a particular demographic group (column)
Source: 1996 Housing and Vacancy Survey Data Files.

living in dilapidated buildings earn very low incomes. Similarly, 61.6 percent of those living in dwelling units with five or more maintenance deficiencies earn very low incomes. Compared to all households in the city, a much higher proportion of households experiencing severe housing quality problems are comprised of single-person households with children, persons not in the labor force, recipients of public assistance, persons receiving housing subsidies, and, to a lesser extent, immigrants. One group that is not overrepresented in physically substandard dwelling units is elderly households.

Severe Housing Affordability Problems

Determining what proportion of a household's income dedicated to housing-related expenses is too much is of course fraught with difficulties (Stone 1993). With respect to federal housing programs, prior to 1981, renters who paid more than one-quarter of their incomes for rent were considered to have affordability problems; this proportion was subsequently raised by Congress to 30 percent. For purposes of this chapter a severe affordability problem for renters is defined as occurring when a household pays more than half its gross income for rent.[10] For homeowners, a severe affordability problem is defined as a household paying more than 60 percent of its gross income on housing-related expenses.[11]

In 1996, an estimated 593,652 households in New York City experienced severe affordability problems. As Table 1.11 indicates, the lion's share of these households, 525,736, were renters; only 67,916 were homeowners. Expressed as a proportion of all city households, 18.9 percent had excessively high rent burdens, and 2.4 percent had extremely burdensome homeownership expenses. Although differences in the Census Bureau's methods of imputing incomes and rents for nonrespondents make direct comparisons to 1993 difficult, comparisons based on actual responses to the HVS suggest that the proportion of renter households experiencing severe affordability problems increased slightly between 1993 and 1996. The number of renter households experiencing a severe affordability problem rose by 1 percent; among homeowners, however, severe affordability problems declined by approximately 1.5 percent.

As might be expected given the widely divergent homeownership and renter occupancy rates among the boroughs, the geographic patterns for severe housing affordability problems vary significantly among the two subtenures. In absolute terms, the largest numbers of renters with severe affordability problems lived in Brooklyn and Manhattan, whereas among homeowners severe housing affordability problems were concentrated in Brooklyn and Queens. The highest rate of severe renter affordability problems was in the Bronx, where over one-quarter of all households paid more than half their incomes for rent. Renter affordability problems were least prevalent in Queens (12.5 percent) and Staten Island (7.5 percent). However, among homeowners, the rate of all households experiencing severe affordability problems was highest in Queens (3.6 percent) and in Brooklyn (3.2 percent).

Relatively large clusters of households, in absolute terms, face severe housing affordability problems in the South Bronx; much of Manhattan south of 96th Street as well as Washington Heights; Bedford-Stuyvesant, East New York, Bensonhurst, Flatbush, and Sheepshead Bay in Brooklyn; and Forest Hills and Flushing in Queens. Figure 1.2 shows especially high rates of severe housing affordability exist in the South Bronx as well as Brooklyn's Bedford-Stuyvesant and East New York neighborhoods. Interestingly, severe affordability problems are not necessarily prevalent in the same neighborhoods as severe housing quality problems.[12] Indeed, the sub-borough area with the greatest

FIGURE 1.2
Proportion of Households with Severe Affordability Problems, New York City by Sub-Borough Area

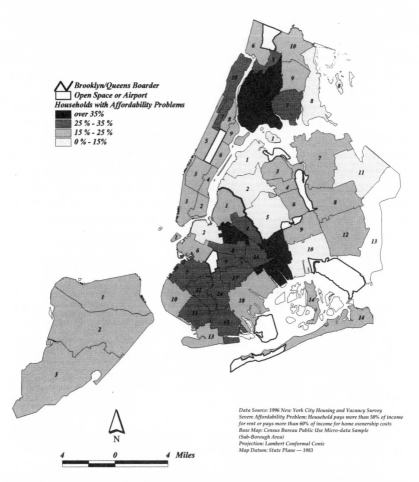

Brooklyn/Queens Boarder
Open Space or Airport
Households with Affordability Problems
over 35%
25 % - 35 %
15 % - 25 %
0 % - 15%

N

4   0   4 *Miles*

Data Source: 1996 New York City Housing and Vacancy Survey
Severe Affordability Problem: Household pays more than 50% of income
for rent or pays more than 60% of income for home ownership costs
Base Map: Census Bureau Public Use Micro-data Sample
(Sub-Borough Area)
Projection: Lambert Conformal Conic
Map Datum: State Plane — 1983

number of households experiencing affordability problems is the relatively affluent Upper East Side.[13]

Despite living in dwelling units subject to rent regulation, tenants of rent stabilized buildings experienced the third highest rate of severe housing affordability problems in the city—28.6 percent. The number of people living in rent stabilized apartments who paid more than half their incomes in rent in 1996 was approximately 290,026, accounting for 55.2 percent of all tenants with severe affordability problems. The highest rate of households paying more than 50 percent of their incomes in rent was in other rent regulated housing, where 37.2 percent of tenants experienced severe burdens. The lowest rates of severe housing affordability problems existed among residents of public housing and all owner-occupied subtenures.

From the perspective of public policy, excessive housing cost burdens are less problematic among relatively affluent households than among the poor. Nevertheless, as Table 1.12 shows, severe housing affordability problems are overwhelmingly concentrated among very low income New Yorkers. Despite constituting only 37.4 percent of the City's population, very low income households comprise 94.5 percent of all renters who pay more than half of their incomes in rent and 69.0 percent of all homeowners who pay more than 60 percent for shelter. Just over one-fifth of all renters with severe housing affordability problems are single-person households with children, 67 percent have no one in the labor force, 50 percent receive public assistance, and about one-third receive housing subsidies. More than one-half of all households with severe affordability problems are foreign born.

The Incidence of Severe Housing Problems in New York City

In 1996, 735,819 households, or more than one-quarter of all households in the city, endured one or more severe housing problems. Between 1993 and 1996 the proportion of households experiencing one or more severe housing problems increased by more than 0.5 percent.[14] Because the vast majority of severe housing problems concern affordability, the patterns for affordability predominate in Tables 1.11 and 1.12. In terms of absolute numbers, Brooklyn and Manhattan have most of the city's severe problems; in relative terms, the highest incidence of severe housing problems is in the Bronx. Similarly, rent stabilized housing has the largest share of severe housing problems, although the highest rate, by far, is in *in rem* housing, where over half the residents pay more than half their incomes in rent or live in substandard conditions. The lowest rates of severe housing problems exist in owner-occupied housing and in public housing (largely because federal rules limit rents to 30 percent of income).

Severe housing problems are predominantly the problems of poor New Yorkers. Very low income households constitute 37.4 percent of New York's population. Nevertheless, almost nine out of ten households that experience one or more severe housing problems earn very low incomes. Among all very low income households, over one-half have severe housing cost burdens or live in poor quality housing.

THE SHORTAGE OF AFFORDABLE RENTAL HOUSING
IN NEW YORK CITY

As the previous section demonstrates, although not insubstantial, severe housing quality problems have been dwarfed in recent years by problems of affordability. In a recent article, Nelson (1995) has examined national housing statistics and concluded that although there exists a net shortage of affordable units for certain extremely low income households, when all low income households who would be eligible for federal housing assistance are considered as a group this shortage disappears. Nelson interprets these results as supporting more stringent targeting requirements for federal housing assistance.

In an effort to compare New York City's affordable housing "shortage" to the nation's, we replicate her methodology using data from the 1996 Housing and Vacancy Survey. Our analysis uses as its universe all New York City households with incomes less than the adjusted median income level for the New York metropolitan area. The median income level is adjusted for household size. Each household whose income was less than the area median income was placed into an appropriate income decile based on the ratio of its income to the median income level for a household its size.[15] A housing unit was deemed affordable for a household in a given income decile if the unit rented for less than 30 percent of the upper bound of that income decile.[16] The 30 percent affordability standard was chosen based upon its use in determining appropriate tenant rent contributions for federally assisted housing.

Table 1.13 shows, for each income decile, the number of households, "affordable" occupied rental units, "affordable" vacant rental units, and the resulting surplus or shortage of rental housing.[17] These data show a substantial shortfall of affordable rental housing in New York City. The largest deficit exists for households earning the lowest incomes. For the 178,872 households in the lowest income decile, there were 47,779 affordable rental units in New York City. Of these 47,779 units, only 187 units were vacant. Thus the shortage of affordable rental housing for these poorest households was 130,876 units. Each of the bottom four income deciles exhibits a shortage of affordable housing units. Beginning with the fifth income decile (that is, households earning between 41–50 percent of the area median income) a surplus of affordable rental units exists. Nevertheless, the acute affordable housing shortage at the lowest income deciles more than offsets the surplus at relatively higher income deciles, resulting in an aggregate shortage of

TABLE 1.13
Estimated Affordable Rental Housing Shortage/Surplus in New York City

Income Decile[1]	Number of Households	Number of Affordable Occupied Units	Number of Affordable Vacant Units	Total Affordable Units	Surplus (Shortage)	Cumulative Surplus/ (Shortage)
0–10%	178,872	47,779	187	47,996	(130,876)	(130,876)
11–20%	259,329	134,822	2,272	137,094	(122,235)	(253,111)
21–30%	245,224	112,470	5,081	117,551	(127,673)	(380,784)
31–40%	188,113	149,703	4,440	154,143	(33,970)	(414,754)
41–50%	168,911	289,692	10,137	299,829	130,918	(283,836)
51–60%	174,089	348,291	19,964	368,255	194,166	(89,670)
61–70%	156,099	303,667	16,070	319,737	163,638	73,968
71–80%	150,049	206,863	10,607	217,470	67,421	141,389
81–90%	137,986	98,599	5,781	104,380	(33,606)	107,783
91–100%	113,786	67,778	2,819	70,597	(43,189)	64,594

Source: 1996 Housing and Vacancy Survey Data File.
1. Percentage of adjusted (by family size) area median income.

affordable rental units for households that earn less than 50 percent of the area median income.

As expected, the finding that the most severe affordable housing shortage in New York City is present at the very bottom of the income distribution is consistent with Nelson's results for the entire United States. However, Nelson finds that there is a cumulative affordable housing *surplus* nationwide for households with incomes less than 50 percent of the median income; the ratio of affordable rental units to households with incomes below 50 percent of the median is 1.03. In this respect, New York City's housing market is demonstrably different from the national housing market. In New York City there is a cumulative affordable housing *deficit* of 283,836 rental housing units for households earning less than 50 percent of the median area income. The ratio of affordable rental units to very low income renters is 0.73.

This estimated shortfall of affordable housing units underestimates the magnitude of the housing affordability problem in New York City. Many of the apartments characterized as "affordable" in this analysis are not actually occupied by low- and moderate-income households. Indeed, of the 756,613 housing units that were affordable to households with incomes below 50 percent of the area median, 267,207 were occupied by households earning incomes above this level. Therefore the real shortage of affordable housing for very low income households would, in reality, be closer to 551,043 units.[18]

The shortage of affordable housing in New York has contributed to the growth of homelessness. Along with a host of other factors, such as deinstitutionalization of the mentally ill without appropriate alternative support networks, increased use or abuse of controlled substances and the breakdown of family networks, the gap between what New Yorkers can pay and the housing that is available has caused many New Yorkers to live in shelters or on the street. Estimates of homelessness among New York residents vary widely. In a recent report (City Planning Commission 1995), the city indicates that it shelters about 7,000 single adults and 5,700 homeless families each day. Culhane, Metraux, and Wachter (see chapter 8 in this volume) show that when one analyzes shelter admissions for an entire year rather than just a single day, the number of persons or households in New York that utilize City facilities annually is considerably higher. For example, in 1995, 24,153 single persons and 13,302 families used these facilities. Neither of these sets of numbers account for people who are either doubled up with friends or relatives or who live on the streets and do not avail themselves of the city's services or shelters.

RACIAL AND ETHNIC DISPARITIES

In New York City, as elsewhere in the nation, many housing market outcomes differ based on whether the household happens to be composed of members of certain racial and ethnic minority groups. One particularly important housing market outcome is where the household lives and whether that household's choices have been constrained by racial or ethnic discrimination. As Table 1.14 indicates, in 1996 black and Hispanic households were not distributed evenly throughout the city. Figures 1.3 and 1.4 demonstrate pictorially areas of racial and ethnic concentration in the city. Sub-borough areas with the highest proportions of black households include Brooklyn's Bedford-Stuyvesant, North Crown Heights, Ocean Hill/Brownsville, and East Flatbush as well as Manhattan's Central Harlem. Hispanic households formed disproportionately high proportions of the residents of Washington Heights and Mott Haven.

The method most often used by social scientists to assess housing segregation is the index of dissimilarity, which measures what proportion of a metropolitan area's population would have to move to achieve an even distribution of minority groups throughout the area. A high level of segregation is generally thought to be indicated by an index value above 60. Among the twenty-three metropolitan areas in the United States with the largest black populations in 1990, the average index of dissimilarity was 74.5, down slightly from 78.8 in 1980. In New

TABLE 1.14
Race and Immigrant Status by Borough

Householder	City	Bronx	Brooklyn	Manhattan	Queens	Staten Island
White	1,308,987	89,274	349,283	417,699	343,278	109,453
	47.1%	21.7%	42.9%	59.3%	48.1%	79.8%
Black	669,089	134,912	283,250	98,224	142,309	10,395
	24.1%	32.8%	34.8%	14.0%	19.9%	7.6%
Non-Puerto	306,730	60,129	55,398	86,860	98,688	5,655
Rican Hispanic	11.0%	14.6%	6.8%	12.3%	13.8%	4.1%
Puerto Rican	286,535	114,176	79,964	51,335	34,428	6,632
	10.3%	27.7%	9.8%	7.3%	4.8%	4.8%
Asian	195,931	10,166	40,525	48,281	92,360	4,599
	7.0%	2.5%	5.0%	6.9%	12.9%	3.4%
Other	13,075	3,118	5,124	1,544	2,915	375
	0.5%	0.8%	0.6%	0.2%	0.4%	0.3%
Total[1]	2,780,349	411,775	813,544	703,943	713,978	137,109
	100.0%	100.0%	100.0%	100.0%	100.0%	100.0%
Immigrants[2]	1,227,674	197,318	391,982	249,832	364,097	24,445
	44.3%	47.9%	48.2%	35.5%	51.0%	17.8%

Source: 1996 Housing and Vacancy Survey Data File.
1. Universe: All occupied units.
2. A household is defined to be an immigrant household if the householder was foreign born and both of his or her parents were foreign born. For purposes of this analysis a person born in Puerto Rico is considered foreign born.

York, the index value in 1990 was 78, essentially unchanged from 1980 (Yinger 1995, 112). Brooklyn and Queens are the most segregated boroughs according to this measure. For the twenty metropolitan areas with the largest Hispanic populations in the United States, the average index value was 48.9 in 1990. In New York, the index took on the value of 54 (Yinger 1995, 113). Thus among blacks, the level of segregation in the New York metropolitan area is high in absolute terms, although not terribly higher than the national average for large metropolitan areas. Segregation among Hispanics, however, is considerably more moderate.

High levels of segregation between whites and blacks and between non-Hispanic whites and Hispanics might be explained by several factors, including income disparities among whites and nonwhites, different preferences for neighborhood racial and ethnic composition, and illegal discrimination. In New York, as well as the nation, a correlation exists between income and race or ethnicity. For example, according to the Housing and Vacancy Survey, in 1995 the median income among white non-Hispanic households was $36,500 compared to $24,400 among black households and $17,000 among Puerto Rican households, the largest of the city's Hispanic groups. Since low cost

FIGURE 1.3
Proportion of Black Households, New York City by Sub-Borough

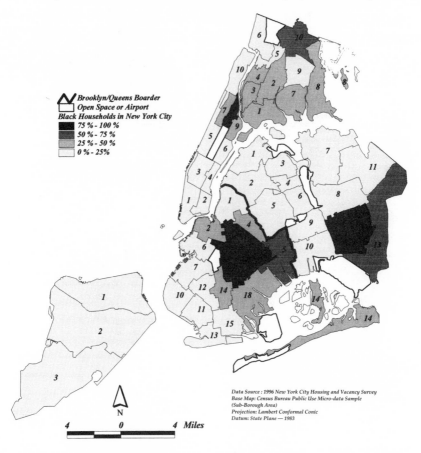

Brooklyn/Queens Boarder
Open Space or Airport
Black Households in New York City
■ 75 % - 100 %
  50 % - 75 %
  25 % - 50 %
  0 % - 25%

Data Source : 1996 New York City Housing and Vacancy Survey
Base Map: Census Bureau Public Use Micro-data Sample
(Sub-Borough Area)
Projection: Lambert Conformal Conic
Datum: State Plane — 1983

N

4   0   4 Miles

housing is frequently located in certain geographic areas of the city, one
might expect to find that lower incomes contribute to segregated housing patterns. Although income may play a role in housing segregation,
several studies in other metropolitan areas suggest that this role is actually quite limited (Schill and Wachter 1995). Similarly, different preferences among white and nonwhite households for neighborhood racial
and ethnic composition may explain at least a portion of New York's
segregated housing patterns (Schill 1996).

Substantial evidence suggests that discrimination against black
and Hispanic households may limit their choices in the housing market.
The most direct method of estimating the incidence of discrimination

FIGURE 1.4

Proportion of Hispanic Households, New York City by Sub-Borough Area

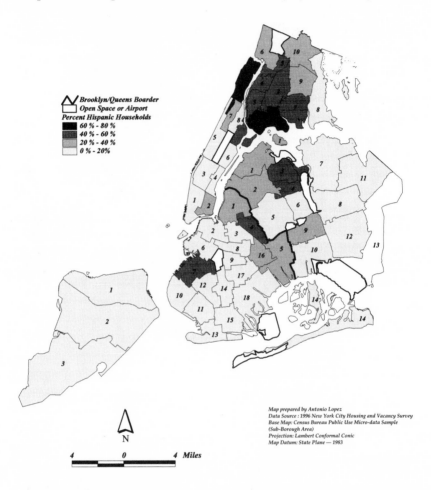

Map prepared by Antonio Lopez
Data Source : 1996 New York City Housing and Vacancy Survey
Base Map: Census Bureau Public Use Micro-data Sample
(Sub-Borough Area)
Projection: Lambert Conformal Conic
Map Datum: State Plane — 1983

is through the use of matched testers. Pairs of individuals—one minority and one majority—are sent separately to the offices of real estate agents or landlords, posing as apartment seekers. These testers are matched with respect to most characteristics other than race or ethnicity so that discrimination can be inferred from differential treatment.

In the mid-1980s, the New York City Commission on Human Rights investigated discrimination by real estate agents in four of the city's boroughs. In eighteen of thirty-two separate investigations, the city determined that probable cause existed to believe that discrimination had occurred. Only three agents or landlords were conclusively found not to discriminate, with the remaining investigations suspended because of broker suspicion, tester error, or other administrative problems (Webber undated).

The Human Rights Commission testing investigations likely overstate the prevalence of discrimination in New York City because one of the criteria for selecting the agents to be tested was the existence of allegations of discrimination. More systematic data, however, can be obtained from the Housing Discrimination Study (HDS) conducted by the Urban Institute in 1989. The study involved 3,800 fair housing (matched tester) audits in twenty-five metropolitan areas (Turner et al. 1993). The results of this study demonstrate the persistence of discrimination in the housing market. The HDS authors used econometric techniques to obtain national estimates of the likelihood that black or Hispanic persons would encounter discrimination in housing-related transactions. Based upon the national sample, they concluded that 53 percent of black renters and 59 percent of black homebuyers could be expected to encounter one or more incidents of discrimination. Among Hispanics, the expected incidence of discrimination was 46 percent for renters and 56 percent for homebuyers.

Relatively small sample sizes make it difficult to draw conclusions about rates of housing discrimination in individual cities included in the HDS. Nevertheless, the authors oversampled a subset of the cities, including New York. According to the authors, the proportion of blacks who encountered comparatively unfavorable treatment in the New York housing market ranged from 40 percent to 48 percent (Yinger 1991, 43–53). Between 53 percent and 61 percent of Hispanic home seekers in the New York metropolitan area sample had similar experiences. Econometric studies based on the HDS data also suggest that the incidence of discriminatory acts in New York was greater than many other metropolitan areas included in the sample (Yinger 1991, 55–59).

Existing research supports the proposition that substantial discrimination against racial and ethnic minorities exists in the New York City housing market. Discrimination by actors in the housing market limits the housing opportunities available to minority households and, in so doing, affects not just their housing conditions, but their health and welfare as well as social mobility.

Regardless of its cause, racial and ethnic disparities in housing outcomes exist in New York. The homeownership rates among black households (25 percent) and Hispanic households (13 percent) are much lower than the 40 percent homeownership rate for whites. Furthermore, as Table 1.15 shows, the incidence of severe housing quality

TABLE 1.15
Severe Housing Problems in New York City: Racial and Ethnic Disparities

All Income Groups	Unit Has Five or More Maintenance Deficiencies	Unit Is in Dilapidated Building	Renter Pays More Than 50% of Income for Rent	Owner Pays More Than 60% of Income for Housing	Occupant Has Affordability or Housing Quality Problem
White Households	1.6%	0.7%	15.0%	3.1%	20.7%
Black Households	6.9%	1.3%	20.8%	2.4%	30.1%
Puerto Rican Households	8.3%	1.4%	28.0%	1.0%	34.7%
Hispanic Non-Puerto Rican Households	7.6%	1.9%	24.9%	1.3%	34.4%
Asian Households	2.5%	1.2%	14.9%	3.3%	22.4%
Very Low Income Households					
White Households	2.3%	1.0%	45.4%	7.7%	58.1%
Black Households	9.8%	1.5%	47.2%	3.7%	56.8%
Puerto Rican Households	11.2%	1.8%	50.0%	1.0%	55.2%
Hispanic Non-Puerto Rican Households	10.3%	2.4%	52.1%	1.4%	60.8%
Asian Households	3.9%	1.5%	48.7%	5.9%	59.9%

Source: 1996 Housing and Vacancy Survey Data Files.

problems is much higher among black and Hispanic New Yorkers as compared to white households. For example, 0.7 percent of white households live in dilapidated buildings compared to 1.3 percent of all black and 1.4 percent of Puerto Rican households. Similarly only 1.6 percent of all white households live in buildings with 5 or more maintenance deficiencies compared to 6.9 percent of black households and 8.3 percent of Puerto Rican households. Severe affordability problems also disproportionately affect minority renters. Rent burdens of 50 percent or more affect 15.0 percent of white households, 20.8 percent of blacks, and 28.0 percent of Puerto Ricans.

Given the income disparities between New York City white households and its nonwhite and ethnic minority population, one would expect differences to exist in rates of homeownership, affordability, and housing quality. Therefore, Table 1.15 also contains the incidence of severe housing problems for very low income households, those earning less than 50 percent of the area median income. The proportional disparities among whites and nonwhites with respect to the incidence of severe housing quality problems actually widen among the very poor. The differences between whites and nonwhites with respect to the incidence of severe affordability problems, however, narrow a bit.

It is difficult to draw conclusions about the relationship between race and housing outcomes without using multivariate techniques. In recent research, Rosenbaum has used the Housing and Vacancy Survey to analyze the impact of race and ethnicity upon the housing and neighborhood attributes of recent movers in New York City. In one recent article (Rosenbaum 1994), she constructed a sample of housing units that had experienced a change of occupancy between 1978–1981, 1981–1984, or 1984–1987. Using logistic regression techniques to control for a wide variety of building and household characteristics, she found that compared to white households, blacks and Hispanics were more likely to move to apartments with three or more housing maintenance deficiencies and to neighborhoods they characterized as fair or poor. A separate study using data from 1991 (Rosenbaum 1995) found that compared to whites, housing disparities existed for a variety of Hispanic subgroups such as Puerto Ricans, Dominicans, and Central Americans. Among Asians, however, no significant difference existed with respect to the likelihood of living in an apartment with three or more housing maintenance deficiencies. Rosenbaum further found that each racial and ethnic group other than the Chinese had a lower probability than whites of being a homeowner.

Regardless of its cause, disparities among white and nonwhite households, particularly those that contribute to high levels of racial and ethnic housing segregation, are likely to have an enormous impact on the health, safety, and welfare of city residents. Since the 1970s, cities throughout the nation have experienced a sharp increase in the geographic concentration of poverty. Kasarda's analysis of census data for the largest one hundred cities in America indicates that the number of extreme poverty tracts—census tracts in which 40 percent or more of the residents earn incomes below the federal poverty level—jumped from 751 in 1970 to 1,954 in 1990 (Kasarda 1993a, 263). The population living in these extreme poverty tracts doubled during the period. In New York City, the number of extreme poverty tracts increased at an even faster rate than the national average. From 1970 to 1990, the number of extreme poverty tracts jumped from 73 to 276; by 1990, 952,484 people, or 13 percent of the city's population, lived in these neighborhoods (Kasarda 1993b, 4–39).

As Massey and Denton (1993) have demonstrated, high levels of housing segregation among racial and ethnic minorities make them especially vulnerable to living in neighborhoods of concentrated poverty. Given the disproportionately higher rates of poverty experienced by blacks and Hispanics as compared to whites, segregation acts to concentrate and intensify poverty. One can observe this relationship between race and residence in New York City. In 1990, of the 952,484 people residing in extreme poverty tracts in the city, 409,271 were non-Hispanic black individuals and 459,099 were Hispanic (Kasarda 1993b, 4–41).

Living in communities of concentrated poverty has enormous social consequences for New York City's minority residents. Typically, these communities have high rates of infant mortality and crime (Citizens Committee for Children of New York 1995). Proximate employment opportunities have typically diminished as have other forms of economic activity. In addition, several sociologists have argued that living in communities of concentrated poverty can generate behavioral adaptations that impede social mobility. For example, Wilson (1987) has argued that children who grow up in environments with few working role models develop weak attachments to the labor force. Lacking employment opportunities and the appropriate socialization to seek work, youths will frequently engage in deviant or illegal activities to earn income and gain status, thereby further distancing themselves from middle-class norms. These behaviors are reinforced by peer groups. Activities that are likely to assist them in obtaining employment and social mobility, such as graduating from high school, are stigmatized rather than valued (Massey and Denton 1993, 167).

Since 1987, social scientists have repeatedly tested Wilson's hypothesis that growing up in a neighborhood of concentrated poverty will generate "concentration effects." Although the precise causal mechanism remains a matter of debate, studies testing the theory demonstrate a consistent relationship between social and spatial isolation on the one hand, and high rates of teenage childbearing, school dropout, and welfare dependency on the other (Anderson 1991; Brooks-Gunn et al. 1993; Clark 1992; Crane 1991; Osterman 1991).

CONCLUSION

Housing is critical to the health, well-being, and prosperity of New York City and its residents. The absence of adequate housing can make it difficult or impossible for families to achieve stability in their lives. At its most elemental, housing or the lack thereof can affect one's health by subjecting people to dangerous or disease-promoting conditions. Where one resides frequently can circumscribe one's opportunities for living in a safe environment, obtaining an adequate education, and acquiring gainful employment. Housing can also consume so much of a household's resources as to leave it unable to pay for other necessities such as food, health care, or clothing. Excessive housing costs may also limit economic activity in the city, by making it difficult for businesses to attract a skilled workforce at competitive wages.

In many respects, New York City has made important strides over the past two decades in improving its housing. Thousands of units of housing have been rehabilitated through the creative use of government subsidies and partnerships among government, business, and community groups. Housing quality, at least as measured by the Census Bureau, is better today than at any time this century. Nevertheless, enormous housing and housing-related problems remain. A significant proportion of New York City's population cannot obtain housing and is forced to live in shelters or temporary accommodations. A much larger share of the population, disproportionately poor, live in decent housing, but pay excessive proportions of their incomes for rent or homeownership costs. Finally, housing market forces, including racial and ethnic discrimination, restrict the ability of many New Yorkers to move to neighborhoods where they would be able to obtain good schools for their children and access to jobs and economic opportunities for their families.

NOTES

The authors would like to thank Scott Susin for his assistance in preparing this chapter.

1. The Housing and Vacancy Survey is conducted by the Census Bureau every three years under contract with the City of New York. The survey is representative of all housing in the city and collects information about the physical characteristics and occupant characteristics of this housing stock.

2. In the HVS, 46.8 percent of all households failed to disclose their incomes, and 6.3 percent of renter households failed to disclose their monthly contract rents. For the 1996 HVS, the Census Bureau used other demographic information to impute incomes and rents for households in which incomes and/or rents were not reported. The Census Bureau applies similar imputation techniques in all of its other periodic surveys.

3. For expositional purposes, we treat population and the number of households as affecting the demand for housing. However, we recognize that housing market outcomes such as market rents surely affect population and the number of households.

4. A household is defined to be an immigrant household if the householder was foreign born and both of his or her parents were foreign born.

5. Using unimputed incomes only, the median household income of New Yorkers was $25,200 in 1995.

6. One study estimated that New York City's financial commitment to housing exceeded the combined expenditures of the next fifty largest cities in the United States (Berenyi 1989).

7. In addition, the median house value of the nation, New York City metropolitan area, and New York City itself were $78,300, $209,000, and $189,600, respectively (U.S. Department of Commerce 1990).

8. The methodology for this analysis of "severe" housing problems is similar although not identical to the "worst case" problem methodology described in U.S. Department of HUD (1992).

9. The median income for a family of four in the New York metropolitan area in 1995 as calculated by HUD was $49,100. The metropolitan area, as defined by HUD for purposes of calculating housing subsidies, comprises the five counties that make up the City of New York, as well as Rockland and Putnam counties (U.S. Department of HUD 1995).

10. This benchmark is used by several other housing analysts such as Nelson (1995). Rent, as used in this context, is contract rent.

11. These expenses include property taxes, mortgage payments, and utilities. The 60 percent threshold was adopted by Nelson (1995).

12. The correlation coefficient between the rate of severe affordability problems and severe quality problems is 0.43.

13. Given the high rents in this sub-borough area relative to the rest of the city, there is some question as to whether the choice by households to spend high proportions of their incomes for housing there should be characterized as a problem.

14. To allow a comparison between 1993 and 1996 numbers, only unimputed incomes and rents were used to compute the rates of severe housing problems.

15. Median household incomes were adjusted for family size according to HUD Section 8 income thresholds. For the New York, NY, PMSA the adjusted median income for a four-person household is $49,100.

16. To estimate whether a housing unit's rent is affordable, one needs to make certain assumptions about the household size that would be appropriate for that unit. As in Nelson (1995) this paper utilizes the standards set forth in 26 U.S.C. 42(g)(2)(C). A studio apartment is assumed to house one person, a one bedroom is assumed to house 1.5 persons, with each additional bedroom housing another 1.5 persons. Rent, as used in this context, is contract rent.

17. To be consistent with Nelson's presentation of her results, each affordable occupied and vacant rental unit in each income decile is affordable for incomes equal to or below the highest adjusted income level in the decile and not affordable for the highest adjusted income level in the previous income decile.

18. Even this estimate of the shortage of affordable rental housing for households with incomes below 50 percent of the area median may understate the actual magnitude of the problem. A large number of owner occupants, 67,916, pay more than 60 percent of their incomes for housing expenses.

REFERENCES

Anderson, Elijah. 1991. "Neighborhood Effects on Teenage Pregnancy." In *The Urban Underclass*, ed. C. Jencks and P. Peterson. Washington, D.C.: Brookings Institution.

Austrian Roth & Partners. 1995. *1994 Manhattan Land Indexes*. New York: Austrian Roth & Partners.

Berenyi, Eileen B. 1989. *Locally Funded Housing Programs in the United States: A Survey of the Fifty-one Most Populated Cities*. New York: New School for Social Research.

Blackburn, Anthony J. 1995. *Housing New York City: 1993*. New York: Department of Housing Preservation and Development.

Brooks-Gunn, Jeanne, et al. 1993. "Do Neighborhoods Influence Child and Adolescent Development?" *American Journal of Sociology* 99:353.

Citizens' Committee for Children of New York. 1995. *Keeping Track of New York's Children*. New York: Citizens' Committee for Children.

Clark, Rebecca L. 1992. *Neighborhood Effects on Dropping Out of School among Teenage Boys*. Discussion Paper. Washington, D.C.: Urban Institute.

Crane, Jonathan. 1991. "The Epidemic Theory of Ghettos and Neighborhood Effects on Dropping Out and Teenage Childbearing." *American Journal of Sociology* 96:1226.

Finder, Alan. 1995. "Success of Housing Program Rests on Economy." *New York Times*, May 2, B-3, col. 1.

Hamilton, Rabinovitz & Alschuler, Inc. 1998. The Making of a New Community: An Update on Residential Conversion Activity in Downtown New York. New York: Alliance For Downtown New York, Inc.

Hevesi, Dennis. 1997. "A Pillar of City Housing: Tax Relief." *New York Times*, February 16, Sec. 9, 1.

Kasarda, John D. 1993a. "Inner-City Concentrated Poverty and Neighborhood Distress: 1970 to 1990." *Housing Policy Debate* 4:253.

———. 1993b. "Inner-City Poverty and Economic Access." In *Rediscovering Urban America: Perspectives on the 1980s*, ed. J. Sommer and D. Hicks. Washington, D.C.: U.S. Department of Housing and Urban Development.

Kober, Eric. 1996. Telephone interview.

MarketSource. 1997. *Key Rates*.

Massey, Douglas S., and Nancy A. Denton. 1993. *American Apartheid: Segregation and the Making of the Underclass*. Cambridge: Harvard University Press.

National Real Estate Index. 1995.

Nelson, Kathryn P. 1995. "Whose Shortage of Affordable Housing?" *Housing Policy Debate* 5:401.

New York City Department of City Planning. 1998. Unpublished table entitled, "Number of Housing Units Based on Building Permits Issued, by Borough and by Type of Housing, for New York City: 1988–1997."

New York City Department of City Planning. 1995. *Proposed Consolidated Plan, Federal Fiscal Year 1995*. New York: Department of City Planning.

———. 1993. *Socioeconomic Profiles: A Portrait of New York City's Community Districts from the 1980 & 1990 Censuses of Population and Housing*. New York: Department of City Planning.

———. 1992a. *Demographic Profiles: A Portrait of New York City's Community Districts from the 1980 & 1990 Censuses of Population and Housing*. New York: Department of City Planning.

———. 1992b. *New Housing in New York City 1992*. New York: Department of City Planning.

New York City Housing and Vacancy Survey Data Files. 1993.

New York City. 1997. *New York City Greenbook*.

New York City Rent Guidelines Board. 1997. *Housing Supply Report*.

———. 1995. *Housing NYC: Rents, Markets and Trends '95*. New York: Rent Guidelines Board.

New York State Division of Housing and Community Renewal. 1993. *An Overview of New York State's Rent Regulated Housing*. New York: DHCR.

Osterman, Paul. 1991. "Welfare Participation in a Full Employment Economy: The Impact of Neighborhood." *Social Problems* 38:475.

Pozdena, Randall Johnston. 1988. *The Modern Economics of Housing.* New York: Quorum Books.

Real Estate Board of New York. 1992. *Housing in New York: A Continuing Crisis.* New York: Real Estate Board.

Rosenbaum, Emily. 1995. "Racial/Ethnic Differences in Home Ownership and Housing Quality 1991." Paper presented at the 1995 Meeting of the Population Association of America in San Francisco.

————. 1994. "The Constraints on Minority Housing Choices, New York City 1978–1987." *Social Forces* 72:725.

Rosenberg, Terry J. 1995. *Updated Poverty Tables for New York City with March 1994 Current Population Survey Estimates.* New York: Community Service Society.

R. S. Means. 1997. *Square Foot Costs.*

Salins, Peter D., and Gerald C.S. Mildner. 1992. Scarcity by Design. Cambridge: Harvard University Press.

Schill, Michael H. 1996. "Local Enforcement of Laws Prohibiting Discrimination in Housing: The New York City Human Rights Commission." *Fordham Urban Law Journal,* 23(4):991.

Schill, Michael H., and Susan M. Wachter. 1995. "Housing Market Constraints and Spatial Stratification by Income and Race." *Housing Policy Debate* 6:141.

Stone, Michael E. 1993. *Shelter Poverty: New Ideas on Housing Affordability.* Philadelphia: Temple University Press.

Turner, Margery Austin, Raymond J. Struyk, and John Yinger. 1991. *Housing Discrimination Study: Synthesis.* Washington, D.C.: U.S. Department of Housing and Urban Development.

U.S. Department of Commerce, Bureau of the Census. 1998. Unpublished table entitled, "1996 New York City Housing and Vacancy Survey Losses from the Inventory."

U.S. Department of Commerce, Bureau of the Census. 1996. *Population Estimates for Cities in the United States.*

U.S. Department of Commerce. Bureau of the Census. 1995a. American Housing Survey for the New York-Nassau-Suffolk-Orange Metropolitan Area in 1995. Washington, D.C.: Author.

U.S. Department of Commerce. Bureau of the Census. 1995b. American Housing Survey for the United States in 1995. Washington, D.C.: Author.

————. 1994. Housing and Vacancy Survey Data File Documentation.

————. 1960, 1970, 1980, 1990. Census of Population and Housing. Washington, D.C.: Government Printing Office.

U.S. Department of Housing and Urban Development. 1992. The Location of Worst-Case Needs in the Late 1980s: A Report to Congress. Washington, D.C.: U.S. Department of HUD.

Webber, Karen. No date. Systemic Report: Fair Housing Assistance Program Type II, HA-14607. New York: New York City Commission on Human Rights.

Wilson, William J. 1987. The Truly Disadvantaged: The Inner City, the Underclass and Public Policy. Chicago: University of Chicago Press.

Yinger, John. 1995. Closed Doors, Opportunities Lost: The Continuing Costs of Housing Discrimination. New York: Russell Sage Foundation.

————. 1991. Housing Discrimination Study: Incidence of Discrimination and Variation in Discriminatory Behavior. Washington, D.C.: U.S. Department of Housing and Urban Development.

CHAPTER 2

REVIVING NEW YORK CITY'S HOUSING MARKET

Peter D. Salins

New York City's housing conditions, already inferior to those of most other American cities, are destined to get worse in the decades ahead because there are just not enough new homes or apartments being built to accommodate the housing needs of new families and offset the deterioration of existing housing units. According to the most recent published report on New York City housing conditions, in a *good* year New York's housing stock loses nearly 14,000 dwelling units; in the most recent period, it lost over 18,000 units. At the same time, unlike other large eastern and midwestern cities, New York's household population is actually growing—between 2,500 and 9,000 households per year recently (Blackburn 1995). That means New York needs to add between 12,000 and 17,000 dwellings to its housing stock each year just to stay even. If housing conditions are to be improved and housing prices reduced, twice that number must be added. Why? Because New York has among the nation's oldest and most deteriorated housing stock, and to substantially upgrade its quality, much of it should be replaced. Assuming an average viable dwelling unit life of about sixty-five years, ideally 1.5 percent of New York's housing stock (approximately 42,000 dwelling units) should be retired each year. Could many of these units be substantially renovated instead? Probably not. In the case of most of New York's oldest dwellings—tenements and modest apartment houses built in upper Manhattan and the inner-tier neighborhoods of Brooklyn, Queens, and the Bronx—the cost of renovation is too high, and the likely housing product too inferior, for renovation to be worthwhile.

In the last decade, residential construction in New York City has not even come close to meeting the city's housing needs. Even in the best years for residential construction in the mid-1980s, only 12,000 to

16,000 dwellings were added, many of them developed and subsidized publicly (Blackburn 1995). In 1994, just 4,010 private residential building permits were issued in New York City, a city with nearly three million dwelling units, and 30 percent of these permits were issued in Staten Island, New York's smallest and most uncharacteristic borough (U.S. Department of Commerce 1982–94). Although the city's resurgent economy has led to a doubling in the annual number of building permits issued (see Schill and Scafidi, chapter 1 in this volume), even this level of housing production is significantly below the levels necessary to maintain and expand the city's housing stock.

If low rates of housing development and replacement persist, existing dwellings will inevitably become even more overcrowded, harder to find (which translates to higher rents), and more deteriorated than they are today. While the failure to build new housing hurts all New Yorkers, its greatest hardship is visited on the city's most vulnerable residents, the poor, who must live in the worst of the city's dwellings and neighborhoods.

For a city not experiencing population decline, New York's record of housing production is abysmal, by any possible reckoning. In proportion to its population, economic importance, and grandiose self-image New York builds fewer housing units and maintains its existing housing stock more poorly than all but the most derelict of American cities. When New York is compared with the other central cities of America's ten largest metropolitan areas, as indicated in Table 2.1, only three had a lower rate of new residential construction than New York, and every one of these places—unlike New York—had a declining rate of population growth in the last decade (U.S. Department of Commerce 1995 and 1982–94). Even Boston and Chicago, with declining populations, have seen more housing built than New York. The best explanation for New York's poor showing is that the city is strangling its housing market in a web of regulation and government intervention unmatched in any other large city.

New York is one of only four large cities to retain rent regulation, under rules initially imposed during World War II and never removed. In fact, the scope of regulation was significantly extended in 1969 and 1974. Even compared to the handful of other rent regulated places, New York's regulatory rules are more constraining, and more strictly applied than elsewhere. New York City's Zoning Resolution, accruing special districts, special regulations, certifications, overlays, exceptions, bonuses, and housing quality standards continuously since its adoption in 1961, is the most complex and housing-unfriendly development ordinance of any large city. Since 1975, New York has been the only major city to force most new development—housing and commercial—

TABLE 2.1
Housing Construction Rates, Ten Largest Metropolitan Central Cities

| City | Housing Permits per 1,000 Dwelling Units | | | | | % Pop. Growth 1980–92 |
	1994	1990	1986	1982	1985–94	
Dallas	9.85	5.91	27.79	26.47	129.99	12.9
Los Angeles	1.78	9.10	19.88	4.40	98.27	17.5
Houston	7.66	2.97	17.70	22.44	92.39	6.0
San Francisco	2.89	3.28	6.21	3.70	40.18	7.3
Boston	1.04	1.11	10.00	1.61	38.55	-2.0
Chicago	2.28	2.86	3.09	3.82	24.75	-7.9
New York	1.34	2.29	3.26	2.50	22.29	3.4
Philadelphia	0.64	1.11	3.05	2.33	15.46	-7.9
Washington	0.75	1.32	2.30	1.55	14.69	-8.3
Detroit	0.94	1.54	0.50	2.58	9.09	-15.9

Source: U.S. Department of Commerce (1982–94).

through a punishing gauntlet of procedural review. Since 1977, New York has been the only place to apply a municipal environmental regulation more stringent than required by its state or the federal government. Since 1985, New York has been the only American city whose government spends its own tax levy resources to compete against the privately owned low cost housing sector as developer and subsidizer. And since 1987, New York has been the only place to institutionalize a discriminatory property tax system that levies higher taxes on apartment houses than any other large American city.

Given the cascading set of new or stricter rules applying to the production or operation of housing in New York City since the 1960s, it should come as no surprise that New York's housing production has fallen steadily over the last three decades, as indicated in Table 2.2. In the early 1960s New York's private developers were building over 45,000 dwellings a year, more than enough to replace housing losses, accommodate population growth, and upgrade housing quality. Thirty years later, housing development (including subsidized dwellings) has slowed to an annual trickle of 7,500 units. Taking into account the flow of annual housing losses and modest population growth, the balance of housing supply and demand has gone from a surplus of 28,500 units in the early 1960s to a shortfall of nearly 17,000 in 1994.

Why should New Yorkers care about the city's housing production shortfall? Because its two most likely consequences are extremely harmful to New York's livability and economic prospects. To the degree that New York's households are captive, as most of the poor are, the failure to build and upgrade housing will make the city's existing housing scarcer,

TABLE 2.2
Annual Change in New York City Housing Stock

Year	Dwelling Unit Additions	Dwelling Unit Losses	Household Gain or Loss	Net Housing Additions
1960–64	45,900	13,300	4,100	28,500
1965–69	27,900	8,600	8,700	10,600
1970–74	19,400	11,200	–19,000	27,200
1975–79	16,500	27,000	–12,000	1,500
1980–84	10,500	23,800	10,100	–23,400
1985–89	11,600	14,800	9,100	–12,300
1990–94	7,500	18,300	3,100	–13,900
1994	4,000	18,300	2,500	–16,800

Source: New York City Housing and Vacancy Surveys (Sternlieb and Hughes 1976; Stegman 1985; Wolkoff 1988; Blackburn 1995).

more expensive, and more deteriorated. On the other hand, if New York's households are able to move away (or choose not to move in), the city's neighborhoods and economy will be further eroded. While a city's demand for housing is largely a product of its economic vitality, the reverse can also be true: a city's economic vitality is enhanced when it possesses a high-quality, reasonably priced housing stock.

Immigrants—especially illegal ones—represent a group uniquely disadvantaged by New York's dearth of housing construction. As the most captive of the city's households, they put up with the worst of its housing conditions so they can gain membership in the bottom of its labor force. But as their squalid living conditions attract public attention, demands for code enforcement rise. Ineligible for rent controlled apartments, and unable to afford decent ones, immigrants will be forced to hide or move out of the city.

The deficiencies of New York's regulatory system and housing policies have long come under critical scrutiny both by economists and in publicly commissioned studies (Rapkin 1966; Mayor's Rent Control Committee 1969; Rand 1970; Sternlieb 1972; Lett 1976; Mayor's Commission 1977; Roistacher 1991; Salins and Mildner 1992; and Urstadt undated). All of the studies have more or less accurately identified the major impacts that rent control has had on New York's housing, but they also varied widely as to the desirable or necessary degree of reform required. The early studies (Rapkin, Rand, Sternlieb) led to limited reforms of New York's oldest and most rigid form of rent regulation: rent control. In 1970 the New York City Council adopted the Maximum Base Rent system, permitting modest annual rent increases for rent controlled apartments until a fair "base rent" was achieved, and in 1974 the New

York State Legislature, as part of the Emergency Tenant Protection Act, moved vacant rent controlled apartments into the Rent Stabilization system. The only major public official sufficiently persuaded by the raft of critical reports and studies to actually propose phasing out rent regulation altogether was Governor Nelson Rockefeller, who persuaded a reluctant State Legislature in 1971 to adopt comprehensive vacancy decontrol—for both controlled and stabilized dwellings. This reform was short-lived, however—its repeal was enacted by the Legislature in 1974 with the support of Rockefeller's successor, Malcolm Wilson.

What has not been sufficiently understood, by either the critics or the politicians, is the way these regulations and policies interact and reinforce each other in a negative way to undermine that incredibly delicate and fragile system that is the New York City housing market. And that— not regulatory nuisances per se—is what New Yorkers are up against: the inexorable decline of the vitality of their city's housing market.

Housing markets are generally metropolitan in scope. When the housing market is thwarted in one metropolitan jurisdiction, housing demand and supply is simply displaced to neighboring jurisdictions. When the housing market is inhibited in the central city, housing activity is displaced to the suburbs. In many American metropolitan areas central city housing market demand is weak because of declining population and economic activity. New York, however, is a city still experiencing some population growth, and many of its neighborhoods, both in Manhattan and the outer boroughs, are desirable enough to sustain a flourishing housing market if they were permitted to. But because of New York City's regulatory barriers, almost all of the New York region's new housing is now being built in its suburbs.

A housing market is not just a collection of residential buildings; it is a hugely complex process. In a properly functioning urban housing market the rational economic behavior of housing suppliers and consumers operates to assure:

- a continuous stream of additions to the housing stock numerous enough to accommodate new household formation and to replace obsolete or deteriorated dwellings (in New York City, that would mean building about 40,000 new units a year)
- continuous movement of households through the housing stock as their needs, desires, and pocketbooks dictate
- continuous investment in maintaining or enhancing the quality of the existing stock
- a continuous process to remove (or renovate) the deteriorated and obsolete housing stock

Above all, a well-functioning housing market depends on the correct pricing of the housing stock, from the top of the market to the bottom, to send the right signals to all housing market actors, both suppliers and consumers, to make sure that their individual economic rationality is congruent with housing market vitality.

New York's rent, zoning, development, and environmental regulations, and its other housing policies, hobble all four components of a vital housing market—they keep new housing from being built, they provide disincentives to maintenance and reinvestment, they freeze much of the household population in place, and they keep obsolete housing from being removed. The primary mechanism by which public sector intervention curtails the normal operation of the housing market is the aggressive mispricing of much of the housing stock. Out of three million dwellings in New York's housing stock, 53 percent have their prices and operations determined by one or another public agency; and by far the largest component of this publicly priced stock (37 percent) is the 1.1 million apartments subject to rent regulation. The rest comprises 165,000 New York City Housing Authority apartments, 295,000 shallow subsidy units (mainly benefiting from State and federal financing subsidies like those embedded in New York's Mitchell-Lama Program, or rent subsidies available under the federal Section 8 program), and 23,000 apartments operated by the city after tax foreclosure (Schill and Scafidi, chapter 1 in this volume).

In spite of all the government-managed price fixing, New York's housing is no bargain, especially for the poor and near poor. Whether measured by rent-to-income ratios or in comparison with housing prices in other cities, only traditional public housing is cheap. According to the 1993 Housing and Vacancy Survey the poorest rent controlled tenants (those with 1993 household incomes under $10,000) pay 57 percent of their income in rent, other rent regulated (that is, rent stabilized) poor tenants pay 84 percent, and even tenants in city-owned tax foreclosed apartments pay 72 percent. In fact, overall, the 28 percent of all renters not protected by one or another format of public sector rent setting devote exactly the same share of their income to pay for housing as the 72 percent who do benefit: 31 percent (Blackburn 1995). Nevertheless, even absent any aggregate benefit, government intervention in pricing the housing stock causes major distortions in the housing market at the level of individual apartments, buildings, and neighborhoods, creating a random and perverse distribution of household windfalls and hardships.

The best metaphor to characterize a housing market is to liken it to a vast game of musical chairs. Housing developers are the people supplying the chairs; housing consumers occupy the chairs, and housing prices are akin to the musical signals that make people change seats. New York City's regulatory and other housing policies spoil New York's housing musical chairs game by keeping chairs from being added and taken away, and by not allowing the music to play often enough for people to change their seats.

The granddaddy and archvillain of New York's regulatory ensemble is rent regulation, but not only for the reason most studies usually cite: its impact in accelerating the rate of housing deterioration—an especially acute issue for rent controlled dwellings. Nor is rent regulation's problem that it causes landlords to lose money, the most common complaint of the real estate industry; maybe it does sometimes, but if most landlords lost too much money, there would be no housing. To the degree that New York's public officials worry about rent regulation at all, it is to make property owners whole (with, for example capital improvement rent increases, annual guidelines reflecting the cost of housing operation, and so forth); but that does not get to the heart of rent regulation's negative impacts on the housing market. The real damage of rent regulation is done by the very features that are the most popular: in fact, the entire rationale for having rent regulation at all is keeping the price of rental housing below market levels, and allowing tenants to remain in their apartments as long as they like, regardless of their landlord's wishes.

Keeping prices as low as possible doesn't—in the case of rent stabilization—even result in very low prices; New York's stabilized rents are higher than most cities' unregulated ones. But stabilized prices are almost always the wrong prices, prices different from what an unregulated housing market would charge; and rent regulation has its most egregious impact on the middle and upper end of the market, where the price differential between market and regulated rents is greatest. This has two undesirable effects: it reduces the demand for new housing, and it misallocates the existing housing stock. If regulated tenants in Manhattan, Riverdale, or Forest Hills moved to newer, better apartments—or bought them—the increment of additional rent or carrying costs they would have to pay would far exceed the increment of housing improvement. This demand factor is more important than the prospect of future regulated rents in discouraging construction of new mid- and high-priced housing. At the same time, the cessation of movement among the musical chairs exacerbates shortages in the low end of the stock, shortages that cannot be responded to by private housing suppliers because of the costs of regulation and the incomes of the low-end tenants.

While rent regulation's impact on housing demand is to some extent speculative and not easily documented, its misallocation effects are readily apparent in a variety of mismatches between household and apartment characteristics in the regulated stock. Because many small households preempt regulated apartments, overcrowding (as indicated by more than one person per room) is more prevalent in unregulated apartments (9.8 percent) than in rent controlled (3.3 percent) or post-1947 rent stabilized ones (7.5 percent) (Blackburn 1995). Because holding on to a regulated apartment requires skill and the ability to time or defer moves, more privileged demographic groups have a distinct edge, undermining the ostensible equity objective of the regulatory system. As a result, 73 percent of rent controlled and 58 percent of post-1947 rent stabilized apartments are occupied by whites (who comprise only 41 percent of all renter households) and a greater percentage of high income (72 percent) than low income (50 percent) single households occupy regulated apartments (Blackburn 1995).

The other destructive housing market feature of rent regulation is its stringent tenure protection. Tenants have every economic incentive to stay put, and very little incentive to move. Any move by a regulated tenant, even to a smaller or less desirable apartment in the city, will probably result in a higher rent. The longer a tenant has lived in a particular apartment, the more likely this is to be the case. This, as much as below-market rents, keeps housing turnover low. This, as much as below-market rents, gives landlords a disincentive to maintain their properties at optimal levels. And this feature, tenure protection, makes it impossible to remove dwellings from the housing stock after they have lost most or all of their value.

The low turnover rate generated by tenure protection is frequently cited by rent regulation advocates as a distinct benefit, generating allegedly greater socioeconomic integration, neighborhood stability, and apartment maintenance than there might be under conditions of higher turnover. Yet, New York is among the most spatially segregated of large American cities, has seen many of its formerly stable neighborhoods deteriorate, and, as documented by the *American Housing Survey*, has inferior dwelling unit conditions by contemporary American urban standards.

The combined impact of the New York housing market's below-market prices and low turnover is to frustrate the normal dynamics of housing "filtering," the term housing economists use to describe the process by which decent housing is made available to low- and moderate-income households in most urban communities. The filtering model posits that the development of new housing for middle- and upper-income families leads inevitably to lower housing prices and greater housing availability throughout the local housing market through a

TABLE 2.3
Rental Housing Characteristics for Five Large Cities, 1991

City	Median Rent 2 BR Apt ($)	Median Apt. Age (years)	Median Tenure (years)
New York	563	48	5
Los Angeles (1989)	651	31	4
Chicago	538	43	2
Atlanta	539	19	1
Houston	475	15	1

Source: U.S. Department of Housing and Urban Development, American Housing Survey: New York, Chicago, Atlanta, Houston,1991; Los Angeles, 1989.

chain of vacancies. Much like a high rate of new automobile production and purchase leads to an upgrading of the quality of the entire automobile fleet as all motorists trade up to newer and better cars, a high rate of housing production should lead all households to have access to newer and better dwellings. Conversely, a low rate of housing production, by the logic of the filtering model, must result in most households occupying older and inferior dwellings. Unless, that is, households can filter out of the city altogether into newer and better housing in the suburbs. Thus, if New York does not create a housing environment that encourages filtering within the city, it risks both a decline in housing conditions and the outmigration of its most upwardly mobile familes.

But even when and if New York City and State were to end "rent regulation as we know it," an eventuality that was seriously considered by the New York State Legislature in 1997, but put off at least until the year 2003, the rest of New York's regulatory apparatus would come into play. Opponents of rent regulation hope that absent its debilitating impact, more housing would be built, but their optimism may not be warranted. Unless they are reformed, other New York housing interventions might cancel much of the salutary impact of rent deregulation.

There are only three possible places where new housing can be built: on vacant or underutilized land, in established neighborhoods by infill or replacing existing structures, or in areas where obsolete housing is removed. Among the most logical sites for new residential development would appear to be somewhere in the 15,000 acres of land (7 percent of New York's land area) that New York's planners have designated for manufacturing, especially considering that manufacturing employment has declined by 160,000 jobs per decade since the end of World War II and shows no sign of reversing course anytime soon. But before building can take place on underutilized manufacturing sites (many of them along the waterfront, in choice Manhattan locations, or in vast open tracts in Queens, Brooklyn, and Staten Island), each manufacturing area where new housing might be developed has to be rezoned for residential development, because New York is one of the few places in the country that reserves manufacturing zones exclusively for industry. The city's planning leadership today actually wants to do this. But it is no easy task.

To begin with, each affected area needs a separate environmental impact assessment which can be a costly proposition. Sometimes such assessments are paid for by potential developers, but only in contemplation of the most desirable sites. Then the proposed rezoning must wend its way through New York's Uniform Land Use Review Process (ULURP), where it is almost certain to trigger objections by development opponents. ULURP is a review protocol, mandated by New York City's charter, that gives local communities and other affected interests the power to scrutinize and make recommendations regarding land use and development proposals needing dispensation from zoning or other regulations. In the unlikely event that the rezoning emerges unscathed from ULURP and doesn't become bogged down in court challenges (usually justified by some defect in the environmental and ULURP protocols), each change must be approved by the City Planning Commission and the City Council, where political mobilization can derail the proposal. The present planning administration has, with dogged persistence, managed to rezone five districts from manufacturing or restrictive mixed-use to residential or commercial (which allows for residential)—two in Manhattan, and one each in Brooklyn, Queens, and Staten Island. Each rezoning took more than two years and millions of taxpayer and developer dollars to consummate (according to information supplied by the New York City Planning Department). Although the city's planners are continuing their piecemeal rezoning efforts, wresting housing sites wholesale from New York's obsolete industrial landscape would be an enormously costly and time-consuming undertaking.

There are also substantial obstacles to housing development in established neighborhoods. There is a better than even chance that any potential site is in one of the city's thirty-eight special zoning districts—districts designed to preserve or promote particular building types, activities, and amenities—or in one of the city's forty-four historic districts, or near a wetland (New York has 580 miles of shoreline, not to mention countless streams, ponds, marshes, and springs), or on a brownfield (in addition to industrial areas this can apply to any former gas station site or drycleaning establishment), or on a lot with one or another restrictive quirk. Even when it lies in Staten Island, that quintessentially suburban part of New York, the place where one-fifth of all private housing was built between 1991 and 1995, a housing site may need a "school seat certification," a requirement in South Richmond that makes developers prove that the schools have enough room for the additional students that new housing might bring. In almost any New York neighborhood, developers have to negotiate with city officials and the site-specific opponent du jour on a site-by-site basis. Like rezoning, each development proposal, even after negotiation, needs an environmental assessment and has to undergo review in the Uniform Land Use Review Process. Obviously, housing development does take place—4,000 dwellings worth in 1994—but only by the hardiest of developers, pitching to the most affluent of market segments. Given the obstacles, the pace of development quickens only in the most robust of economic times.

Some of the most obvious and desirable of potential housing development sites are in the wastelands of housing devastation, where the city has acquired thousands of structures on hundreds of acres through tax foreclosure, the locations of the city's voluminous *in rem* portfolio, now comprising nearly 30,000 apartments. As things stand, private developers of market-priced housing often find it harder to build there than in established neighborhoods. If they purchased properties with partially occupied buildings, they would be barred from tearing down the structures or massively renovating them because tenure protection rules prevent them from relocating the remaining tenants. But the issue is moot, in any case. New York City has long been reluctant to sell its tax-foreclosed properties to the highest bidder, and since the early 1980s has implemented a policy of turning over city-owned residential property—vacant or occupied—to selected private owners and developers only with stringent restrictions and targeted subsidies, setting aside all *in rem* properties as "community" housing resources. Thus, in the short run, New York spends hundreds of millions of dollars each year to operate *in rem* housing at a loss—and in the long run, *billions*—subsidizing nonprofit and private developers, under several city-sponsored and funded programs, to redevelop these properties with expensively renovated apartments offered to eligible tenants at below-market rents.

The thousands of dwellings already developed under this program have unquestionably revitalized sections of East New York, the South Bronx, and Harlem. But even this impressive accomplishment further destabilizes New York's housing market because the new housing raises the "wrong price" problem again. Subsidized development competes with low-end private apartment buildings in attracting the limited number of responsible, working, moderate-income families willing to live in these neighborhoods. Thus, the unsubsidized stock becomes the housing resource of last resort, mainly occupied by the poorest and most irresponsible households, hastening its demise. The city can, of course, then add this new increment of failed housing to its costly development portfolio, but if someday the city tires of or can no longer afford this role, it will once again be faced with housing wastelands orphaned by both the private and public sectors. In any case, experience shows that the kinds of subsidies New York uses to underwrite redeveloped *in rem* housing are unsustainable over the long haul, making it likely that much of this redeveloped stock will also fail. It is certainly premature to conclude that the city-subsidized revitalization of New York's worst neighborhoods has been a mistake, but the effort should be viewed as at best a limited—and not necessarily durable—substitute for a vigorous unsubsidized housing market.

In addition to the housing development hurdles posed by New York's zoning, environmental, procedural, and public development policies, prospective developers of new housing continue to face construction costs from 5 to 15 percent higher than those prevailing in other parts of the region imposed by building codes riddled with numerous outdated or unreasonable requirements and unnecessary disabled access and seismic provisions. New York City's construction and fire safety standards, for example, are far more stringent than those in New York State's model building code. The requirements for making residences accessible for the physically handicapped (who constitute a minuscule fraction of all households), which are applicable to every single home or apartment, are stricter than the federal government's. And the code's earthquake-proofing provisions make no sense in a city that has never experienced a serious earthquake.

If that were not enough, prospective developers, landlords, even homeowners who propose to renovate the older stock, continue to face the prospect of complying with punishing asbestos and lead paint abatement requirements, and a whopping increase in their property taxes. Owners of unprofitable rental buildings who think they can save them by selling their apartments as co-ops or condos continue to face a restrictive New York State co-op and condominium conversion law.

Those developers undaunted by the city's regulatory exactions must market their newly constructed dwellings burdened by a property tax system that discriminates against co-ops, condos, and new owner-occupied housing, and even more, against rental housing, regardless of vintage, as well as exorbitant water/sewer assessments. While the effective property tax rate for older one- and two-family homes in New York is under 1 percent of their market value, the rate for newer homes approaches 2 percent (the average suburban rate), the rate for co-ops and condos is around 4 percent, and the effective tax rate for multifamily rental properties is 5 percent. By comparison, apartments in Chicago pay property taxes under 3 percent of their market value; apartments in Houston, Washington, Seattle, Dallas, and Boston pay around 1.5 percent; and taxes on apartments in California cities are under 1 percent (Mildner 1991)

New York's discriminatory property tax classification scheme is driven by two unworthy notions: a willingness to exploit the city's ostensibly "captive" property owners, and a belief that New York must bribe middle-class homeowners in the outer boroughs to stay in the city. Unfortunately, multifamily housing is not really captive. The tax structure assumes that, with their tenants protected by rent regulation, multifamily rental property owners must "eat" the high taxes. What happens, instead, is that current tenants "eat" the high taxes in deferred maintenance, and future tenants "eat" them when they confront the limited and unsatisfactory housing choices of New York's crippled housing market. New York's answer to extortionately high taxes on multifamily housing has been to offer tax abatements to new apartment houses. But these abatements merely postpone the economic pain because they expire gradually over ten years. These abatements, incidentally, are conditioned on having the buildings that benefit submit to rent stabilization, effectively canceling the exemption from rent regulation available to new rental developments.

As things stand, rational housing actors in the city's housing market find themselves trapped in a regulatory and policy maze where every contemplated avenue of escape leads to a dead end or subjects them to another economic penalty. In the end, however, the system harms New York's residents more than its property owners and developers. Rent regulation induces owners of existing rental housing to undermaintain or abandon their properties, and developers of new housing to build in other places. Other costly and time-consuming regulations and high property taxes only make these problems worse. This causes a housing shortage that makes ending rent regulation unthinkable, and it also tempts the municipal government to become the houser of last resort. As the city goes into the housing business, more private competitors abandon their buildings, more residential property stays off the tax rolls, and low-income tenants not lucky enough to qualify for a subsidized apartment face a tighter and costlier housing market, which reinforces the cycle of public intervention.

How did New York ever build so much housing in the past, when the city added anywhere from 20,000 to 100,000 dwellings a year to the stock? The city certainly did not accumulate three million housing units by building 4,000 units a year. Much of the present stock, of course, was publicly developed or subsidized, more than anywhere else in America. But the private sector had a much easier time not so long ago. Rent regulation may date back to the World War II, but its scope was substantially expanded in the 1970s. The city's environmental rubric is just a few decades old, and is more strictly interpreted now than originally. The zoning ordinance keeps adding districts, and conditions, to the fairly basic 1961 resolution. Landmark districts have been added over the years. ULURP is a product of a 1975 Charter revision. The city's *in rem* housing policies, and capital program, are only a decade old.

TABLE 2.4

Selected Landmarks of New York Housing Market Intervention

Year	Policy
1942	Rent Control introduced as part of U.S. Emergency Price Control Act
1947	National rent controls lifted—New York's retained for all apartments occupied before 1947
1961	Passage of major revision to the 1916 Zoning Resolution
1965	Creation of Landmarks Preservation Commission with power to designate historic districts
1967	Introduction of first special zoning district
1969	Rent Stabilization introduced to regulate rents on all apartments not under Rent Control
1971	New York State legislates "vacancy decontrol" for all controlled and stabilized apartments
1971	National wage, price, and rent controls imposed under President Nixon
1974	Emergency Tenant Protection Act repeals vacancy decontrol
1975	1975 Charter reform mandates Uniform Land Use Review Process (ULURP)
1976	Passage of (New York) State Environmental Review Act (SEQRA) mandating environmental review of all discretionary zoning changes
1976	Introduction of New York City Housing Quality Program setting housing design standards
1977	City Environmental Quality Review (CEQR) introduced by mayoral executive order
1981	Introduction of zoning rules for residential loft conversions
1985	Koch Administration introduces "Housing New York" plan to rehabilitate *in rem* housing
1987	Assessment Act of 1987 introduces property tax classification system
1987	New York City Local Law 58 mandates apartment design standards for the disabled
1993	New York State passage of "luxury decontrol" for apartments with rents exceeding $2,000 and tenant incomes exceeding $250,000
1997	New York State passage of the Rent Regulation Reform Act of 1997 reducing income threshold of luxury decontrol to $175,000, enacting more generous vacancy bonuses and requiring tenants to deposit rents in court after second adjournment of a holdover action.

The time has come for New Yorkers to revive their housing market by ending this counterproductive set of interlocking regulations and policies, an imperative if they want New York to retain its place as America's premier metropolis. To do so they must embrace at least five fundamental changes in the city's housing regulations and related policies.

1. *Deregulate all rents.* A half-century of rent regulation is more than enough. The deregulation proposals that the New York State Legislature seriously considered—and rejected—in 1997 might have proven an effective way of ending rent controls painlessly. The transition would have been managed through a policy of "vacancy decontrol plus." The "plus" describes provisos that immediately deregulated all luxury apartments, "luxury" encompassing much lower rents and incomes than the current luxury decontrol policy; that transitional regulatory protection be restricted to current leaseholders with absolutely no succession rights, even for close relatives; that no apartments retain regulatory protection after ten years. Rent deregulation by itself may not be enough to revive New York's housing market, but it would go a long way toward making the revival possible. Deregulation would stimulate new housing demand and competition among housing suppliers, triggering enhanced maintenance, lower rents, and rising vacancy rates. An open, market-priced rental housing stock would also obviate the need for other market-inhibiting regulations and the restriction on co-op and condo conversion, and might increase the appeal of homeownership.

2. *Scale back the procedural gauntlets* through which much new housing development—especially new development involving large or unusually configured projects—must navigate to get approval. A good place to begin would be to scrap the city's own environmental regulation overlay, the City Environmental Quality Review (CEQR), which is both redundant with, and more restrictive than, the State's environmental review procedure, the State Environmental Quality Review Act (SEQRA), especially since CEQR is legitimated only by mayoral order. Just as CEQR magnifies and exceeds the development obstacles of state environmental rules, so do the city's building codes; and the city's disabled access requirements are more unreasonable than recently enacted federal ones. As a general policy, New York City should eliminate all housing regulations that go beyond state and federal standards that are more than adequate to protect New Yorkers. That still leaves ULURP, another unique New York City development hurdle. Because it is embedded in the charter, its elimination cannot be envisioned any time soon. But ULURP only af-

fects projects that require special permits because they depart from the regular terms of the zoning resolution; the easiest way to end ULURP's jurisdiction is to liberalize the city's zoning. Therefore, New York should enact a comprehensive rezoning as described below.

3. *Comprehensively rezone.* The best place to begin would be to rezone for residential development all appropriately situated manufacturing areas free of serious environmental hazards. Many manufacturing zones are unlikely to attract residential development, but waterfront areas in and around Manhattan would be appealing, along with large open, but underutilized, tracts in the further reaches of the other boroughs. In existing residential zones, density and other restrictions should be replaced with simple aesthetic standards (like height restrictions) that protect neighborhood scale and character. Most special district designations and rules should be eliminated, especially when they constrain new housing development as in Manhattan's East Side and Staten Island's South Richmond. Whatever the details, the objectives of rezoning should be to make more sites available for residential development, and to make most residential development "as-of-right."

4. *Get the city out of the real estate business.* All new tax-foreclosed properties should be auctioned, or their tax liens sold; all existing *in rem* properties should be transferred to private ownership—with few if any strings—as expeditiously as possible. With the elimination of rent regulation, purchasers of structures—even partially occupied ones—could tear them down and build new housing (as well as commercial structures) in their place. With the city no longer offering subsidized low-rent apartments in competition with privately owned ones next door, and with the demise of rent regulation leaving private landlords free to choose their tenants and charge market rents (but also feeling real competition from other nearby private housing entrepreneurs), many of New York's badly rundown neighborhoods might be revived.

5. *End property tax discrimination.* The system of property classification that discriminates against multifamily housing should be scrapped, and all properties made subject to the same effective tax rate. Given current property values and revenues, that would require a uniform rate of around 2 percent of market value. The greatest winners would be commercial properties in Manhattan (which might stimulate the commercial office market, and the economy generally), but right behind them would be multifamily residential properties, both owner occupied and rental. This would, in conjunction with the other proposed policy changes, stimulate a housing boom in the

city's more attractive apartment house precincts. Lower tax rates on new luxury apartments would also make tax abatements unnecessary; abatements represent another kind of tax discrimination, and they expire after a decade, making tax abated apartments less marketable over time. In the city's poorer neighborhoods, lower property taxes would make economically marginal properties more viable, reduce abandonment, and make redevelopment of already abandoned properties more attractive. The losers, obviously, would be owners of existing one- to three-family houses in the outer boroughs. But even they may gain in the long run. The city's liberalized regulatory environment should loosen the housing market across the board, offering present and potential homeowners wider selection and higher quality, perhaps even lower prices in some cases. And by ending the long-running contract between the city and its homeowners whereby the city stints on municipal services in exchange for letting homeowners stint on property taxes, homeowners might demand—and get—decent schools and other services for their appreciated tax dollars.

New York City today is at a critical housing policy crossroads. For the first time in decades, an agenda of comprehensive reform might actually be feasible because of fresh political and economic forces in play in New York and elsewhere in the United States. Reform-minded administrations now govern City Hall and Albany; there is a new appreciation of free markets and governmental reinvention from coast to coast; and New Yorkers might be ready to take drastic measures to revive their city's stagnant economy. But housing reform cannot be enacted piecemeal. As the debate surrounding the recent failed legislative attempt at ending rent controls proved, the city cannot end rent regulation until developers build more new housing. Developers will not build more new housing until the city ends rent regulation, lowers property taxes, and changes its zoning laws. The city will not lower property taxes until its tax base grows, and it cannot change the zoning laws until it changes its environmental laws. It cannot change the environmental laws without angering environmental advocates and securing state approval. At the end of the housing market day it does not really pay to change anything at all unless everything changes. The alternative to changing everything is to change nothing. And if nothing changes, the city government of New York is left with the punishingly costly role of being the developer and housing subsidizer of last resort, and the people of New York are left living in America's oldest and shabbiest housing. On the other hand, if New York's politicians exhibit the

courage and foresight to dismantle the city's oppressive housing policies, all New Yorkers will benefit. Middle- and high-income New Yorkers will soon be able to live as comfortably as their peers in Seattle or
Chicago. Poorer New Yorkers will, at a minimum, inherit some decent,
inexpensive apartments vacated by families above them on the income
ladder. But also, they may be surprised to find that, as the current housing regime's high costs and restrictive rules are curtailed, some builders
will come forward and build unsubsidized new housing for low- and
moderate-income families.

Can we be sure that dismantling New York City's housing regulations will motivate developers to build more, or enough more to make
a difference? Maybe not, but we do know that in the past, a regime of
fewer and less onerous housing regulations resulted in more housing
being built. And there is little downside risk in any case. A lighter regulatory burden can, at a minimum, make New York's housing less expensive, can motivate New York's landlords to better maintain their
rental properties, can guide New York's tenants and owners to make
more economically rational discretionary housing decisions, and can
more fairly allocate New York's existing housing stock.

REFERENCES

Blackburn, Anthony J. 1995. *Housing New York City, 1993*. New York: City of
New York Department of Housing Preservation and Development.

Lett, Monica. 1976. *Rent Control: Concepts, Realities, and Mechanisms*. New
Brunswick, N.J.: Rutgers University Center for Urban Policy Research.

Mayor's Commission. 1977. *The Effects of Rent Control and Rent Stabilization in
New York City*. New York: The Commission.

Mayor's Rent Control Committee. 1969. *Rent Control and Its Impact on Housing in
New York City*. New York: Mayor's Rent Control Committee.

Mildner, Gerard C. S. 1991. "New York's Most Unjust Tax." *NY: The City Journal*
vol. 1, no. 4 (summer 1991).

Rand Institute. 1970. *Rental Housing in New York City*. New York: Rand Institute.

Rapkin, Chester. 1966. *The Private Rental Housing Market in New York City, 1965*.
New York: New York City Rent and Rehabilitation Commission.

Roistacher, Elizabeth A. 1991. *Reforming Residential Rent Regulations*. New York:
Citizens Budget Commission.

Salins, Peter D., and Gerard C. S. Mildner. 1992. *Scarcity by Design*. Cambridge: Harvard University Press.

Stegman, Michael A. 1985. *Housing in New York: Study of a City*. New York: New York City Department of Housing Preservation and Development.

Sternlieb, George. 1972. *The Urban Housing Dilemma: the Dynamics of New York City's Rent-Controlled Housing*. New York: New York City Housing and Development Administration.

Sternlieb, George, and James W. Hughes. 1976. *Housing and Economic Reality: New York City 1976*. New Brunswick, N.J.: Rutgers University Center for Urban Policy Research.

Urstadt, Charles, ed. Undated. *Final Report, 1994 Gubernatorial Transition Housing and Community Development Committee* (unpublished and confidential).

U.S. Department of Commerce, Bureau of the Census. 1995. *Statistical Abstract of the United States, 1995*.

———. 1982–94. *Housing Units Authorized by Building Permits*.

Wolkoff, Michael A. 1988. *New York State Project 2000 Report on Housing*. Albany: Nelson A. Rockefeller Institute of Government.

CHAPTER 3

THE CONTRIBUTION OF PUBLIC-PRIVATE PARTNERSHIPS TO NEW YORK'S ASSISTED HOUSING INDUSTRY

Kathryn Wylde

Shortly after his election, Ronald Reagan convened a Presidential Commission to lay the groundwork for cutbacks in federal spending on housing production programs, ushering in the era of public-private housing partnerships. The limitations of a federal housing strategy in which "partnership" was a euphemism for transferring public obligations to the private sector were noted by David Rockefeller, whose family had been among the earliest limited profit investors in decent and affordable housing for New York's working poor.

In January 1981, Rockefeller brought President Reagan to New York and used the occasion to announce his own version of a housing partnership in which the resources of the private sector would supplement—not supplant—the government's role in funding affordable housing. The president did not leave before committing federal participation in the New York City Housing Partnership. Over the next few years, $30 million in what would be the last of the federal Urban Development Action Grants became the catalyst for production of more than $1 billion in new homeownership housing through Rockefeller's New York City Housing Partnership.

David Rockefeller found common cause with James Rouse, David Maxwell, Franklin Thomas, Mitchell Sviridoff, and others with the vision to find a silver lining in the federal budget crisis. Pulling together the threads of the community development movement of the 1960s and the privatization initiatives of the 1980s, they saw the opportunity to reorganize the nation's assisted housing industry to respond to political and fiscal realities. It was time to replace high-cost, top-down federal housing production programs with a new "partnership" approach that would leverage scarce public dollars and be more responsive to the needs of America's cities and to low income communities.

A decade later, the nation's assisted housing industry is dominated by a network of institutionalized partnerships whose primary task is to package and channel multilayered public and private financing into local housing and community development initiatives. These partnerships are typically structured as nonprofit "intermediaries" that provide the horizontal and vertical connections among community-based organizations, banks, builder/developers, investors, foundations, and all levels of government. The primary tools of their trade are the Community Reinvestment Act, the Community Development Block Grant, the HOME program, Low Income Housing Tax Credits, and the Empowerment Zone/Enterprise Communities initiatives. This new network has largely displaced the traditional constituency for federally subsidized housing (large-scale developers, public housing contractors, syndicators, investment bankers, and the construction trades), few of whom were prepared to participate in programs that involved at-risk private investment and limited profits.

The "partnership approach" has allowed local and state governments to stretch their resources and maintain a flow of housing production in poor neighborhoods during a period of federal retrenchment. By ceding substantial control over project design, construction specifications, and income targets, public programs have attracted private sector expertise and resources into the affordable housing field. Banks and developers with their own funds at stake collaborate with nonprofit organizations and government to keep costs down. Although no systematic empirical studies have compared the costs of housing built by public/private partnerships in the 1980s and 1990s to earlier housing programs, in many instances the cost to the taxpayer of a subsidized housing unit is lower today, in real dollars, than it was ten years ago. Moreover, the discipline of the marketplace and oversight by private investors has improved both the quality and prospects for long-term maintenance of assisted housing.

THE NEW YORK EXPERIENCE

Nowhere have the themes of public-private partnership and community development been more effectively interwoven than in the neighborhood rebuilding initiatives carried out in New York City over the past fifteen years. Since 1980, New York City and New York State have put up $5 billion in cash, free land, and tax abatements, matched ɔy another $5 billion in private loans and equity investments. This collaborative effort, together with an increase in demand for housing fueled by a burst of immigration (New York City Department of City Planning 1996), has produced or preserved an estimated 200,000 units of housing, reversing decades of economic decline in low-income communities across the five boroughs (New York City Housing Partnership 1994). An infrastructure of community-based nonprofit development organizations, for-profit developers and builders, financial institutions, and many national, regional, and local intermediaries are participants in a predictable, consistent system for development, ownership, and management of housing in the five boroughs.

With its reputation for red tape and high costs, New York City was an unlikely place for an efficient, public-private housing delivery system to emerge. A number of factors have contributed to its leadership role in this new era. For one thing, the housing crisis hit New York earlier than most places. New York's private affordable housing industry all but disappeared in the 1970s, when the cost of new construction went over $35 a square foot and increasingly large numbers of city residents could no longer afford the price of an unsubsidized home or apartment. Total production of housing shrank from an average of 37,000 units per year in the 1960s to 17,000 and 10,240 in the 1970s and 1980s, respectively (New York City Rent Guidelines Board 1997). Homebuilders moved to the suburbs and major developers, union contractors, and the organized construction trades redirected their attention to hotels and office buildings. Increasingly, residential construction and renovation work was left to nonprofit groups and small developer/builders.

Like many cities, New York entered the 1980s with a significant inventory of vacant land and abandoned buildings. But unlike most of its urban counterparts, New York enjoyed a resurgence of population growth, largely attributable to foreign immigration. Most important, this growth included many upwardly mobile people. Between 1980 and 1990, according to a study by Citizens Housing and Planning Council, the number of middle-income households (earning over $40,000) in New York City grew from 658,040 to 1,041,925, or an increase of about 384,000 households (Citizens Housing and Planning Council 1995). The result was a new demand for affordable housing from people who could afford to pay a significant share of their housing costs and support private debt.

New York capitalized on this market for moderately subsidized housing by employing homeownership and mixed-income development programs financed largely by the private sector. In the South Bronx, for example, block after block of new homes, colorful gardens, and ornamental wrought iron fences have replaced rubble-strewn lots and razor wire barricades. An emerging African American and Puerto Rican middle class, bolstered by the influx of Asian, Caribbean, Russian, and Latin American immigrants, reestablished property values in many of New York's inner-city neighborhoods.

At the other end of the economic spectrum, New York was the first place where the phenomenon of family homelessness captured media attention and public sympathy. Exposure of poor conditions in city shelters and welfare hotels led to a surge of advocacy efforts aimed at eliminating homelessness. By the mid-1980s, both the city and the state were committing significant funds to build and operate temporary and permanent homeless housing with little federal support. New York's federally funded public housing system was uniquely healthy and unwilling to accommodate homeless households, forcing the city and the state to develop locally funded housing alternatives with nonprofit organizations. While other cities were preoccupied with maintaining a deteriorated inventory of public housing for their poorest residents, New York was using federal emergency shelter payments to leverage private development of temporary shelters and requiring assisted housing developers to incorporate a set-aside of apartments for the homeless in mixed-income projects.

Perhaps the most important factor in New York's emergence at the forefront of the public-private housing movement was the relative strength and pace of the city's economic recovery from near bankruptcy in the 1970s. New York was in a position to invest its own money in homegrown, flexible public-private housing programs at a time when other cities and states still had to depend on a dwindling stream of highly restricted federal dollars. The city opened its capital budget to housing in 1982, with a $14 million allocation for street and sewer work associated with the construction of single-family homes. The city and the state also agreed to direct more than $500 million in surplus revenues from sources such as lease payments from the development of Battery Park City and refinancing of the debt of the Municipal Assistance Corporation into its housing production programs. By the end of the decade, the city was self-funding most local housing production and preservation activity at $400–$500 million a year, spending more than the next fifty largest cities in America combined (Berenyi 1989).

Freed from stringent federal program rules and income guidelines and from congressionally mandated Davis-Bacon requirements to pay prevailing wages to laborers and federally prescribed site and neighborhood standards, the creative energy of the city's assisted housing industry was unleashed. For the first time in memory, subsidies could be tailored to the needs of particular neighborhoods and sites, rather than having to fit local projects into the federal mold. The city's inventory of property and capital programs provided the raw material for a giant urban housing laboratory that attracted talent and energy from throughout the country. The role of community-based nonprofit and for-profit companies grew as the evidence came in that housing economics were enhanced by local ownership and management. Banks and investors became full partners in a system where the city's housing agency had the discretion—and good sense—to negotiate programs and projects that could sustain private investment or be readily modified if risk factors changed. There was never a federal production program that incorporated these elements.

There have been false starts and failed ventures, but the measure of New York's success is the fact that property values in the city's low-income communities have risen dramatically over the past decade—by as much as 300 percent in some communities. A notable example is Charlotte Street, where ranch homes that sold for $53,000 in 1984 now have current resale values in excess of $180,000. There is also a proliferation of entrepreneurial activity and institutional investment in neighborhoods where only the government had invested in development for the previous half century. Public-private housing initiatives have generated new relationships between low-income communities and the private sector that are spilling over into economic development, health care, small business growth, and job creation (Schwartz 1997). As banks, developers, and other investors have come to better understand neighborhood markets and to establish relationships with community leaders, they have been more willing to provide financing for business development in these areas.

New York's Public-Private Delivery System

New York's affordable housing industry has three distinct and largely self-contained sectors that produce and renovate assisted housing. First, there are a handful of private developers and syndicators that build or restore approximately 1,500–2,000 units a year in large, mixed-income projects with tax exempt financing, tax credits, FHA insurance, and tax abatements. Second, there are construction managers and bonded contractors who build and renovate public housing and other fully funded government programs, amounting to another 3,000 units of new or rehabilitated housing a year. Finally, the greatest production and renovation activity (6,000–10,000 units a year) comes out of an infrastructure of nonprofit development groups, intermediaries, community development lending institutions, small private developers, homebuilders, and contractors—all of whom share a neighborhood focus, work on a small scale, and utilize a blend of public and private resources. This last group holds tremendous promise for a sustained, cost-effective urban housing delivery system and is the subject of this chapter.

The economic structure of public-private partnership housing transactions is often quite complicated, involving multiple sources of equity and debt and broad allocations of risk. For example, development of low-income housing by nonprofit sponsors typically requires philanthropic seed funding from foundations or intermediaries to cover predevelopment costs. Construction and permanent financing must be obtained from a combination of sources that typically include banks, all levels of government, and private equity from individuals or the proceeds of tax credit syndication. For rental housing, operating subsidies are frequently necessary. Aside from local real estate tax abatements, the federal government has been the primary source of operating subsidies. The virtual elimination of incremental federal Section 8 subsidies has meant that federal HOME funds and the Low Income Housing Tax Credit must be used to capitalize operating reserves as well as pay for development costs of rental housing. For homeownership housing, the downpayment and credit history of individual purchasers are the foundation of a financial structure that includes public grants (CDBG, HOME, or local sources) to write down development costs, as well as tax abatements, tax exempt mortgage loans, and conventional bank mortgages. The central role of nonprofit intermediaries in virtually every partnership transaction is a direct consequence of the requirements associated with packaging and administering this layered, multisourced financing.

COMMUNITY DEVELOPMENT CORPORATIONS

Over the past two decades, New York City's housing delivery system has undergone a revolutionary change in focus and composition. Slum clearance and high-density development have given way to community-based planning and development, characterized by preservation, rehabilitation, and in-fill new construction at a neighborhood scale. This change was precipitated by the community development movement of the 1960s, seeded by the Ford Foundation and others, through which residents of low-income communities have become more sophisticated stakeholders in the assisted housing industry (Halpern 1995). The new direction was reinforced by the growing influence of private lenders and small developers, whose inclination was to take incremental risk and develop at more modest scale than was the case with government renewal and redevelopment programs.

Today there are more than 200 nonprofit community development corporations (CDCs) in New York City that own and manage 50,000 units of low- and moderate-income housing. These groups, primarily through advocacy intermediaries like the Association for Neighborhood Housing Development and the Community Training and Resource Center, exercise significant influence over city housing policies, including neighborhood planning, disposition of city-owned property, and capital budget priorities.

The City Charter revisions of 1975 and 1989 reinforced the role of communities in the land use planning and approval processes and, thereby, created a political arena in which local organizations could articulate community priorities and negotiate a greater role for themselves in neighborhood development. In 1975, New York State began funding the operating costs of local housing organizations through the Neighborhood Preservation Companies Program. This helped to move groups that started as community organizers and tenant advocates more firmly into development and ownership of low-income housing. In other localities, federally funded Community Development Block Grants (CDBGs) became the fuel for the community housing movement. Ironically, the result was often a lack of production orientation and discipline. Because New York City's CDBG funding was almost entirely diverted to support city staff and the repair costs of tax foreclosed (*in rem*) property, community-based nonprofit organizations in New York did not have this source of operating support and were forced to take an entrepreneurial approach as housing developers to support themselves.

The performance and longevity of CDCs was erratic for the first twenty years of their existence. During the past decade, however, their status and role in the housing industry grew, largely as a result of financial and technical assistance and political clout provided by the emergence of two national intermediaries, the Local Initiatives Support Corporation and the Enterprise Foundation. In 1987, LISC and Enterprise set up the city's first standardized, high-volume production program delivered through CDCs. The program involved the rehabilitation of vacant, city-owned buildings. The intermediaries provided a backstop that enabled CDCs to become general partners of hundreds of small projects financed through a combination of city and federal HOME dollars and the syndication of federal Low Income Housing Tax Credits.

Economies of scale in development and syndication were achieved through the wholesale nature of the relationship between government and the intermediaries. LISC and Enterprise selected the nonprofit developers, helped identify contractors, packaged financing, and enforced program requirements. As a result, the average predevelopment period for projects sponsored by CDCs was reduced from more than four years (application to project construction) to less than ten months, and the annual volume of CDC production increased from fewer than one hundred units a year to more than 1,000. Currently, CDCs are playing an expanded role in the purchase and renovation of occupied city-owned buildings and, under contract with the city, in early intervention with privately owned, distressed properties in their neighborhoods (see Braconi, chapter 4 in this volume).

The city's reliance on nonprofit groups as owner/managers of low- and moderate-income housing has had mixed results. While some of the larger groups have institutionalized a sophisticated property management system and strong professional staffing, others are struggling with their buildings and end up contracting out management to for-profit companies (Turetsky 1993). Some of the neediest communities have the least community development capacity. In Harlem, for example, the CDC movement was significantly retarded by the historically heavy-handed role of the now-defunct Harlem Urban Development Corporation, a state agency governed by a board of local elected officials.

CDCs in Harlem and some other communities still operate in a political environment that does not encourage the type of strong professional leadership required to sustain successful community development organizations. An illustration is the Consortium for Central Harlem Development (CCHD), a nonprofit initiative organized to carry out comprehensive redevelopment in the Bradhurst renewal area of Harlem. CCHD received enormous public and private investment but failed to produce the hoped-for results, in terms of physical development or community empowerment. Conversely, there are strong and seasoned CDCs in the South Bronx and Brooklyn that have run out of development opportunities in their own neighborhoods but are unable to expand into other needy communities because of parochial turf considerations. A good example is Los Sures, one of the strongest Latino-led CDCs, which has rebuilt its community in Williamsburg, Brooklyn, but been rebuffed by political forces when it has sought to extend its reach into other, undeserved Latino areas.

Looking ahead, CDCs that have depended on revenues from development of low-income housing will have to look for new sources of support if they are to survive the slowdown in production that will inevitably come with budget cuts. It is unclear whether housing management and services, as opposed to development, will sustain the interest of the current quality of leaders and staff. Even where development opportunities exist, the deep government subsidies that enabled local nonprofit groups to step into the role of developer are largely unavailable. Most CDCs will not be able to assume the financial, construction, and market risks associated with privately financed development. There is also concern as to how the current inventory of CDC-owned rental housing will fare as a result of the termination of Section 8 operating subsidies and the loss of benefits that many tenants will experience as a result of welfare reform (see Schwartz and Vidal, chapter 9 in this volume). In contrast to private landlords, CDCs depend on the good will of the communities they serve and are likely to be held at least partially accountable by their neighborhood constituencies for the impact of losses in public funding over which they have no control.

CDCs are grappling with these issues and looking beyond housing for the answers. Despite a spotty track record in the past (Schill 1997), new initiatives are under way to engage CDCs in retail and business development. CDCs are also being tested as a possible delivery mechanism for other services, including social welfare, day care, and employment training and job brokerage services. As the nation seeks more efficient ways to stretch scarce public resources and attract private investment to meet the needs of low-income communities, the community-based housing delivery system is a likely vehicle.

THE ROLE OF INTERMEDIARIES

New York City has used national and local intermediaries to design, administer, and help finance its most successful housing development programs. Development has become increasingly complex as a result of regulatory impositions and the multilayered financing required in the post-1980 partnership era of subsidized housing. The housing intermediary helps to package and track development projects, extending the capacity of government and facilitating the achievement of ambitious public policy objectives at a time when the budget and staff of public agencies is limited.

Intermediaries have been largely responsible for organizing private sector participation in the city's housing programs. Their institutional presence gives banks, investors, and developers confidence that public commitments will survive changes in elected administrations. Through memoranda of understanding, the City Department of Housing Preservation and Development (HPD) has used intermediaries to co-administer its development programs. This has permitted the city to avoid the inflexibility of the regulatory, procurement, and political encumbrances of a government agency, while not losing control of the development process or tying up sites and subsidies with individual developers.

The New York City Community Preservation Corporation (CPC) was the city's first *financial* intermediary, working with New York officials and communities to structure community reinvestment opportunities on behalf of a consortium of participating financial institutions. CPC was established in the mid-1970s to finance the upgrading of older apartment buildings in target preservation neighborhoods. It helped create and implement the city's Participation Loan Program for upgrading of private apartment buildings, using a blend of private and federal CDBG funds. CPC's role included helping to formulate the tax abatement and rent restructuring laws that made private lending to low-income, rental housing possible. CPC was also the intermediary that helped create and administer the Vacant Buildings Program in the 1980s, using a blend of private and city capital dollars to renovate the city's huge inventory of tax foreclosed vacant apartment houses. CPC has also been a vehicle through which pension funds, insurance companies, and the national secondary market have provided long-term capital to finance multifamily mortgages in low-income areas. In the past few years, several banks have also set up community development corporations and joined CPC as financial intermediaries, working directly with HPD to structure programs and underwrite projects.

The New York City Housing Partnership was the city's first *development* intermediary, organized in 1982 to help create and manage an affordable homeownership production program with the city. The Partnership forged a constituency of builders and banks to reestablish a homebuilding industry in inner-city neighborhoods. It was successful in generating new sources of federal and state funding and in securing private sector financing commitments to support what became the city's New Homes Program. The success of the Partnership-assisted initiative contrasted with the city's failed efforts to attract qualified homebuilders or private lenders to participate in an earlier homeownership program HPD had attempted on its own, using federal Section 235 subsidies. More than 13,000 homes and apartments, valued at more than

$1.5 billion, have been built and sold under the Partnership program. Three-quarters of the financing has been provided in the form of private equity and uninsured bank loans.

In the mid-1980s the most prominent national intermediaries, LISC and Enterprise, established major development programs with HPD along the lines of the Housing Partnership model, but applied to rental housing and rehabilitation rather than new construction. They brought philanthropic funds to seed low-income and homeless housing projects being developed by CDCs, raised equity through syndication of Low Income Housing Tax Credits, and established an oversight capacity to supervise and monitor the development activities and portfolios of dozens of CDCs. Since 1987, the programs of these intermediaries have resulted in rehabilitation of some 11,000 units, with more than $500 million in private funds generated by syndication of federal tax credits.

The value of intermediaries has been demonstrated in a variety of rehabilitation initiatives. The city's 1988 effort to launch a Small Home Rehabilitation and Sale Program to renovate and sell city-owned, tax foreclosed one- to four-unit buildings ran into delays and high costs. The program was recrafted as CityHome, with the Community Preservation Corporation advancing construction loans and the Enterprise Foundation coordinating development and marketing through nonprofit organizations. While still a labor-intensive and expensive program, several hundred city-owned buildings have been successfully renovated and sold since the intermediaries got involved. Enterprise also helped eliminate the interagency gridlock that stymied development of small, nonprofit projects in the early years of the State Housing Trust Fund and Homeless Housing Assistance programs.

Besides LISC and Enterprise, other national organizations have played intermediary roles in New York's housing industry. For example, the Industrial Areas Foundation established church-based initiatives in East Brooklyn and the South Bronx that have produced more than 3,000 affordable homes with a combination of public and private funding under the Nehemiah Program. ACORN established community-based mortgage counseling services and sponsored a development program that rehabilitated and sold more than a hundred abandoned houses in Brooklyn. New York City Neighborhood Housing Services, under the sponsorship of the national Neighborhood Reinvestment Corporation, has organized private and public financing for home improvement and rehabilitation initiatives.

Local nonprofit housing organizations have also undertaken intermediary roles to accommodate the demands of public-private funding sources and to respect the prerogatives of local residents and neighborhood-based institutions. The Urban Homesteading Assistance Board (UHAB) functions as an intermediary for tenant cooperatives, providing technical assistance and, increasingly, helping to structure and administer rehabilitation of city-owned buildings being purchased by residents under HPD's Tenant Interim Lease Program. The Community Service Society and the Parodneck Foundation have played an intermediary role with HPD and Chase Bank on behalf of tenants in distressed, privately owned rental buildings that are being acquired and upgraded with a combination of private and public funds through the Ownership Transfer Program.

Most recently, New York City has introduced intermediaries into the renovation and disposition of tax foreclosed, occupied buildings—for years the single most costly and poorly managed of the city's housing activities. A three-track initiative is focusing on geographic clusters of *in rem* buildings that are being turned over to tenant cooperatives, neighborhood entrepreneurs, and nonprofit CDCs. Through intermediaries, HPD hopes to achieve a "wholesale" approach to disposition that will more efficiently return the remaining stock of *in rem* buildings to private/nonprofit ownership and management.

NEIGHBORHOOD ENTREPRENEURS

For many years, opportunities for community participation in the assisted housing industry were limited to the construction workforce and the nonprofit sector. Local entrepreneurs seldom had the experience, bonding, union affiliations, or financing to qualify as contractors, developers, or owner-managers of government-funded projects. As a result, housing dollars flowed through low-income communities with little residual economic benefit in terms of business development and neighborhood employment.

The era of public-private partnerships opened up new opportunities for local contractors and developers, as smaller projects were financed through intermediaries with more flexible requirements and greater emphasis on reducing project costs. The first wave of opportunities went to recent immigrants, local property owners, and small contractors who established themselves as a second-tier residential construction industry specializing in moderate rehabilitation work. This emerging industry relied primarily on financing from the Community Preservation Corporation.

Despite the fact that assisted housing development was concentrated in minority communities, it was not until the end of the 1980s that Black and Latino entrepreneurs began to gain a share of the City's affordable housing business. In 1988, the Housing Partnership organized the first City program to bring minorities into the homebuilding industry, the Neighborhood Builders Program. The Partnership provided technical and financial assistance to minority firms seeking to move up to builder-developer status. Mortgage insurance from the State of New York Mortgage Agency (SONYMA) on construction loans and veteran homebuilders who served as a backstop for minority firms provided the credit enhancement these companies needed to secure bank loans. Over the succeeding decade, eighteen companies owned by blacks and Latinos have built more than $100 million in new housing through the Neighborhood Builders Program.

The growing role of black churches in the housing delivery system has also accelerated opportunities for neighborhood and minority entrepreneurs, as church-sponsored CDCs insisted on full minority participation on development teams and put their institutional assets on the line as a credit enhancement for minority companies. Church-based and minority-led CDCs do not share the adversarial relationship with their local for-profit sector that characterized many community development initiatives of the 1960s. Among mainstream CDCs, economic empowerment for low-income communities historically meant expanding opportunities for nonprofit institutions. Minority leaders, on the other hand, are dedicated to nurturing a for-profit, entrepreneurial sector within their communities. The federal Empowerment Zone, with strong minority leadership, will offer an opportunity to forge a new generation of public-private initiatives dedicated to making sure that minorities residing in low-income neighborhoods are employers as well as employees.

As might be expected for small companies experiencing rapid growth, the failure rate among minority-owned developers has been high. This is seldom due to a lack of technical skills, but is rather the consequence of being undercapitalized and overextended in terms of both debt and management capacity. Without access to conventional credit, minority contractors often incur enormous tax liens with interest accruals that ultimately force them out of business. None of the public loan funds created to assist these contractors has been successful. Joint ventures with majority companies, on the other hand, typically provide the minority partner with limited opportunities for growth and no recognizable track record for future business.

The Regional Alliance for Small Contractors, as well as borough and community-based local development corporations and a few programs sponsored by financial institutions, has developed programs to assist minority contractors. The entrepreneurial sector of the community housing movement, however, still lags far behind the nonprofit sector in terms of capacity, access to financing, and political support. For African American and Latino contractors, in particular, market share in New York's construction industry remains small.

In addition, public ownership of much of the real estate in low-income communities has also made it difficult for local and minority entrepreneurs to acquire an asset base. Over the past twenty years, the city owned up to 65 percent of the residential property in Central Harlem. The Giuliani Administration is attempting to get properties back into local private sector hands through a new initiative known as the Neighborhood Entrepreneurs Program. Using its Neighborhood Builders Program as a model, the Housing Partnership is the intermediary working with the city to renovate and transfer ownership of occupied *in rem* buildings to neighborhood-based property management companies. An interesting outcome of this initiative has been to encourage partnerships at the community level between entrepreneurs and nonprofit organizations. Initially, when the Partnership hired nonprofit groups to provide social welfare and employment services to tenants, neighborhood entrepreneurs objected to bringing a potential adversary onto the team. After working together on tenant orientation, services, and temporary relocation, however, many of these same entrepreneurs came to value the nonprofit role and voluntarily retained the organizations to provide tenant services after building rehabilitation.

LEVERAGING PRIVATE DOLLARS

New York's public-private partnerships have achieved volume and scale by attracting private investment in the form of both equity and debt financing. Most of the development has taken place in low-income communities where vacant city-owned land and buildings were located. Ironically, these were the same areas that suffered from massive disinvestment by private property owners and financial institutions during the 1960s and 1970s. The proactive role of banks and other private investors in helping to finance rebuilding efforts in these communities can be credited to three factors: (1) enactment of the federal Community Reinvestment Act (CRA) of 1978, together with related federal and state mortgage disclosure and fair lending laws; (2) incentives put in place by government to reduce risk and to enable banks and other private investors to earn a market rate of return; and (3) the resurgence of homeownership activity in inner-city neighborhoods, offering banks a standardized and familiar source of business activity with predictable takeout from the national secondary mortgage market.

Under the CRA, federally insured depository institutions must respond affirmatively to the credit needs of service areas from which they draw deposits, including minority and low-income communities. Bank regulators have recently promulgated more rigorous standards for CRA compliance that will rate institutions on the basis of actual lending and investment activity. Although New York is headquarters for more than 400 banks, only about two dozen institutions are active originators of community development or government-assisted loans, led by Chase Manhattan, Fleet, Citibank, Bank of New York, Dime, and Republic. Others gain CRA credit by participating in lending consortia organized by intermediaries. For example, Neighborhood Housing Services provides pooled financing for home improvement lending and downpayment assistance. The Community Preservation Corporation offers banks the opportunity to invest in multifamily mortgages or construction loans through lending pools or participation in loans to individual projects that rely on CPC's expertise for underwriting and loan administration. Foreign and wholesale institutions have also been tapped, most significantly in the SONYMA-insured investment facility known as GRAND (for Global Reinvestment in Affordable Neighborhood Development). An initiative of the Housing Partnership and Bankers Trust, GRAND has raised over $100 million from international financial institutions for the purchase of participation interests in construction loans originated and serviced on a conventional basis by real estate lenders.

Although CRA opens the door to bank financing, it does not require that banks subsidize development or take extraordinary risks with depositors' funds. As a result, bank loans for community development are typically proffered at market rates and on strict business terms. This means that government incentives are often required to mitigate risk and enhance affordability of housing developed through public-private partnerships. Cash subsidies, tax incentives, mortgage insurance, and indemnification from liability for lead and other contaminated conditions are some of the inducements the city has used to encourage bank investment. Programs have also been structured to provide latitude for response to changing market conditions and unanticipated construction problems, including subordination of public liens to private debt and flexible income targets. When banks put their own funds at risk, the city has also allowed them to control the projects' budgets and manage both public and private funds.

New York's rental housing programs have been structured to leverage bank loans and equity investment. The highest ratio of public to private investment in rental housing (1:1) has been achieved in preservation programs (for example, the Participation Loan Program) that involve moderate renovation of privately owned apartment buildings and where public dollars represent no more than 50 percent of total project cost. For projects involving substantial rehabilitation of vacant buildings and a mixed-income tenancy with a portion of units set aside for homeless households (for example, the Vacant Buildings Program), the ratio of public to private investment was closer to 2:1. Programs utilizing the federal Low Income Housing Tax Credit to finance rehabilitation of vacant buildings for low-income households (for example, LISC and Enterprise) have achieved public to private investment ratios of 2.5:1.

Homeownership programs have proven the most successful means of generating maximum private investment in residential redevelopment of blighted areas. Since 1980, the city's subsidized housing industry has increasingly shifted its focus from the production of rental housing and limited dividend cooperatives to small homes and condominiums. Among the reasons for this change is that single family homes cost less to build and require less public subsidy than multifamily construction. Owner-occupied housing also has the advantage of a built-in subsidy amounting to about $20,000 per unit, on account of the deductibility of home mortgage interest from income taxes. Through the national secondary mortgage market (Fannie Mae and Freddie Mac), home loan originators are assured access to an infinite supply of mortgage capital at lower rates and more favorable terms than rental housing. The city's homeownership development programs (for example, New Homes and Nehemiah) secure 80 percent of their required financing from private sector sources, including homeowner equity and institutional loans. Moreover, the ongoing property improvements contributed by resident-owners cause appreciation in neighborhood property values and generate further private investment in the surrounding area.

Housing development also leverages economic benefits beyond the dollars invested in construction. According to the U.S. Department of Commerce, each dollar spent on housing construction in New York generates an additional $1.95 in private sector economic activity in the region. A report of the New York Building Congress, "Fastrack to Recovery," found that each job created on a construction site resulted in a total of 2.23 jobs in the metropolitan region. A cost-benefit analysis of the Housing Partnership New Homes Program found that every $1 of city investment resulted in a long-term economic benefit of $12.46, including incremental tax revenues, infrastructure improvements, and the purchase of goods and services triggered by homebuilding and sales.

REPLICABILITY AND THE CHALLENGES AHEAD

New York City is distinguished from other localities by the size of public investment in housing and the extent to which intermediaries and private lenders play a significant role in the design and administration of the city's development programs. The volume and strength of New York's housing accomplishments reflect the fact that both local government and all sectors of the development community have recognized the value of partnerships and have learned how to use them. New York's success in leveraging private sector participation and regenerating neighborhoods suggests that its approach should be a model for other cities.

In summary, the key elements of New York's public-private partnership approach to community-based housing development and neighborhood renewal have included the following:

- Housing programs that have been restructured to limit profits and more effectively apportion risk and responsibility among the public, private, and nonprofit sectors using intermediaries as program administrators
- Government agency staff and nonprofit organizations that have assumed the upfront political risk and the cost associated with planning, public review, site selection, environmental review and compliance, and subsidy approvals
- Private builder-developers and contractors who have taken on the economic risk for containing construction costs, repayment of project loans, and timely sales or leasing
- Banks and other investors that have helped design programs and projects for which they could provide financing and expertise
- The use of local, state, and private funds to finance housing, in place of highly restrictive and bureaucratic HUD programs, which has resulted in lower costs, expedited project approvals, and participation by small, low-cost contractors

New York City has successfully used its housing development programs as a stimulus for private reinvestment and economic integration of many of its most blighted residential neighborhoods. However, economic development has not kept pace with the residential rebuilding programs. As a result, New York finds itself without the strategy for job creation and business development required to mitigate the impact of federal and state cutbacks in welfare, Medicaid, and housing programs that will disproportionately impact low-income communities. This, in turn, puts the public and private housing investment at serious risk.

It is also important to note the limitations of public-private partnerships in financing housing for very low-income households. In the absence of federal Section 8 subsidies or alternative forms of rental assistance for households living below the poverty line, there is no means to sustain private investment in rental housing for this population. In a high-cost area like New York, the Low Income Housing Tax Credit is insufficient to develop housing for households earning less than 50 percent of median income. As a result, the continued application of private equity or debt financing as a component of low-income housing development depends on federal assistance for the poorest segment of the population.

The challenge ahead is to adapt the resources of the community development movement and the network of public-private partnerships to the task of building a new urban economy that is less dependent on public funding. The federal government's effort is focusing on the Empowerment Zone and Enterprise Community initiatives. Intermediary organizations are devising their own strategies for helping their constituencies cope with the new fiscal reality. One example is the Retail Initiative launched by LISC, through which CDCs become co-owners of supermarkets with private investment capital raised by the national organization. In New York City, LISC and Bankers Trust, with Ford Foundation funding, have organized a fund through which CDCs can purchase retail franchises on behalf of neighborhood entrepreneurs. The New York City Partnership, a business organization, is raising $100 million from private investors to provide catalytic seed funding for urban economic development. The first project is the construction of new retail space on blighted shopping corridors in redeveloping neighborhoods, using a HUD grant and federal loan guarantees to bring commercial rents in at a level affordable in the local retail markets. The builder-developers, lenders, and owners of these projects will be the experienced private developers, banks, and CDCs that have joined forces to carry out housing partnership programs.

The thrust of these new national and local initiatives is to use the community-based, public-private housing delivery system as the primary agent for the transition of neighborhood economies toward greater self-sufficiency. The housing infrastructure is uniquely positioned to help design and deliver a new generation of social welfare and employment programs that are less costly and better coordinated than the current systems. Organizing services around where people live will help eliminate the redundancies and inefficiencies that public bud-

gets can no longer afford. The future of cities under the new fiscal realities will depend on the successful convergence of the community empowerment and privatization movements, a direction that has already
been charted by the nation's community-based housing industry.

REFERENCES

Berenyi, Eileen B. 1989. *Locally Funded Housing Programs in the United States: A
Survey of the Fifty-one Most Populated Cities.* New York: New School for Social Research.

Citizens Housing and Planning Council. 1995. The Urban Prospect.

Halpern, Robert. 1995. *Rebuilding the Inner City.* New York: Columbia University Press.

New York City Department of City Planning. 1996. *The Newest New Yorkers
1990–1994.*

————. 1992. *The Newest New Yorkers: An Analysis of Immigration into New York
City during the 1980s.*

New York City Housing Partnership. 1994. *Building In Partnership: A Blueprint
for Urban Housing Programs.* New York: New York City Housing Partnership.

New York City Rent Guidelines Board. 1997. "Housing Supply Report."

Schill, Michael H. 1997. Assessing the Role of Community Development Corporations in Inner-City Economic Development. *New York University Review of Law and Social Change* 22:753–81.

Schwartz, Alex, Bill Traylor, and Michael Bornheimer. 1997. *The Economic Impact
of New York City's Housing Investments.* New York: Local Initiatives Support
Corporation.

Turetsky, Doug. 1993. *We Are the Landlords Now: A Report on Community-Based
Management.* New York: Community Service Society.

CHAPTER 4

IN RE *IN REM:* INNOVATION AND EXPEDIENCY IN NEW YORK'S HOUSING POLICY

Frank P. Braconi

In rem is an unfamiliar term to most housing policy analysts in Washington and elsewhere, but in New York it resonates even with moderately informed members of the general public. That is because over the past eighteen years the city's *in rem* housing program has had a profound impact on its poorer neighborhoods and their residents. It has been the crossroads at which some of the most intense ideological battles over social policy have been fought and where the city's housing policy has scored its most dramatic victories and endured its most distinctive failures.

In rem is a legal term that derives from the Latin, meaning "against the thing." Technically, it refers to legal sanctions against property rather than individuals, specifically foreclosure actions on real estate for tax delinquency. In the vernacular of municipal government it is used to refer to the huge stock of tax foreclosed housing, both vacant and occupied, that is owned and managed by the city. More broadly, the term has come to connote the entire matrix of policies and programs directed at financially distressed private housing.

During the span of a single year in the late 1970s, New York City became the manager of nearly 40,000 occupied apartments, creating what was, in effect, the second-largest public housing authority in the country. The decision to assume that enormous responsibility was taken in response to a cycle of housing disinvestment and abandonment that had left some communities resembling the bombed-out cities of World War II. The intervention reflected New York's expansive view of the responsibilities of municipal government but also dramatized the city's chronic inability to acknowledge unpleasant social realities until exigency forces an improvised response. During the ensuing years the *in rem* program, shaped by constituency pressures, institutional inertia, and political expediency, became an expensive symbol of all that New York's progressive housing tradition had sought to avoid.

DISINVESTMENT AND RESPONSE: ORIGINS OF THE *IN REM* PROGRAM

The *in rem* program was New York's desperate response to the wave of disinvestment and housing abandonment that swept through many of its neighborhoods during the late 1960s and 1970s. Although New York is not the only city to have suffered housing abandonment (a 1979 GAO report found that 113 American cities suffered from building abandonment), several factors contributed to its particularly virulent form in New York and to the city's distinctive attempt to counter it.

The problem of building abandonment first aroused the concern of housing experts in the mid-1960s, by which time the underlying causes were already long standing. Disinvestment had been going on for some time but was manifested in a gradual deterioration in maintenance and services that was imperceptible except through statistical surveys. Only when the most advanced stage of disinvestment—abandonment—became plainly visible did the problem attract widespread attention. Significant housing abandonment began around 1963, and between 1965 and 1968 the city lost about 100,000 housing units (Kristoff 1970). The number of abandoned and boarded-up structures citywide increased from about 1,000 in 1961 to 7,000 in 1968.

Rates of abandonment peaked during the 1970s. Losses to the city's housing inventory approached 40,000 units annually in the years between 1970 and 1978, dropping to about 27,000 annually between 1978 and 1981 and to 23,000 annually between 1981 and 1984 (Stegman 1988). The loss rate dropped to 13,600 during the mid-1980s due to the combined effects of a surging economy and real estate values, mass immigration, the advent of community reinvestment banking, and the development of public anti-abandonment programs, including the *in rem* program itself.

The fundamental cause of housing abandonment was demographic change and the steady impoverishment and depopulation of many inner-city neighborhoods. As middle- and working-class whites sought more attractive housing options and neighborhood environments in quasi-suburban areas of the city or in adjacent suburban counties, black and Puerto Rican migrants replaced them in the city's older, more densely built neighborhoods. Denied the economic opportunities afforded their Euro-American predecessors, these minorities tended to have lower incomes and far higher rates of joblessness, making it more difficult for owners of marginal rental buildings to collect rents commensurate with building maintenance and operating expenses.

While racial prejudice accelerated the exodus of white working families out of the South Bronx, northern Manhattan, and central Brooklyn, a similar process also took place in neighborhoods that experienced little or no racial change, such as Harlem and Bedford-Stuyvesant. Seeking the same types of housing and neighborhood amenities as their white counterparts, the vanguard of a growing black middle class began departing those communities, eventually leaving behind a distilled strata of poor that has been termed "the urban underclass."

The sequence of racial change and urban impoverishment was generic to most older American cities and resulted in a similar marginalization of the older housing stock. But several factors that were characteristic of New York City contributed to a particularly intense form of housing disinvestment.

One factor was the city's unusual dependence on rental housing. New York's housing stock was (and still is) comprised two-thirds of rental housing and one-third of owner-occupied housing, nearly the reverse proportion of any other large city. That makes the city's housing stock more sensitive to profit and loss calculations, as absentee investors are more likely to be aware of, and act upon, bookkeeping judgments than are owner-occupants. Likewise, renters are more likely to resist paying for long-term investments in upkeep than are those who own the housing they live in.

A second factor was New York's propensity for undertaking large-scale housing development projects, which, while improving housing conditions for thousands of families, undermined the marginal private rental stock (Schwartz 1993). New York's program of public housing development far exceeded, even in proportional terms, that of other cities, pulling the most stable working tenants from less desirable private housing. Publicly assisted private housing had a similar effect, as when the massive Co-op City Mitchell-Lama project facilitated a sudden exodus of working-class families from the South Bronx.

Another factor was the city's system of rent regulation. The weight of the evidence suggests that it was a contributing, but not the primary, cause of housing abandonment (Rent Guidelines Board 1991). Some flexibility in rent setting was permitted by the regulatory authorities, but it was not enough to offset fully increases in operating costs. Between 1971 and 1981 heating oil prices increased by 430 percent and overall operating costs of apartment buildings in New York City rose by 131 percent, whereas the cumulative permitted rent increase for rent controlled apartments was 106 percent and for rent stabilized apartments 81 percent (Stegman 1985). Those years coincided with the period of peak housing abandonment.

The turbulence surrounding the city's rent regulation laws during the late 1960s and early 1970s dramatized the growing concern about building abandonment and how that concern was often subordinated to broader political considerations by both city and state legislators. Major liberalizations of the regulatory system were enacted in 1970 (the Maximum Base Rent system for adjusting rents) and in 1971 (vacancy decontrol), while regulatory controls were vastly expanded in 1969 (rent stabilization) and in 1974 (termination of vacancy decontrol). Property owners seeking regulatory relief found allies among academic and institutional critics concerned about housing disinvestment, while pressure for strengthening controls was exerted most effectively by representatives of middle-class neighborhoods where little abandonment was occurring (Mildner and Salins 1992).

While the city's rent regulation policies were vacillating between liberalization and restriction in response to countervailing political pressures, its housing agency was initiating a series of programs aimed at injecting desperately needed capital into financially starved low-income housing. In 1962 the city created the Municipal Loan Program, which provided low-cost public loans to qualifying properties for rehabilitation purposes. Although the Municipal Loan Program ended with a corruption scandal in 1971, its successors, the Participation Loan and Article 8-A programs, have become major instruments for leveraging public rehabilitation funds and are principal weapons against housing disinvestment. In 1973 the New York City Rehabilitation Mortgage Insurance Corporation (REMIC) was created to insure mortgages and hence to facilitate private lending in low-income neighborhoods. REMIC was an important financing tool until the State of New York Mortgage Agency (SONYMA) became active in the multifamily insurance market.

One of the most effective responses was the establishment of the Neighborhood Preservation Program in 1973. Utilizing a "carrot and stick" approach field workers operating out of "preservation offices" in five distressed neighborhoods (it was later expanded to other communities) identified buildings with serious maintenance code violations and encouraged landlords to apply for rehabilitation assistance or suffer the legal consequences. The program helped educate private owners about public rehabilitation programs and also served as a training ground for a number of housing activists who later assumed important executive roles in government, nonprofit, and private sector housing development.

Another anti-abandonment strategy, aimed at reducing the frequency of rent arrears among welfare recipients and improving their housing conditions, was worked out in conjunction with the city's Human Resources Administration (HRA) in 1978. Under that proposal, HRA proposed to expand its use of two-party rent checks (requiring the endorsement of both tenant and landlord in order to be cashed) for public assistance tenants in targeted housing; in return, owners would pledge to meet housing code standards and to participate in an intensified code enforcement program. The proposal was endorsed by major housing organizations but was opposed vigorously by welfare advocacy and social service organizations (Bernstein 1983). Opponents successfully lobbied the federal Department of Health, Education, and Welfare to deny the city permission to implement it.

Code enforcement and rehabilitation initiatives, even when financed with new federal Community Development Block Grant (CDBG) funds, were not sufficient to significantly stanch the epidemic of abandonment that was raging during the mid-1970s. By that time only a massive new income support program for the ghetto poor or direct subsidies to their landlords could have averted wholesale housing loss. Yet, when the Nixon Administration proposed a dramatic shift in federal housing support toward rent subsidies for families in private housing, the city was unenthusiastic. In congressional hearings Mayor John Lindsay expressed his concern that the proposed subsidies would cause rent inflation in low-income housing (which, of course, was exactly what was needed), and when the city received its first allocation of Section 8 Existing rent certificates, the Beame Administration sought to target them to residents of state- and city-financed public housing projects in order to reduce city subsidies to those developments.

In 1976 the city took its first major step toward becoming the owner of the last resort. Local Law 45 was enacted, shortening the period of tax delinquency required before the city could foreclose multifamily properties from three years to one. The new Koch Administration hoped that quicker vesting would encourage tax compliance or, at the least, allow the city to intercept buildings before they were completely deteriorated. At that time the majority of multifamily properties the city was vesting had already been abandoned by landlords and tenants alike. The new foreclosure policy resulted in more vestings of still-occupied buildings, but the city quickly realized that few legitimate housing investors were participating in its subsequent building auctions. Most of the buildings sold quickly lapsed into tax and mortgage arrears, and they were either abandoned or repossessed by the city (Green 1979). A moratorium on residential building sales was declared in 1978; when auctions were resumed in 1980 the program emphasized small buildings for which owner-occupancy was usually a condition of sale.

The inevitable result of the new vesting and sales policy was the accumulation of troubled buildings in the city's portfolio. The city's inventory of *in rem* buildings skyrocketed from 2,500 in September 1976 to 9,500 in September 1978 and by 1979 included some 40,000 occupied and 60,000 vacant apartments. In order to better manage this immense inventory responsibility was transferred from the Department of General Services (DGS) to a reconfigured housing agency, the Department of Housing Preservation and Development (HPD).

THE IMPROVISED HOUSING AUTHORITY: THE CITY AS MANAGER

HPD's efforts to gain control of its sudden, dilapidated empire were nothing short of heroic. When the agency assumed management responsibilities, most of the properties were in horrendous physical condition, the occupancy rate in *occupied* buildings was less than 40 percent, and rent collections were running at about 36 percent of billings. At the outset HPD did not have accurate data on how many buildings were in its charge, whether they were occupied or vacant, or whether the tenants of record were actually still living in the apartments (Leventhal and Raymond 1979).

The agency's early efforts focused on cataloging the inventory, computerizing records, consolidating buildings, and addressing critical maintenance needs, particularly heating problems. A comprehensive physical survey of the inventory was launched, aimed at gauging the occupancy and maintenance condition of the buildings, verifying tenancy, and establishing rent payment records. The HDA had operated a Division of Relocation Operations responsible for relocating tenants displaced through Urban Renewal or other government programs, and the unit was expanded to conduct consolidation operations in *in rem* buildings. During the first five years of HPD management, 7,448 families were relocated and over 1,900 buildings were emptied and demolished or boarded up. The consolidation operations raised the occupancy rate of centrally managed buildings to over 85 percent by 1984.

The abysmal rent payment rate in city-owned buildings apparently angered and embarrassed Mayor Ed Koch, and he ordered HPD officials to attach the highest priority to raising rent collections. The deteriorated condition of the buildings and DGS's lax approach toward collecting rent and providing services had fostered "negligent, if not belligerent, attitudes toward rent payment among some tenants" (Leventhal 1979). To facilitate tenant payments HPD established a network of Manufacturers Hanover branches and check-cashing outlets where tenants could pay their rent bills in person, and created the Tenant Legal Affairs Unit (TLAU) to initiate legal action against residents who failed to pay rent. Through 1983 the TLAU served some 25,000 three-day eviction notices and repossessed over 5,000 apartments. The unit also worked with the Department of Social Services to identify public assistance recipients who were in rent arrears; within a year either two-party rent checks or direct vendor payment rent checks were being issued for some 1,100 public assistance recipients living in city-owned buildings. Such efforts eventually raised rent collections to over 87 percent.

For the day-to-day management of the stock HPD established eleven neighborhood offices, out of which real estate managers could coordinate the activities of superintendents, handymen, and contractors. When HPD assumed responsibility for *in rem* housing, routine maintenance was performed by some 2,800 superintendents, most of whom were part-time employees. The agency began a program of consolidating and upgrading its superintendent workforce, reducing the number of superintendents by 1,100. Major repairs were performed by independent contractors through open-market orders (OMOs). The number of OMOs issued by HPD rose from 47,000 in 1979 to 64,000 in 1982. Between the winter of 1979 and the winter of 1981 the percentage of occupied *in rem* buildings without heat on any given day was reduced from nine to two, and the median time required to restore heat was cut from 14 days to three. Overall, the number of tenant complaints received by the agency's Central Complaint Bureau decreased from 56,000 in 1979 to 13,400 in 1983.

As valiant as HPD's initial efforts to gain control of the inventory were, once the agency settled into a long-term management role the inevitable bureaucratic rigidity and indifference set in. Efficiently managing a huge, severely deteriorated inventory scattered haphazardly throughout a third of the city is a virtually impossible task. Furthermore, the city's elaborate purchasing rules made procurement of simple maintenance items and services expensive and time consuming. Maintenance conditions in *in rem* housing remained far below the standards of most of New York's rental housing (see Table 4.1). HPD's Bureau of

TABLE 4.1
Housing Maintenance Deficiencies, *In Rem* v. All Rental Housing, 1991

Condition	In Rem	All Rental
Maintenance deficiencies		
1 or more	89.1%	54.4%
3 or more	54.0	17.3
Additional heating needed	38.0	20.9
Heating breakdown (four or more times)	22.9	9.9
Cracks or holes in wall/ceiling/floor	66.4	23.9
Broken plaster	35.5	13.2
Rodents present	76.9	32.4

Source: 1991 Housing and Vacancy Survey.

Vacant Apartment Repairs (BVAR), in particular, was cited for inefficiency and waste. When the agency's operating budget was cut back in the early 1990s, maintenance problems multiplied.

As the 1980s progressed, narcotics trafficking in *in rem* housing became a significant maintenance and safety problem. Through bribery and intimidation, drug gangs took over numerous *in rem* apartments, creating dangerous environments in many buildings. HPD's narcotics unit removed a remarkable 1,300 drug dealers from *in rem* buildings between April 1988 and September 1989, in the process pioneering methods of thwarting housing-based drug dealing (Vance 1994) that have been replicated nationwide.

During the 1990s legal and environmental considerations increased the pressure on HPD's management practices. A state court ruling associated with the *Mattie Lacks v. City of New York* litigation would subject all *in rem* housing to New York's Housing Maintenance Code, complete compliance with which HPD claims would require rehabilitation of the entire portfolio at a cost of $10 billion. The agency has also grown increasingly concerned about the proliferation of lead poisoning liability suits, which can expose the city to huge financial judgments. In one case the family of a child who suffered lead poisoning while residing in an *in rem* apartment was awarded $10 million.

Operating the *in rem* stock proved to be extraordinarily expensive and has been the source of long-standing friction between the city and the federal Department of Housing and Urban Development (HUD). The federal Community Development Block Grant (CDBG) program was created under the Housing and Community Development Act of 1974, and the city began receiving federal funds through it in 1975. When the city ceased auction sales of occupied *in rem* buildings, it made an emergency request to HUD for permission to use $41 million of its CDBG funds for *in rem* maintenance and management. That request

TABLE 4.2
HPD Occupied *In Rem* Inventory and Sales by Program, 1980–1996

Year	Total Inventory	TIL	Sales by Program POMP	CMP	Other	Total
1980	46,420	85	0	0	0	85
1981	43,867	254	516	102	758	1,630
1982	44,046	1,027	222	725	293	2,267
1983	43,667	1,521	964	306	258	3,049
1984	46,361	575	825	303	232	1,935
1985	51,764	410	1,001	492	554	2,457
1986	53,243	413	582	581	136	1,712
1987	52,160	325	554	153	30	1,062
1988	51,849	1,024	0	111	76	1,211
1989	49,998	542	644	309	88	1,583
1990	48,998	740	2,228	457	21	3,446
1991	45,478	1,429	1,085	472	21	3,007
1992	43,607	1,212	930	275	37	2,454
1993	41,315	1,127	1,725	622	38	3,512
1994	38,964	655	855	216	40	1,766
1995	39,112	1,054	198	630	833	2,715
1996	34,474	1,183	0	0	3,144	4,327

Source: New York City Department of Housing Preservation and Development.

was approved, but when the city sought to use $100 million for the program the following year, HUD denied permission, ruling that such use of funds was contrary to the statutory language authorizing the program. After vigorous lobbying by members of New York's congressional delegation, Secretary Patricia Harris authorized use of the funds to cover *in rem* expenses other than fuels and utilities, conditional on the city's commitment to return the buildings to private ownership. Vice President Walter Mondale personally telephoned Mayor Koch with the news of the Administration's decision.[1]

At the time of its 1979 request, HPD was predicting that the *in rem* inventory would grow to include 10,450 occupied buildings containing 83,000 housing units. Those workload projections were not borne out; as shown in Table 4.2, a peak inventory of about 53,000 occupied units was reached in 1986. As the cost of operating the inventory increased, however, and federal appropriations to the CDBG program were curtailed, the share of its Community Development funds the city spent on *in rem* operations rose to about two-thirds. Many other CD-eligible programs were squeezed out, including rehabilitation programs for the private stock.[2]

During the period spanning the city's 1991 to 1994 fiscal years spending on HPD's property management operations reached their maximum, averaging $294 million annually. Rent collections over the period averaged about $85 million, leaving an operating deficit of about $209 million annually (an additional $100 million per year was spent on *in rem* building rehabilitation through the city's capital budget). Community Development funds covered about $165 million of that annual deficit. On a per-unit basis the operating deficit averaged about $5,000 per year, or $400 per month, as against residential rent collections that averaged $167 per month. In 1995, contract rents in *in rem* housing averaged only $229 per month.

The principal reason rents remained so low is that impoverished tenants have become increasingly concentrated in *in rem* buildings during the years of city ownership and thus have little ability to pay. Between 1981 and 1992 the median income of *in rem* tenants *declined* from $6,865 to $6,420, while the proportion on public assistance rose from approximately 30 percent to 65 percent. This deterioration in the income mix of *in rem* buildings was a direct result of the city's homeless policies.

As family homelessness emerged as a major social problem during the early 1980s, the Koch Administration, under intense pressure from the advocacy community, the media, and the courts (Kirchheimer 1990), desperately sought permanent housing resources into which homeless families could be placed. Meeting disinterest by private housers and resistance from the New York City Housing Authority,[3] the Administration focused on HPD's inventory and in 1983 adopted a policy of filling all vacancies in *in rem* buildings with referrals from the city's shelter network. The decision to use *in rem* housing as the city's "housing of the last resort" greatly complicated subsequent management and disposition efforts. Between 1987 and 1995 the city placed almost 13,000 homeless families into *in rem* buildings, representing about 40 percent of all homeless families relocated to permanent housing.

Homeless families in New York city are drawn almost exclusively from the ranks of the welfare poor, a fact that the homeless advocacy community has attempted to downplay over the years. Advocates have sought to distance the homeless in the eyes of a generally sympathetic public from the politically unpopular welfare issue, while quietly pressing for higher welfare grants through the courts.[4] Although it proved to be a successful public relations strategy, it also blurred the relationship between welfare policy and homelessness and has not led to an open and honest political debate on either. This strategy accorded with the "grand compromise" on welfare policy that held at the national level for thirty years: public policy would make no educational or work demands of welfare recipients, but in return government would be free to pursue a least-cost system of income maintenance for the nonworking poor.

The "housing, housing, housing" mantra of advocates for the homeless during the 1980s should more appropriately have been "welfare, welfare, welfare," since family homelessness in New York City has been a direct and predictable outcome of the state and city's unrealistically low welfare grants. Since New York's AFDC grants were bifurcated in 1975, creating separate "basic grants" and "shelter allowances," the real value of the shelter allowance has eroded by 40 percent.[5] Between 1981 and 1991 the supply of private rental apartments affordable to a welfare family of three in New York City declined by nearly 60 percent (Braconi 1993). The monthly grant of $286 for a family of three is nearly $100 less than what the Rent Guidelines Board calculates is the average cost of operating a rent stabilized apartment. Given the enormous gap between economic rents and the shelter allowance, the mystery is not why 5 percent of the city's welfare families become homeless each year, but why the rest do not.

With options for placing homeless families in private and conventional public housing thus limited, the *in rem* stock served as the relief valve for the state and city's myopic welfare policy.

BIRTH OF A CONSTITUENCY: *IN REM* DISPOSITION PROGRAMS

From the outset it was anticipated that city ownership of abandoned and tax-delinquent buildings would be temporary. In early 1979 the agency projected that dispositions would begin to exceed vestings by 1982 (Leventhal 1979), but the disposition process quickly proved to be more difficult and expensive than anticipated. Indeed, one of the fundamental miscalculations the city made in organizing its *in rem* program was its failure to anticipate how intensely politicized the disposition process would become.

In 1979 HPD projected that annual dispositions of occupied *in rem* housing units would reach 13,500 by 1982, with nearly 10,000 coming through its newly created Division of Alternative Management Programs (DAMP). In fact, dispositions reached only 4,490 in fiscal 1982 and for the first three years of the program totaled more than 15,000 below projections. Even further off the mark were projections regarding the per-unit cost of rehabilitation work prior to disposition. In 1979, the agency projected a weighted average unit cost of $3,887; in reality, the rehabilitation costs have spiraled ever upward, topping $35,000 per unit by 1990.

Upon taking control of the *in rem* inventory in 1978, HPD established an array of disposition programs geared toward utilizing virtually any potential source of alternate ownership. Three core approaches survive to this day: tenant ownership, local nonprofit ownership, and private for-profit ownership. A fourth, continued public ownership under the auspices of the New York City Housing Authority, faded as the authority increasingly resisted bailing out the city to its own financial detriment.

Tenant ownership has been the most ambitious of the disposition routes, by far the most favored by housing advocacy groups and, when viable, by the tenants themselves (Cotton 1993, 1996). While many of the city's housing policies have drifted toward a pervasive paternalism, tenant ownership has been one of the few areas where the poor have been encouraged to take responsibility for shaping their environment. By supporting the program and encouraging tenant involvement the advocacy community has generally played a constructive role. Although the concept appeals to social policy conservatives as well, it has never been a favorite of the professional bureaucracy at HPD, which tends to see more expansive social policy goals as a diversion from the agency's production-oriented mission.

Tenant ownership has been pursued mostly through the Tenant Interim Lease (TIL) program of the DAMP. Originally, the program was intended for rapid out-take of the "better" buildings in the *in rem* inventory, especially those that had high occupancy rates and required relatively little predisposition renovation. In its original plan, HPD anticipated per-unit rehabilitation costs of only $1,000 in TIL buildings. Among the conditions of sale were that 60 percent of the tenants residing in the building sign a resolution seeking ownership, and that they would be willing to raise rents, if necessary, to meet projected expenses. During an eleven-month interim period a tenants' association would manage the building and receive technical assistance and classroom training from the Urban Homesteading Assistance Board (UHAB), a citywide nonprofit organization operating under contract to HPD. If the tenants' management performance passed HPD's review, the building would be sold to a legally constituted tenant cooperative corporation for $250 per dwelling unit. In many respects the program, especially in its early years, worked as designed; in the first three years, 111 buildings containing 2,887 apartments were sold to residents. Many of those buildings became showcases for tenant empowerment and islands of stability in otherwise devastated communities. By 1996 over 600 *in rem* buildings had been sold to their residents through the TIL program.

During the 1990s, unfortunately, some of the early TIL co-ops ran into financial difficulties and many are now vulnerable to *in rem* foreclosure themselves. Those difficulties are, in part, a legacy of the financial illusions of both housing activists and city policy. The anti-landlord rhetoric of advocacy groups misled tenant cooperators about the precarious financial realities of operating low-income housing in the city, leading to initial rents that were set too low and to a chronic unwillingness of tenant-comprised co-op boards to implement sufficient rent increases. For its own political and financial reasons the city could not admit to the essential worthlessness of most *in rem* buildings and so overassessed TIL buildings for property taxes and, for years, clung to the ludicrous policy of requiring 40 percent of the profits from resold apartments to be "returned" to the city.[6] Moreover, budget constraints and disposition urgency led the city to set rehabilitation scopes for the early generation of TIL buildings that were far too modest.

In more recent years rehabilitation budgets for TIL buildings have been equalized with those of other disposition programs, but new factors have emerged to constrain the program. Most importantly, potential tenant co-ops must now be drawn from a hard-core pool of *in rem* properties, many of which have languished in city ownership for years and have been populated with very low-income, often multiproblem, formerly homeless families. This affords tenant organizers with a less competent and cohesive roster of residents from which to recruit association or co-op board members. Tenant organizers also report that drug-dealing operations in many buildings intimidate tenants into disinvolvement and focus the energies of the more upwardly mobile on leaving.

The second mainstay of the disposition effort has been the nonprofit sector. The mechanism for turning city-owned residential buildings over to private nonprofit companies actually predated HPD, having been created in 1973 under the auspices of the HDA. Although the particulars of the program have changed along with its acronym (the Community Management, Neighborhood Ownership Works, and Neighborhood Redevelopment programs under the Koch, Dinkins, and Giuliani administrations, respectively), the essentials of the approach have remained the same. Nonprofit community groups, usually organized under Article 11 of the State Private Housing Finance Law, manage a cluster of buildings for two or three years under contract to the city, and eventually purchase the buildings for a nominal sum or turn them over to a tenant cooperative. In the interim the buildings undergo moderate rehabilitation; the scope of work has tended to be expansive as the buildings were originally selected from among those least ready for quick dispositions to tenants or to the for-profit sector. The program has put many buildings into the hands of capable and dedicated community groups, although HPD has often voiced concern about the capacity of the nonprofit sector to handle the volume of work the advocacy community would have thrust upon it. Through 1996, dispositions to nonprofit organizations accounted for only about 23 percent of all *in rem* building dispositions. Indeed, HPD officials have often grown impatient with the pace at which community groups move toward assumption of ownership; program redesign during the Dinkins Administration was geared toward giving experienced for-profit contractors more authority to do fast-track rehabilitations.

The nonprofit approach to privatizing *in rem* buildings is a descendant of the limited dividend housing movement, which has a long and varied history in New York (Birch and Gardner 1981; Robbins 1984). This approach eliminates the purely speculative elements of private housing investment and theoretically lowers rent levels by limiting profit margins (whether to 7 percent, 6 percent, or zero). But a number of observers, including some from within the not-for-profit community, have questioned whether community ownership has demonstrated any clear cost efficiencies when compared to the for-profit model. Like those sold through TIL, some of the buildings transferred to not-for-profit organizations have run into financial problems. Initial rents, especially in the early generation of buildings, were set quite low and have failed to keep up with escalating operating costs. Although they are generally treated favorably for tax purposes, rising water and sewer charges after 1988 have hit them particularly hard.

The third and most controversial leg of the disposition triad has been for-profit disposition, most of which has been through the Private Ownership and Management Program (POMP). The program was favored by HPD officials because it allowed them to achieve high outtake volumes working with experienced for-profit contractors and managers, but it was the target of unrelenting criticism from the advocacy community during its thirteen-year life. Although intakes into POMP were eventually terminated by the Dinkins Administration, they were nevertheless the workhorse of the city's disposition efforts during the Dinkins years, accounting for nearly half of the 12,400 units disposed of between 1990 and 1993.

Under POMP the housing agency selected for-profit management firms, most of which were also construction contractors, from a prequalified list. These firms managed agreed-upon buildings for a period of one year under contract to HPD, during which time they were responsible for making repairs and removing code violations. Originally, the buildings were selected from among the least deteriorated of the *in rem* portfolio, but the quality of buildings targeted for the program declined dramatically during its course. Prior to 1988 per-unit rehabilitation costs ranged from about $1,700 to $4,600, after which the cap on renovation expenses was raised from $5,000 to $12,000 per unit. The expenses were paid for with CDBG, federal Section 17, or city capital budget funds. If the firm's management performance was acceptable, it was given the option to purchase the buildings for $2,500 per unit. To deter short-term speculation, the buildings were appraised at the time of sale and the difference between the purchase price and the appraised value was recorded as a contingency lien on the property that could be called if the terms of the sales agreement, which included a ten-year ban on resale and a fifteen-year prohibition on co-op conversion, were violated. As in other DAMP programs, a rent restructuring was implemented prior to sale and the apartments were placed under rent stabilization upon out-take.

Private low-income housing developers were ambivalent about the program (Citizens Housing 1989). Many felt that the buildings were too run down, and populated by a tenancy that was too uniformly poor, to offer attractive investment opportunities. Drug dealing and other management problems made some skeptical that the buildings could be stabilized without significant budgets for security and social services. Those who were enthusiastic were usually motivated more by the hope of long-term appreciation than by the prospects for immediate operating profits. The professional housing community, including many leading figures in the not-for-profit development sector, generally viewed the program as a necessary and manageable component of the disposition effort. Grassroots advocacy groups, however, were unremittingly hostile to it.

The opposition of some leftist advocacy groups to POMP was, at root, ideological. Those activists portrayed for-profit ownership as fundamentally inconsistent with the provision of low-income housing and sought in the *in rem* program a means of socializing, or "not-for-profitizing," the preponderance of the city's low rent housing infrastructure. That perspective often exaggerated the likelihood of "gentrification" in very low-income neighborhoods and elevated perpetually low rents to a position of primacy among social policy goals. More moderate elements of the housing community regarded any income mixing that might gradually come about through private owner rental practices as socially beneficial, and stressed the need for low-income housing subsidies whatever the form of ownership.

Like too many policy debates, the POMP controversy took place without the benefit of much hard, quantitative evidence. The most thorough study of the program was conducted by the New York City Comptroller's Office (Holtzman 1991), but the significance of its conclusions was mostly in the eyes of the beholder. Critics pointed to the numerous code violations found in some of the buildings and to an alleged overreliance on eviction proceedings to stabilize building rent rolls. Defenders of the program, including HPD, focused on the generally good maintenance records of the majority of the properties surveyed, on the disproportionately high number of homeless families accommodated in POMP buildings, and on the owners' excellent record of property tax payments. The Dinkins Administration's decision to terminate the program was celebrated by tenant advocates but dismayed the professional housing community and some senior HPD officials.

By the early 1990s the city was spending over $100 million annually in capital budget funds to rehabilitate and dispose of occupied *in rem* properties. The ten-fold growth in per-unit renovation costs reflected, in part, the city's financial ability to fund more complete and sounder rehabilitation scopes. It also reflected, however, the politicization of the disposition process and the growing power of tenant and community group constituencies.

The contentious process of occupied building disposition contrasted markedly with the rapid mobilization undertaken to recycle vacant *in rem* buildings after 1986. Administratively, the vacant property programs were organized by HPD's development arm out of the agency's 100 Gold Street headquarters, rather than by its property management division at 75 Maiden Lane.[7] The bureaucratic culture in the development unit was, by virtue of its mission and its staff expertise, geared more toward construction efficiency and production volume, and because there were no tenants in place, it was far less constrained by constituency pressures. No tenant ownership program was established, giving the private development community a far greater role. Several massive clusters of vacant buildings were transferred to sophisticated, citywide nonprofits and rehabilitated using large, private sector construction management contractors.[8] Disposition to smaller, community-based nonprofits was accomplished by utilizing the services of the Enterprise Foundation and the Local Initiatives Support Corporation (LISC) as intermediaries, which provided tax-credit financing and management and technical expertise. The workhorse of the program, however, was the Vacant Building Program, which recruited private sector contractor-managers to rehabilitate and own small clusters of buildings. Essentially an adaptation of the PLP moderate rehabilitation program, the Vacant Building Program blended city and private funds and, by preserving private sector cost incentives, achieved high production volumes and low per-unit costs. The program proved to be immensely popular with private developers and potential residents alike, with managers regularly receiving over one hundred applications for each apartment available for rent. Overall, the vacant-building disposition effort accomplished the gut rehabilitation of some 40,000 housing units within seven years, a record that ranks among the most successful urban redevelopment initiatives in the country's history.

Toward the end of the Dinkins term the growing fiscal crisis ended the period of massive city spending on new housing development, and the requirements of the *in rem* disposition program began to squeeze other desirable community development efforts out of the budget. Repeated cuts in HPD's operating budget diminished the agency's property management capacity, and even the most vocal advocates of public sector appropriation of low-income housing began to reconsider the desirability of indefinite city ownership of *in rem* buildings. In 1993 the city quietly began a moratorium on new property vestings.

PRIVATIZATION WITHOUT TEARS: THE GIULIANI DIRECTION

By the time the Giuliani Administration took office, shrinkage of the city's *in rem* portfolio had assumed a new urgency. Mounting budget pressures forced deep cuts in HPD's expense budget and the city began to bump against the municipal debt ceiling set by the State Constitution, constraining its ability to use capital budget funds for *in rem* rehabilitation or any other housing development purpose. The *Mattie Lacks* case threatened to force the city into a more expensive standard of *in rem* maintenance while the number of lead paint liability suits mushroomed. After the Republican sweep in the 1994 congressional elections, even the future of the Community Development Block Grant program—for years the lifeblood of the *in rem* program—seemed uncertain.

During the 1993 mayoral election campaign Rudolph Giuliani made it clear that he would aim to reduce the *in rem* inventory; he was particularly critical of Dinkins's decision to phase out the POMP program. Many expected that his administration would adapt the Vacant Building Program to achieve maximum disposition to the for-profit sector, utilizing the organizational infrastructure and network of contractors that had been established through that program. The administration surprised the housing community, however, when the new Housing Commissioner Deborah Wright unveiled a for-profit disposition initiative, the Neighborhood Entrepreneur Program (NEP), geared toward cultivating locally based, minority-owned housing development capacity. The program enlisted the New York City Housing Partnership as a not-for-profit intermediary to screen applicants and provide technical and other assistance. Participation in the program was limited to smaller construction contractors and housing managers with established ties to targeted neighborhoods. Although participation was not restricted to minority-owned firms, the criteria for developer selection were set to maximize minority involvement. The advocacy community offered perfunctory opposition to NEP that was muted somewhat by the minority-owned business orientation of the program. Within the professional housing community reactions were mixed, with some welcoming the attempt to encourage a minority-owned housing development sector and others fearing that the goal of rapid rehabilitation and disposition could get subordinated to other objectives.

Although the administration also made adjustments to other disposition programs, its most dramatic break with past policy came on the intake side of the ledger. The Dinkins Administration had begun to defer the city's annual boroughwide property vestings in 1993, but the Giuliani Administration amazed the real estate industry when it publicly acknowledged the moratorium in early 1995. The public announcement of a moratorium on *in rem* foreclosures temporarily left the city with no property tax enforcement mechanism and effectively committed the administration to redesigning its policies toward tax delinquent real estate. After months of analysis and internal debate, a new tax enforcement policy was announced in October 1995.

The new policy would generate revenue from tax receivables by selling tax liens to investors, an enforcement approach used by other cities throughout the country and by New York City itself until well into the 1950s. Tax lien sales, however, would be limited to commercial, utility, and high-end residential properties that offered good prospects for repayment and hence would be marketable to investors. Economically marginal residential properties would be channeled through the conventional foreclosure process, but once a judgment of foreclosure was rendered the properties would be deeded to third-party for-profit or not-for-profit owners rather than to the city. The city would consequently stop taking residential properties into its direct ownership (except for unusually deteriorated or unmanageable buildings), hence circumventing its intricate land-use rules and blunting the political pressures that have constrained disposition policy. The new approach was generally well received by the professional housing community. Most encouraging was the plan's emphasis on early intervention and preservation of troubled housing.

During the 1990s housing analysts have grown increasingly concerned that the city is heading for another cycle of low-income housing disinvestment (Citizens Housing 1992; Bach and West 1993). The citywide real estate depression, triggered by the 1987 stock market crash and subsequent economic contraction, punctured the speculative hopes that had sustained many low-income housing investors during the 1980s. Despite a decline in rental building values, property tax assessments continued to increase in low-income neighborhoods while soaring water and sewer fees became a major new source of financial stress. From 1989 to 1995 aggregate property tax arrears for walk-up apartments—the building type most often foreclosed by the city—increased from $28 million to $71 million. Although the population of buildings in serious tax trouble has not increased significantly, about 14,000 endangered buildings have fallen deeper into delinquency. In 1996 federal welfare reform legislation further dimmed the financial prospects of low-income housing.

The Giuliani Administration's *in rem* plan recognizes the need to identify troubled buildings before their problems become insurmountable and for the city to devise assistance packages that address their financial difficulties. There is widespread skepticism, however, that the city will commit the budgetary resources or political capital necessary to reverse the deteriorating financial condition of low-income housing (Schwartz and Vidal, chapter 9 in this volume).

At present any significant plan to preserve private, low-income housing must have two major components. First, a substantial increase in city funding for PLP and Article 8A loans is needed. Those loans not only provide low-cost capital for rehabilitation and renovations that lower building operating expenses, they also provide access to J-51 tax benefits and permit increases in regulated rents. In recent years those programs have treated about 3,500 units annually on combined budgets of about $30 million per year, but there are approximately 350,000 private, rent regulated housing units in the city's poorer neighborhoods. The task of upgrading and assisting all buildings that might benefit from those programs, moreover, was made immeasurably more difficult by Congress's temporary elimination of funding for incremental Section 8 rental vouchers, which are used to mitigate the effects of rent increases on low-income tenants of rehabilitated buildings. Few in the housing industry expect the city to provide the $90 million annually that would be necessary to lower the rehabilitation cycle from one hundred to thirty years.

The second essential component is tax relief. The extraordinary rates of tax delinquency in certain neighborhoods[9] indicate that there is a fundamental bias in the city's assessment practices that leads to an unrealistic tax burden on low-income housing, but it continues to siphon income from marginal properties through property taxes and other charges. Although there is some hope that a less regressive pricing system for water and sewer services can be implemented, militating against property tax relief is the city's budget condition and its need to keep the assessed value of its real estate high for municipal borrowing purposes.[10]

THE AMBITIOUS DETOUR: AN EVALUATION
OF THE *IN REM* EXPERIMENT

In retrospect the Koch Administration's decision in 1978 to intervene directly to prevent continued housing abandonment appears remarkably courageous. The administration was under no legal compulsion to assume responsibility for thousands of residential buildings that were no longer economically viable, but it did so despite the realization that the city's already critical budgetary problems would be exacerbated. At the time the *in rem* program was created, the forces of urban disinvestment had gained such momentum there may have been no short-term alternative to direct city ownership of distressed housing. The program probably did, in fact, prevent the eventual abandonment of the 50,000 or so housing units that were seized during the early years of the program, although the more important factors in stabilizing neighborhoods were the subsequent regional economic boom and the advent of community reinvestment banking.

The disposition programs established under the Koch Administration also had some positive effects, controversy notwithstanding. The Community Management Program and its successors helped to cultivate a useful not-for-profit housing management infrastructure while the Tenant Interim Lease program was one of the few elements of city housing policy that promoted tenant empowerment rather than dependency. The new NEP program, if it is successful in incubating neighborhood enterprise, may also contribute to broader social policy goals. From a pure production standpoint, the disposition effort also accomplished the rehabilitation of some 30,000 housing units, although the cost-effectiveness of *in rem* rehabilitation relative to private sector mechanisms is open to debate.

Once the rate of residential building abandonment slowed to a manageable level and HPD's property dispositions began to offset the number of new *in rem* foreclosures, the city's performance was much less admirable. When the political pressure refocused on homelessness during the early 1980s, the goals of disposing of *in rem* properties and restoring the financial viability of low-income private housing were subordinated to that of relieving the logjam in the city's homeless shelters. Preoccupied with that concern and lulled into complacency by the real estate speculation that artificially sustained private investor interest in low-income housing, the Koch and Dinkins administrations failed to confront the inconsistencies in city policy that generated homelessness and set the stage for a new cycle of housing disinvestment.

Foremost among those inconsistencies was the city's—and state's— perverse welfare policies. The rent allowance provided to public assistance households was, and remains, absurdly inadequate to rent decent housing or to provide owners the cash flow to properly maintain it. The deficiency of the welfare shelter allowance has been the principal cause of family homelessness, in turn distorting all of the city's low-income housing policies. An adequate shelter allowance could have kept the passive welfare poor out of the shelters, leaving social service agencies with more resources to address the problems of seriously dysfunctional homeless families. For a time during the late 1980s, the conditions were favorable for a new political compromise on welfare policy, through which more rigorous work and training requirements could have been bargained for more generous grants.[11] Yet, the city supported higher grants only reluctantly and intermittently and never took the lead in forging a new welfare consensus.[12] Had the *in rem* stock not been available as a captive placement resource, the city would have been forced to address the shortcomings of its welfare policies.

One consequence of policy-generated homelessness has been a deepening of the culture of dependency. Instead of providing a realistic housing allowance and demanding that recipients use it responsibly, the city assumed an open-ended obligation for providing permanent housing for virtually any family that requested it. That commitment became entrenched through council legislation, state regulations, consent decrees, and court orders and understandably encouraged welfare recipients to view subsidized housing as a municipal entitlement. The enormous cost of that commitment led to the city's routine payment of rent arrears for delinquent tenants, further weakening the sanctions that promote financial responsibility.

Another byproduct of homeless policy was an increasing concentration of welfare families in publicly owned and assisted housing. The New York City Housing Authority accommodated city policy to the point where it began to seriously jeopardize the stability of its own housing projects; while limitations on homeless placements into NYCHA may help that agency avoid the ghettoization characteristic of other large public housing authorities, they only further delivered *in rem* housing to that fate. In its size and in its intense concentration of poverty, the city's *in rem* portfolio grew to resemble the notoriously troubled Chicago Housing Authority.[13] An important and ironic difference, however, is that the CHA receives sizable federal operating subsidies while New York must use Community Development Block Grant funds to subsidize its *in rem* operations.

The dissipation of the city's CDBG allocations on *in rem* housing has been one of the most pernicious effects of the program. Cumulatively, the city has spent about $2.5 billion of CDBG funds on the *in rem* program—enough to perform moderate rehabilitations of 250,000 apartments or to fund an untold number of other useful community development initiatives.

While the *in rem* program has drained community development budgets and disguised the effects of counterproductive welfare policies, it has also facilitated the evasion of other needed policy reforms. During the era of massive housing loss, spanning the administrations of mayors Wagner, Lindsay, Beame, and Koch, a coherent program of regulatory relief for distressed housing was never formulated. Each attempt to loosen rent regulations provoked middle-class renter outrage that overwhelmed reform efforts, while the anti-landlord rhetoric of tenant and community activists helped to personalize, and hence obscure, the structural factors promoting housing disinvestment. To be sure, the practices of many "slumlords" were unethical and illegal, but the political culture of the city did not encourage a dispassionate discussion of why unscrupulous landlords seemed to concentrate their activities in a dozen or so impoverished communities. In fact, the economics of low-income housing had deteriorated to the point where few legitimate investors could survive in certain neighborhoods, a reality that was not confronted because it implied the need for costly public subsidies or politically unpalatable rent increases. Once the cycle of abandonment abated, the Koch and Dinkins administrations displayed even less appetite for upsetting rent regulated voters. The Giuliani Administration has sought to make the regulatory bureaucracies more sensitive to the grievances of property owners but opposed efforts in 1997 by Senate Republicans and Governor Pataki to ease rent regulations.

More damaging has been the city's failure to reduce the tax burden on private, low-income housing.[14] During the period of maximum housing loss the city provided no significant tax relief, and, during the first half of the 1990s, as indications of housing disinvestment again became apparent, property tax assessments in the city's poorest neighborhoods increased at three times the citywide rate. The resistance to lowering tax burdens stems from the institutional bias of the financial bureaucracy as well as from the city's chronic budget problems. The primary function of the city's Department of Finance is to generate tax revenues; it has historically resisted recognizing the marginal profitability of low-income rental housing and the essential worthlessness of many residential buildings. Indeed, the city persists in taxing privatized *in rem* buildings, using the need to "return them to the tax rolls" as a justification for disposition, as though the immense subsidies they required when in city ownership can be suddenly transformed into tax-paying capacity upon sale to tenants or private managers. By intercepting financially distressed buildings before they sink into complete abandonment, the *in rem* program thus supported the city's policy of extracting maximum tax revenue from low-income housing.

Any thorough evaluation of New York's *in rem* experiment must take into account not only its direct cost effectiveness, but also the indirect effects of the policies it has helped to perpetuate. Consideration of those indirect effects suggests that, on balance, it has not been a constructive element of the city's housing and social policy. Creation of the *in rem* program as an emergency measure was justifiable; its continuation without substantial modification for seventeen years was not. The program provided a path of least political resistance, allowing the city to defer difficult policy reforms that would have furthered social policy goals and left it less vulnerable to the changes in national policy that are now occurring.

NOTES

1. Manhattan Congressman William Green, in a report to Congress, suggested that the statutory language be clarified to make the *in rem* program specifically CDBG-eligible (Green 1979). That clarifying language was not added until 1992.

2. The Participation Loan Program, for example, was originally funded with CDBG funds.

3. Having prided itself on maintaining a stable tenant mix while public housing authorities in other cities became increasingly ghettoized, the New York City Housing Authority (NYCHA) experienced an alarming loss of working families during the 1980s (Thompson, chapter 5 in this volume). Its resistance to becoming the city's principal source of homeless housing surfaced in a public dispute between Chairperson Sally Hernandez-Pinero and the Dinkins Administration in 1992, resulting in a reduction in NYCHA's annual quota of homeless families and increased authority for the agency to screen placements.

4. The litigation strategy resulted in some gains via the *Jiggetts v. Grinker* suit, which has provided court-ordered increases in the shelter grant for nearly

25,000 welfare families (Galowitz, chapter 7 in this volume), but the Pataki Administration appears intent on removing the statutory basis for this suit.

5. In New York State the basic grant is set statutorily by the legislature while the shelter allowance is set administratively, on a county-by-county basis, by the Commissioner of Social Services, subject to appropriations made by the legislature.

6. The Giuliani Administration eliminated this provision in 1994, allowing the city's share of resale profits to be retained by the co-op as reserves.

7. A small portion of the vacant building rehabilitation effort, mostly for housing exclusively homeless families, was administered by the Division of Property Management, and is generally considered to have been among the least successful of the vacant building disposition programs.

8. The use of large construction managers that were more accustomed to commercial and luxury residential projects resulted in high rehabilitation costs, and the program was later modified to facilitate the participation of smaller housing rehabilitation contractors. The clusters transferred to Phipps Houses, the Settlement Housing Fund, and Catholic Charities, however, set the standards for sophisticated not-for-profit housing management.

9. The Rent Guidelines Board estimated that 44 percent of the rent stabilized housing units in Central Harlem were in significant tax arrears in 1993, as were 38 percent in Washington Heights and 30 percent in the South Bronx.

10. The State Constitution limits the debt of any municipality to an amount equal to 10 percent of the three-year average of the assessed value of its taxable real estate.

11. Under New York State's welfare laws the shelter grant can be raised administratively, sparing legislators the need to make politically awkward votes for higher public assistance benefits. Moreover, until 1996 federal funding formulas ensured that state-city increases in AFDC benefits payments would be matched dollar-for-dollar by the federal government.

12. State government deserves at least as much blame for the missed opportunity. Despite bold rhetoric and a smattering of innovative welfare-to-work programs, Governor Mario Cuomo never elevated welfare policy to a central position on his agenda and, in his final years in office, proposed statutory changes that would have undercut the basis for court-ordered supplemental rent allowances under the *Jiggetts* suit. The inertia of state government on the welfare issue contrasted with the leadership provided at the federal level by New York's Senator Daniel Moynihan and Representative Thomas Downey, who forged the compromise that resulted in the Family Support Act of 1988.

13. As of 1992, the CHA operated 30,812 units of conventional public housing, and 61 percent of its tenants were AFDC recipients. In the mid-1990s, New

York had 43,607 units of *in rem* housing, with about 65 percent receiving AFDC or other public assistance.

14. According to the Rent Guidelines Board, property taxes represent about 22 percent of the operating costs of pre-war, rent stabilized buildings.

REFERENCES

Bach, Victor, and Sherece Y. West. 1993. *Housing on the Block: Disinvestment and Abandonment Risks in New York City Neighborhoods.* New York: Community Service Society of New York.

Bernstein, Blanche. 1983. *The Politics of Welfare: The New York City Experience.* Cambridge: Abt Books.

Birch, Eugenie, and Deborah S. Gardner. 1981. "The Seven Percent Solution: A Review of Philanthropic Housing, 1870–1910." *Journal of Urban History* 7:4.

Braconi, Frank P. 1993. *Quarterly Housing Memo, October 1993.* Citizens Housing and Planning Council of New York.

Citizens Housing and Planning Council of New York. 1992. *Preserving New York's Low-Income Housing Stock.*

———. 1989. *The Housing Network, Part II: Recommendations for Improving HPD's Production and Preservation Programs.*

Cotton, Michele, ed. 1996. *No More Housing of Last Resort: The Importance of Affordability and Resident Participation in In Rem Housing.* New York: Task Force on City-Owned Property.

———. 1993. *Housing in the Balance: Seeking a Comprehensive Policy for City-Owned Housing.* New York: Task Force on City-Owned Property.

Green, S. William. 1979. *Review by Congressman S. William Green of New York City's Community Block Grant Funded Program for City-Owned Abandoned Buildings.* Washington: House Banking, Finance, and Urban Affairs Committee.

Holtzman, Elizabeth. 1991. *Audit Report on the New York City Department of Housing Preservation and Development's Private Ownership and Management Program.* New York: Comptroller of the City of New York.

HPD. 1979–1984. *The In Rem Housing Program: Annual Report.* New York: Department of Housing Preservation and Development, City of New York.

Kirchheimer, Donna Wilson. 1990. "Sheltering the Homeless in New York City: Expansion in an Era of Government Contraction." *Political Science Quarterly* 104:4.

Kristoff, Frank S. 1970. "Housing: Economic Facets of New York City's Problems." In *Agenda for a City: Issues Confronting New York*, ed. Lyle C. Fitch and Annmarie Hauck Walsh. Beverly Hills: Sage Publications.

Leventhal, Nathan. 1979. *Memo to Alan Weiner, Area Manager, Department of Housing and Urban Development, February 28, 1979.* Department of Housing Preservation and Development, City of New York.

Leventhal, Nathan, and Charles Raymond. 1979. *Memo to Mayor Ed Koch, January 12, 1979.* Department of Housing Preservation and Development, City of New York.

Mildner, Gerard C. S., and Peter D. Salins. 1992. *Scarcity by Design: The Legacy of New York City's Housing Policies.* Cambridge: Harvard University Press.

Rent Guidelines Board. 1991. *Rent Stabilized Housing in New York City: A Summary of Rent Guidelines Board Research in 1991.* New York: City of New York.

Robbins, Ira S. 1984. *Reminiscences of a Housing Advocate.* New York: Citizens Housing and Planning Council of New York.

Schwartz, Joel. 1993. *The New York Approach: Robert Moses, Urban Liberals, and the Redevelopment of the Inner City.* Columbus: Ohio State University Press.

Stegman, Michael A. 1988. *Housing and Vacancy Survey, 1987.* New York: Department of Housing Preservation and Development, City of New York.

———. 1985. "The Model: Rent Control in New York City." In *The Rent Control Debate*, ed. Paul L. Niebanck. Chapel Hill: University of North Carolina Press.

Vance, Timothy. 1994. *How to Get Drug Enterprises Out of Housing.* New York: Citizens Housing and Planning Council of New York.

CHAPTER 5

PUBLIC HOUSING IN NEW YORK CITY

Phillip Thompson

Public housing across the country has a number of well-known problems, including poor design, inadequate funding, a large concentration of very poor people, lack of social services for residents, high crime rates, and bad management. New York City Housing Authority (NYCHA) historically has earned a reputation as the showcase public housing authority in the country. However valid this reputation in the past, high rates of resident unemployment, lack of social services, crime, and an outdated management structure have eroded NYCHA's luster. NYCHA faces a difficult and uncertain future.

What made New York's public housing different from many cities was its varied location and mix of working and nonworking families, as well as its superior management. Public housing in cities such as Detroit, Newark, Chicago, and New Orleans is considered "troubled."[1] Common problems include the deteriorated condition of much of their housing stock, cumbersome organizational structures (particularly in maintenance and renovation), major crime and security problems, inadequate funding, and physical and social isolation (U.S. General Accounting Office 1995). New York City can be contrasted with troubled housing authorities in other cities along each of these dimensions.

LOCATION AND DESIGN

Visitors to this nation's large cities soon learn where to look for public housing. Public housing can often be found alongside major expressways, near smokestacks and factory buildings (now often abandoned), or in desolate reaches of the cities—near rail yards and factory storage areas. When found in residential neighborhoods, public housing tends to be densely clustered in slums. A public housing project is often the signifier of a slum, orienting the visitor to what "type" of neighborhood he or she is in. Public housing is frequently far from places of work, inconvenient for shopping, distant from parks or recreation areas, and far from schools or hospitals.

Such poor site selection for public housing is frequently described as a "mistake" (Meehan 1975). However, the location of public housing in such resource-poor neighborhoods throughout the nation is anything but accidental. In most cases, public housing was fiercely resisted by the politically potent private real estate industry from the beginning. As longtime housing analyst Mary Nenno noted, the real estate industry "was able to inject the principle that public housing must operate in a way that would offer no possible competition to private enterprise and must be built to standards restricting design to health and safety rather than attractive livability."[2]

Another factor influencing public housing location was racial segregation. One way of describing the history of public housing is to distinguish the period before public housing became overwhelmingly populated by African Americans fleeing the rural South after World War II, and the period since. Public housing became a way to manage huge influxes of African Americans flooding into cities from the rural South after World War II. As public housing became more black, whites resisted locating public housing developments in their neighborhoods. Politically conscious mayors either located public housing developments in minority neighborhoods, or they were put in isolated areas unlikely to provoke political protests from white voters (Nenno 1996).

NYCHA has both similarities to and differences with this general account of public housing development. NYCHA benefited from its early start in 1935. In fact, public housing began in New York before it became a national program. The nation's second housing project, "First Houses," was built in New York City with "oak floors, brass light fixtures, sunny rooms, and a landscaped courtyard" (Swarns 1995). First Houses is a low-rise 125-unit development built in what was a thriving immigrant working-class community in the Lower East Side of New York. The size was kept small so that tenants would get to know each other, and there was a rigorous screening process to ensure that, in the words of a screening supervisor in 1935, only "the very finest types" would get apartments (Gray 1995). As a result of its design, location, and tenant selection policies, public housing in New York did not start off with a bad reputation.

Public housing has served a variety of functions in the history of New York. Peter Marcuse, an urban planner, has identified at least eight historical patterns in the use of public housing in the city. Public housing has been used as a job creation program (as in First Houses), to placate black rioters in the 1930s (as in Harlem Houses), as war-time workers' housing (such as Red Hook and Fort Green), as veteran's housing, as filler between slums and urban renewal projects, as relocation housing for people displaced by transportation and infrastructure projects, as a way to keep working-class whites from leaving the city, and, finally, to house the minority poor—especially in the 1960s (Marcuse n.d.). Marcuse paints a fascinating historical picture far too rich to discuss here. The simple fact is that early public housing in New York City was occupied primarily by working families and by whites, and avoided the stigma associated with public housing in other cities. It also allowed public housing development in nonminority neighborhoods.

A second factor that facilitated the development of public housing in white neighborhoods was that it was developed mostly on a segregated basis. Segregation was perpetuated in recent decades by NYCHA's "community preference" policy. For example, community preferences, negotiated by Mario Cuomo, then a lawyer in Queens, facilitated the construction of Forest Hills Houses in Queens. The preference policy gave priority to neighborhood residents applying to public housing in their own neighborhoods. This policy had the effect of maintaining (for a while) racial and ethnic segregation within public housing located in segregated neighborhoods.[3] On the other hand, the policy was credited with maintaining social networks and organization within neighborhoods (social capital).

Notwithstanding the construction of several public housing developments in predominantly white neighborhoods, New York City has vast concentrations of public housing located in poor African American and Puerto Rican neighborhoods such as central and East Harlem, the South Bronx, central Brooklyn, and East New York. In addition, NYCHA has large housing developments located in isolated areas, such as the Rockaways. Despite its promising beginning, NYCHA has all the building types and racially exclusionary sites typical of public housing in other cities.

The first column on Table 5.1 shows the proportion of census tracts in New York City that had a majority single ethnic population when the census was taken in 1989. Just over 50 percent of census tracts were majority white at that time. Nearly 30 percent of tracts were majority black. Asians (roughly 10 percent of the total population) and Hispanics (roughly 25 percent of the population) were not as concentrated in census tracts where they were a majority. The second column shows the distribution of NYCHA units in majority ethnic/racial census tracts,

TABLE 5.1
Distribution of Public Housing in New York City by Racial/Ethnic Group
Characteristics of Census Tract, 1989

Racial/Ethnic Majority Group in Tract	Proportion of Census Tracts in City (%)	Proportion of Public Housing Units in Census Tracts (%)	Number of Public Housing Units in Tracts
White	50.3	22.7	38,745
Black	29.7	45.3	89,939
Asian	1.3	0.8	2,442
Hispanic	4.8	3.5	6,345
No Majority	13.9	27.7	44,309

Source: New York City Housing Authority.

and the third column shows the number of units in such tracts. These data show that 22.7 percent of NYCHA's units (a total of 38,745) were in majority white tracts in 1989. This is even more significant after twenty years of decline in the city's white population to a percentage of less than half. Almost half the units, 45.3 percent, were located in majority black census tracts. The remaining units were concentrated, 27.7 percent of the total, in mixed ethnic tracts. The data indicate, for the reasons explained earlier, that NYCHA developments are not all socially isolated. While there are dense concentrations of NYCHA housing in black (and mixed black and Hispanic) neighborhoods, more than 20 percent of NYCHA's units are in majority white neighborhoods.

Public housing design tends to differ depending on the historical forces that created it. Newer public housing developments, such as those in the Lower East Side of Manhattan, conform to the low-rise texture of the neighborhood. This comes after much criticism of other developments—such as those built in East Harlem—where public housing developments rise like mountains, towering over low-rise buildings in the surrounding plateau. Streets between the high-rises resemble dark and narrow caverns. It is tragic that public housing officials are often blamed for the clustering of poor families in high-rises. Public housing planners and architects did not advocate building at such high densities (Marcuse n.d.). Densely clustered high-rises resulted from historically inadequate funding for public housing development, high inner-city land costs, and white hostility to locating blacks in their neighborhoods.[4] That having been said, there are numerous mistakes that were made in the course of constructing public housing high-rises. One such mistake, at least according to some veteran housing managers, was the placement of large apartments on the upper floors of some high-rises. The larger apartments are usually occupied by large families having the most children. Larger families make more use of the elevators than do smaller families, resulting in greater wear and tear on elevators, and more frequent elevator breakdowns. In addition, to the extent that parental supervision is more difficult in large families, vandalism of elevators by unsupervised children may be more likely.

Fortunately, the majority of NYCHA developments are not tall high-rises. Figure 5.1 is a histogram showing the number of stair halls on the vertical axis, and the number of floors on each stair hall on the horizontal axis. As can be seen from Figure 5.1, although NYCHA has hundreds of stair halls over ten stories, the vast majority of stair halls are six stories or less. In a city with the high densities of New York, in contrast to lower-density cities such as Chicago, NYCHA developments are not as out of context with their surroundings.

NYCHA also manages more than 20,000 units in formerly privately owned buildings repossessed by HUD. These buildings are typically scattered, small, low-rise buildings that are organized—"consolidated"—into clusters for management purposes. The consolidated buildings pose a particular problem for NYCHA because they were not built to NYCHA specifications and require specially ordered materials for repairs. In addition, they are scattered and thereby not conducive to NYCHA's centralized high-rise management system. NYCHA has recently privatized management of some of the consolidated develop-

FIGURE 5.1
Number of Stairhalls By Number of Stories in NYCHA Developments

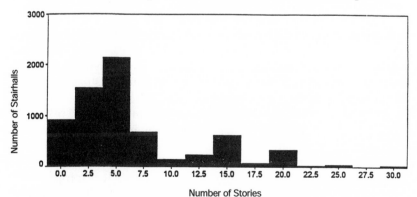

Source: Data from New York City Housing Authority

ments. This is a significant step in part because low-rise, scattered-site housing is the likely pattern for new public housing development—should there be any. NYCHA's privatization of such developments suggests that NYCHA's role in future public housing development might be limited to planning and financial administration.

UNEMPLOYMENT, LACK OF SERVICES, AND CRIME: THE ABSENCE OF SOCIAL CAPITAL IN PUBLIC HOUSING

Numerous scholars have noted the connection between the concentration of poor, nonworking, families in public housing and high rates of crime, school drop-outs, teenage pregnancy, and related ills. Nearly a decade ago, William Julius Wilson wrote that public housing in Chicago concentrated long-term unemployed men, idle teenagers with little future prospects for work, and young women with little incentive to marry these men (Wilson 1987). Combined with the effects of desegregation and affirmative action (increased educational and high-paying job opportunities), which allowed upwardly mobile African Americans to leave inner-city ghettos, an "underclass" of persistently poor people was created (Wilson 1987). Wilson concluded that more than anything, public housing residents needed jobs. Jobs would change behavior by reducing idleness and increasing marriages and the supervision of children (Wilson 1987).

Interestingly, the social benefits of work were foremost on the minds of the early planners of public housing in New York City—residents had to be employed. At that time, in the 1930s, the concern was that idle hands would breed "revolution," not teenage pregnancy (Marcuse n.d.). Although formal estimates are not available, unemployment currently is recognized to be a major problem in NYCHA. NYCHA has over the years developed a number of in-house employment programs, such as plastering, heating, and janitorial services. These programs were uniformly successful, mainly because NYCHA hired graduates of their programs. NYCHA also successfully initiated business development programs that competed for small NYCHA construction contracts set aside for resident-owned businesses. The main area of NYCHA-funded employment is in modernizing public housing projects. NYCHA spends more than $400 million each year to modernize housing developments. The Authority recognizes that these billions spent in construction and the purchase of durable goods, such as refrigerators, represent potentially significant employment opportunities for public housing residents.

NYCHA also encourages contractors to hire public housing residents. However, contractors have several constraints in hiring public housing residents. Most contracts are bid on a competitive basis, and contractors therefore have little slack from which to hire public housing trainees, even if it improves relations with residents on the job. Since 1937, contractors have also been required by federal statute to pay union scale "prevailing wages" (Marcuse n.d.). They are understandably hesitant to hire inexperienced workers at the same rate as experienced workers. In addition, contractors risk confrontations with labor unions when using nonunion labor. In a period of weak demand for construction, labor unions pay close attention to hiring patterns even in small construction jobs. Construction trades have also been historically resistant to racial integration. In short, although NYCHA spends billions of dollars on housing modernization, it employs relatively few public housing residents, and relatively little of that money circulates in the neighborhoods where public housing is located. This is a frequently voiced irritant for public housing residents. Congresswoman Maxine Waters, commenting on similar problems in Los Angeles, recently said that "You should not get people coming from suburban and other places who don't know anything about these housing projects providing service. It angers the public housing residents when they look out their window and they see people who do not come from that neighborhood, they get angry and they do a lot of things. So there should be joint ventures and the people who are working there, no matter what waivers you have to get from the unions . . . you better hire some of those gang bangers who live there."[5]

Douglas Massey, a sociologist, has written a number of articles that show significantly higher rates of crime, school drop-outs, and teenage pregnancy in neighborhoods with dense concentrations of public housing (see, for example, Massey and Kanaiaupuni 1993). Massey maintains that high rates of crime and other inner-city pathologies are the inevitable results of decades of *de facto* segregation of blacks, particularly in public housing (Massey and Denton 1993). Such studies have encouraged HUD to attempt to reduce the concentration of poor blacks in public housing through its Moving to Opportunities Program (MTO). MTO offers "alternative housing choices to low-income families who live in either distressed public housing or areas with high concentration of poverty."[6] MTO is based on evaluations of twenty years of experience in Chicago with the Gautreaux program. The Gautreaux demonstration program arose out of a 1976 Supreme Court decision, *Gautreaux v. Chicago Housing Authority*, that found that the Chicago Authority had discriminated in admitting tenants to public housing. As part of the remedy, the Authority provided more than 5,600 Section 8 certificates to black Chicago residents willing to move into white neighborhoods. In a series of articles, James Rosenbaum documented that suburban participants were more likely than those remaining in Chicago public housing to obtain jobs, graduate from high school, and increase earnings (Rosenbaum 1993).

Critics of deconcentration have observed that minorities are likely to become resegregated in suburbs. John Logan, a sociologist who has studied city-suburban migration in eleven metropolitan regions, recently concluded that as minorities move to the suburbs, they experience the same level of segregation that they left behind (Sengupta 1994); that relocation efforts presume that poor black (and Hispanic) neighborhoods are "not fit places for families and children" (Pollack 1996; Tein 1992), an offensive presumption; that programs such as MTO have little political chance of moving beyond the "pilot" stage, for the same reasons that public housing was segregated in the first place, and that to the extent that programs such as MTO are successful, they will "encourage the most mobile and energetic to leave—the very people who might otherwise take an active role in improving these communities" (Pollack 1996). Logan's observations about the political infeasibility of deconcentration are illustrated by the recent rejection of HUD's proposal to fund $149 million to expand MTO, which was killed by Maryland's liberal Senator Barbara Milkulski—considered one of the strongest supporters of public housing in Congress—after suburban whites protested MTO in Baltimore (Mariano 1994).

While HUD has made desegregation a priority, there is little probability that NYCHA's residents can be dispersed elsewhere in the city and suburbs as a means of deconcentrating inner-city poverty. NYCHA has roughly the same population as the cities of San Francisco or Boston. Given the fierce resistance to even modest public housing development in nearby Yonkers, the notion that significant portions of the NYCHA population could be integrated into Long Island and Westchester is fanciful. Political problems aside, HUD's entire $70 million national MTO budget would have only a minor impact on deconcentrating public housing in New York City.

The segregation thesis also does little to explain the variation in crime and violence among public housing developments. High rates of concentrated poverty do not always, and have not always, resulted in high rates of crime. Robert Sampson, a sociologist, has focused on the social structures—such as family, church, or community organization—that influence individuals not to commit crime or other socially destructive behavior (Sampson 1994). Sampson found that communities with high rates of crime also have high rates of family instability and weak social institutions. Sampson suggests that social breakdown precedes and mediates individual decisions to commit crime (Sampson 1994). Sampson's work suggests that more attention be paid to maintaining and strengthening social networks within and around public housing developments.

Sampson's findings are not new in the history of public housing. As early as the 1950s, public housing officials in New York attempted to create policies to handle the decline in "community consciousness" that they saw as corrosive to poor communities (Marcuse n.d.). The role of social networks—or social capital—in helping public housing residents find jobs, obtain child care, supervise children, and obtain emotional and spiritual support is one of the best understood but least actionable areas in public housing management. One reason for this is a civil rights suit brought by Brooklyn Legal Services, known as the *Davis* case, that resulted in a settlement in 1992 that prohibits NYCHA from granting admission preferences for NYCHA applicants who wish to remain in their neighborhoods. Although NYCHA's "community preference" policy tended to maintain racially and ethnically segregated buildings in segregated neighborhoods, it also allowed for extended families and social networks to develop in NYCHA developments. *Davis* came thirty years too late to have a significant effect on racial segregation. Today NYCHA is nearly completely nonwhite. The suit now seems to integrate various minority ethnic groups, increasing their difficulty in maintaining social ties (social "capital") within buildings.

Early public housing, before it was viewed as a dumping ground for the poor, was built with family rooms, day-care centers, large recreation areas, and other amenities that implicitly recognized and facilitated social capital. HUD's development spending caps now limit such building amenities. HUD, however, at various times has supported tenant "empowerment" initiatives that have included encouraging the formation of independent tenant associations and the appointment of residents to serve on Housing Authority Boards, funding tenants to work with police to eliminate drug dealing in developments and, in some cases, helping tenants to assume management of their buildings (Nenno 1996; U.S. Department of Housing and Urban Development 1992). Unfortunately these efforts have been sporadic and are not systematically evaluated.

Regardless of intent, the lack of attention to the social aspects of residents' lives and the usually token involvement of residents in policy considerations is the managerial equivalent of impersonal functionalism in public housing design. Many housing experts attribute part of the problem to the "silo" approach of the federal bureaucracy. Social services are administered by the Department of Health and Human Services (HHS). Public housing authorities are frequently prohibited from funding social services, and HHS does not coordinate its service delivery with HUD. The result is that broken buildings get help, but residents in buildings often do not. Without enough youth programs or day-care slots, children (who are frequently 60 to 70 percent of a project's residents) turn corridors and stairways into playgrounds. Physical improvements to the buildings do not last, and the public believes its money is wasted (Thompson 1993).

Enhancing social capital is once again being emphasized in local and national public housing policy, particularly as a crime prevention strategy. NYCHA, for example, has begun to conduct criminal background checks on families on the waiting list. This policy harkens back to the days when NYCHA resident committees actually interviewed and screened prospective housing residents. Background checks, combined with a renewed commitment to admitting working families, is a positive response to resident complaints about the deteriorating social fabric within housing developments. However, this policy poses a dilemma for the city. NYCHA's historic success is probably best described as a "social capital" approach that emphasized infusion of job networks (workers) into buildings housing welfare recipients, as well as strict screening of applicants. In precisely these respects, NYCHA was not "public" housing. NYCHA housing was not an entitlement—it was not first come, first serve—and it was not devoted to serving the most needy.

Public housing, therefore, in no way solved the housing crises in New York. Instead it diverted unwanted families into the private housing market. This may have contributed to the crisis of privately owned housing New York City experienced in the 1970s and 1980s (Braconi, chapter 4 in this volume). Private landlords became increasingly unable (or unwilling) to manage their properties, resulting in large-scale abandonment. New York City was forced to take over ownership and management of these buildings through in rem tax foreclosures. In rem housing has many of the same characteristics and problems associated with the most distressed public housing in other cities. The city has spent billions of dollars constructing and renovating more than 50,000 new apartments, basically in response to problems in the private housing market.

In response to the crisis in private and in rem housing, New York City has put pressure on NYCHA to accept homeless families. Today, public housing in New York is less and less an oasis; as an integral part of New York's approach to housing the homeless, it has increasingly been plagued by problems associated with a desperate lack of social services and crime. The social service needs are exemplified by the fact that nearly 15,000 homeless families have been moved into public housing from city-run shelters since 1988, with almost no social service support from the Human Resources Administration (HRA). One out of four new NYCHA tenants comes from the city's shelter system. Many of these new tenants have serious needs for drug treatment, job placement, family life management, educational assistance, youth programs, and a variety of other social services. Despite the special problems associated with the high concentration of troubled families and youth in public housing, there is little coordination in social programming by HRA and NYCHA.

Crime and violence have become the most serious problems in New York City's public housing. Full data on public housing crime rates have not been made available since the merger of the New York City Police Department and NYCHA's Housing Police in 1995. However, data provided by NYCHA show a consistent annual felony rate in the 1990s approaching forty felonies per one thousand residents. Secular data do not do justice to the conditions some public housing residents are forced to endure. Data collected in 1993 showed that NYCHA residents were 20 percent more likely to be murdered and 38 percent more likely to be raped than other New Yorkers (Houppert 1996). There has also been a series of arson attacks in public housing stair halls in recent years. Between 1994 and March 1996, there were at least seventy-nine stair hall fires injuring thirty-four people and killing two residents. NYCHA now estimates that it will spend $150 million to remove apparently dangerous paint from stair halls. This is money that would ordinarily be used for repairs and major appliances (Moses 1996).

A major anticrime initiative begun by NYCHA in 1993 was to install $45 million worth of electromagnetic locks, intercoms, and improved lighting in targeted buildings by March 1996. By 1996, this program was seriously behind schedule—only 23 developments had received renovations while 108 developments were still in the pipeline (Houppert 1996). The reason for this delay apparently was a dispute over payment arrangements and coordinating access to the buildings. In any case, broken locks and the absence of intercoms are blamed for frequent unauthorized access to NYCHA buildings leading to crime—including fires in stair halls. It goes without saying that efforts to improve the social fabric of buildings or recruit working families to live in public housing will be unsuccessful so long as buildings are fundamentally unsafe.

New York City recently combined its housing police with the city police force—at a time when other housing authorities were doing the opposite. Mayor Rudolph Guiliani pledged that the number of officers assigned to patrol 325 public housing developments would eventually double to nearly 300 (Hicks 1995). If this pledge is met, it will constitute an improvement in police coverage of public housing developments. However, some skeptics caution that politically potent neighborhoods might siphon away police once dedicated to public housing to patrol their neighborhoods. Lending credence to this suspicion was the recent announcement by the city that housing officers in the troubled Rockaways developments would be transferred into two local precincts. Diane Tilley, president of the Police Tenant Council in the Rockaways, expressed the fear that "[t]hey may put all the cops in patrol cars and forget about us in public housing" (quoted in Marzulli 1996).

MANAGEMENT

One of the most important issues for a public housing authority such as NYCHA is the selection of tenants. Two contending philosophies, or concerns, have traditionally influenced debates over who should live in public housing. On the one side, some housing advocates maintain that public housing should primarily serve those families most in need of housing—families unlikely to be able to afford housing in the private market. As is well known, since the 1960s public housing has increasingly housed welfare families and decreasingly housed the working poor. Further, these advocates maintain that rent levels for the poor should not exceed 20 percent, or at most 25 percent, of income. Higher rent-to-income ratios deprive poor families of money needed for food, clothing, and other basic necessities (Stone 1993). On the other side, some housing advocates stress the need to mix working and nonworking families within housing developments. Invariably, this means housing some working families that have other options in the private housing market and excluding some nonworking families that lack decent options.

In 1969, then Senator Edward Brooke (R-Massachusetts) successfully passed an amendment to the original Housing Act of 1937 which set all tenant rents in public housing at 25 percent (later raised to 30 percent) of income, with the exception of residents receiving welfare assistance. This had the unintended effect of pushing working families out of public housing, because of what developed into a whopping 30 percent housing tax on income. In response to demands that welfare recipients also not pay more than 25 percent of income for rent, Senator Brooke introduced another successful amendment in 1971 that limited tenant rents of welfare recipients to 25 percent of income. The 1971 amendment also required that welfare benefits not be reduced for recipients (Nenno 1996). The combination of limited rents for welfare recipients and decreasing numbers of working families led to a financial crises in public housing management, and to the neglect of physical upkeep in developments across the country. The recognized need to fund the discrepancy between reduced levels of rental income from welfare recipients and rising operating costs for housing developments led to the establishment of a comprehensive federal operating subsidy for public housing called the Performance Funding System (PFS). PFS became available to public housing authorities in 1975. Between 1971 and 1975, however, public housing authorities lacked adequate funding for operations, causing delays in needed maintenance and other critical services (Nenno 1996; Shuldiner 1994).

Some observers who applaud rent limitations as a means of reducing shelter poverty and reducing incentives for working families to move out therefore support PFS as a means of maintaining public housing and protecting it from the effects of economic downturn. However, Nenno states that, "[w]ith the benefit of hindsight, the 1971 Brooke amendment may have been particularly disastrous for public housing in the long run. By moving to a full-fledged program of operating assistance—tied to the lowest-income tenants—it virtually eliminated the alternative solution to the cost problem—returning public housing to a broad cross-section of families in the lower-income range. The benefits would have been both social and fiscal" (Nenno 1996). It is not clear, however, given the decline in wages of the lower-income workers in the last two decades—combined with rising operating costs—that public housing authorities would have generated sufficient funds to operate effectively.[7]

NYCHA historically maintained a mix of families on welfare, working families, and retirees—one-third each—in public housing. Although there is little systematic research or evaluation to determine the impact of admission policy on housing quality, NYCHA's tenant mix has been widely credited for the unparalleled success of public housing in New York and its traditional vacancy rate of close to zero. NYCHA also pioneered setting rent caps for working families in public housing, after protracted battles with HUD. In a way, NYCHA's history demonstrates that class integration—or more particularly, jobs—is more important for stabilizing neighborhoods than racial integration. Since the

1980s, however, the proportion of working people residing in NYCHA apartments has declined dramatically (see Table 5.2), from 48 percent in 1985 to 30 percent in 1995, partly as a result of the city's policy of placing homeless families in public housing.

In 1994, forty-seven, or 15 percent, of NYCHA's developments had more than 45 percent of their residents on AFDC.[8] In part this concentration of poor families in public housing is due to the effects of increasing family homelessness in the city. Because of the large numbers of homeless families entering NYCHA from city-run shelters, combined with the homeless families already prioritized on NYCHA's 150,000 family waiting list, there have been fewer apartments available for working families.

The impact of the changing tenant base can be seen in the increased portion of NYCHA's operating costs paid by HUD. The last two columns of Table 5.3 show that between 1990 and 1995, HUD increased its operating subsidy to NYCHA—payments to cover the difference between NYCHA's rent receipts and costs of operation—from 40 to 50 percent of the total. Because of PFS, the decline in tenant income does not directly lower the operating budget. However, housing managers frequently note that the changing resident composition has increased vandalism, trash, and other maintenance costs. These changes are not reflected in the PFS funding formula from HUD; NYCHA has more work to do with the same amount of money. This additional burden is on top of monumental increases in workloads resulting from New York City's banning of incinerator use in public housing. Rather than having garbage dropped down a chute for incineration, custodians must now bag, compress, and transport garbage for 650,000 residents to curbside for pick-up. Such changes are also not reflected in the PFS formula, which partly explains why NYCHA is chronically short-staffed in field locations.

For years, pressures have been mounting for a return to NYCHA's traditional preferences for working families. NYCHA's

TABLE 5.2
Proportion of Working Families[1] in New York City Public Housing, 1985–1995

Program	1985	1990	1994	1995
Federal	47%	37%	30%	29%
State	52%	41%	32%	31%
City	68%	57%	44%	44%
All Programs	48%	39%	31%	30%

Source: New York City Housing Authority.
1. A working family is one that does not derive income from public assistance, social security, SSI, etc.

TABLE 5.3
Financial Characteristics of New York City Public Housing, 1990–1995

	Total Operating Expense ($)	Total Operating Receipts ($)	HUD Subsidy ($)	% of Rents	% HUD
1990	804,972,900	482,942,200	302,099,241	62	38
1991	844,791,700	485,091,502	356,271,404	58	42
1992	875,744,000	486,976,077	386,831,333	56	44
1993	921,624,858	486,027,200	417,502,256	55	45
1994	974,012,700	481,772,515	460,945,761	53	47
1995	1,000,639,800	481,460,500	503,041,560	50	50

Source: New York City Housing Authority.

cause was aided with the appointment of Joseph Shuldiner, a former NYCHA General Manager, as HUD's Assistant Secretary for Public Housing. Shuldiner spearheaded a new HUD policy to increase local preferences in tenanting NYCHA apartments to 50 percent of total vacancies. NYCHA soon thereafter announced its intention to use its entire local preference to house working families and submitted a waiver request to HUD in July 1995 to begin implementation of its new preference policy.

Compared to other cities, NYCHA has relatively few developments that would qualify as distressed housing. Using the conventional 40 percent poverty rate as a proxy for high rates of crime and social disorder, Table 5.4 shows that only 27,909, or 15 percent, of NYCHA's units are located in such census tracts. Nonetheless, 27,000 units is larger than all but a few housing authorities in the country. Indeed, one of NYCHA's developments, Beach Houses in the Rockaways, qualified for HUD's HOPE VI program for distressed housing. NYCHA received more than $70 million for building redesign and resident programs for Beach Houses.

TABLE 5.4
Poverty Concentrations in Neighborhoods with Public Housing
in New York City

Proportion of Poor Households in Census Tract	Distribution of Public Housing Units
Less than 10 percent	12,710
10 percent to 40 percent	141,161
Greater than 40 percent	27,909
Total	181,780

Source: New York City Housing Authority.

Despite the absence of management and physical property distress, there are serious and growing problems for NYCHA's property managers, whose jobs have become significantly more complicated with large numbers of distressed and extremely poor residents.[9] Table 5.5 shows that more than one-quarter (27 percent) of the residents of public housing in New York City under 20 years of age were aged 6 or less in 1995. This suggests that NYCHA will confront even greater challenges in the future as these youth reach their vulnerable teenage years. Adjusting to the changing resident population requires, among other things, programs especially designed for youth as well as programs for drug treatment, educational assistance, job training, and anti-crime initiatives. The inability of public housing to provide residents with a sense of physical security in many locations is the most serious problem for management. Broken locks, inoperable intercoms (where they exist), and trash in the hallways are all visible signs of poor management and opportunity for crime. NYCHA's inability to maintain its own schedule for security enhancements and its admittedly slow response to stair hall fires[10] are signs that management is falling behind in its ability to maintain quality housing.

NYCHA admittedly is short-staffed, but a significant part of the problem is caused by NYCHA's management culture. The authority's management style was developed in an era when crime prevention was not a top priority. NYCHA has elaborate twenty-four-hour emergency procedures for elevator outages, for example, but no similar procedures for broken locks or intercoms, although the latter can be more life threatening. Similarly, until the mid-1990s, NYCHA rotated managers every five years to prevent them from developing community networks outside NYCHA that could be used to apply community pressure on NYCHA administrators. This policy effectively blocked the ability of NYCHA managers to develop links with community service providers that would have been useful for needy NYCHA residents.

NYCHA's major organizational initiative has been the decentralization of its management department into nine borough and sub-

TABLE 5.5
Minors in New York City Public Housing, 1985–1995

Age Group	1985	1990	1995
Under 6 years	21.00%	24.60%	27.00%
6 to 13 years	37.00%	39.00%	40.00%
14 to 20 years	42.00%	36.40%	33.00%

Source: New York City Housing Authority.

borough departments. The authority's goal is to establish more power and accountability at its more than three hundred developments (Graziano 1996). However, this will be a long-term process. NYCHA will continue to have difficulty executing its modernization contracts, decentralizing management operations, and creating performance-based evaluation of managers as long as it lacks centralized computer systems. The computer program that NYCHA uses to track billions of dollars in modernization contracts was actually designed for a trucking company and is wholly inadequate. Until 1996, NYCHA's management department operated without a networked computerized bookkeeping system that could track repairs, rent receipts, and other data at the building level. Without adequate information systems to track performance at developments, rewards to managers are allocated on the basis of tests—which do not adequately reflect performance on the job—or through internal patronage.

One distressing sign of lax management is that NYCHA has had a large build-up of more than 6,000 in vacant units in the last few years (see Table 5.6), with more than 5,500 units becoming vacant in just 1994 and 1995. Needless to say, given NYCHA's 124,320 family waiting list, not to mention homelessness, having so many units vacant is a major issue. NYCHA attributes the increase in its vacancy rate to Section 504 regulations implementing the Americans with Disabilities Act (ADA). Section 504, in conformance with the ADA, requires NYCHA to retrofit 5 percent of its apartments for wheelchair access, despite the fact that less than 2 percent of NYCHA's current population (including the waiting list) requires wheelchair access (Graziano 1996). However, it is unclear how many of the vacancies have also resulted from delays caused by the institution of criminal background checks, and how many have resulted from breakdowns in apartment clean-up and retenanting. Apartment warehousing of this magnitude, regardless of cause, is a major human and fiscal expense for the entire city.

Another latent but potentially monumental problem is that the public housing stock is getting older. In 1995, HUD's modernization budget—money used to upgrade existing developments across the

TABLE 5.6
Turnover in New York City Public Housing, 1991–1995

	1991	1992	1993	1994	1995
Households Moving Out	7,981	8,132	7,884	7,854	8,233
Households Moving In	8,125	8,104	7,420	3,449	5,577

Source: New York City Housing Authority.

country—was $2.5 billion. HUD will receive $3 billion in public housing capital funds for 1999. However, public housing's modernization backlog is nearly ten times that amount. NYCHA estimates its own modernization backlog is $6 billion (Graziano 1996). Inadequate funding for building maintenance and repair has been cited as a major factor in causing housing authorities in other cities to become distressed.

The fact that there is no public outcry about NYCHA vacancies reflects a concern over whether NYCHA has the capacity to resolve its management problems and whether NYCHA requires more public oversight and support. One reason why NYCHA receives little public support is that the public knows little about NYCHA, including the housing research and advocacy community. NYCHA's current structure cultivates insularity, inflexibility, and political intrigue. NYCHA has more than 15,000 employees; it is a large bureaucracy with tremendous knowledge and ideas. However, bureaucrats have survived in NYCHA—as in other bureaucracies—not by taking bold initiatives, but instead by making changes on the margins and "playing it" politically safe. The historical source of the problem in NYCHA has been the political nature—and compromised function—of the Authority's Board of Directors.[11] The NYCHA Board has three members appointed by the mayor, one of whom is the chair of the authority. Board members serve full-time and earn more than $100,000 per year. A NYCHA Board appointment is regarded as one of the premier patronage appointments in city government. The large compensation of board members, and its patronage attachment to the mayor, lead to turnover on the Board with each new mayoral administration. In the last ten years, NYCHA has had five Board chairpersons and five general managers (two of those were "acting general managers"). Such politicization and instability at the top of NYCHA reinforces bureaucratic tendencies toward conservatism. It frustrates internal reform efforts—which take time—and breeds cynicism that any chairperson or general manager can change the institution. The most important institutional change that can quickly be made in NYCHA might be to replace the current Board with a larger Board, perhaps of seven members. Board members, with the exception of the chair, should be part-time and have demonstrated expertise in housing or poverty. Board members should also be compensated at a significantly lower rate, and a number of them—perhaps four, and not the chair—should be appointed by the city council. Such a Board structure would allow for greater continuity, less incentive for patronage, and more expertise and outside scrutiny in leading NYCHA into the next century.

LEGISLATIVE OVERHAUL AND NYCHA'S FUTURE

Congressional changes to the public housing program are likely to have a major impact in New York City. The elimination of federal preferences for public housing will enable NYCHA to increase the proportion of working families they admit. The Authority has previously stated that a 50 percent preference for working families would be desirable. However, given the shortage of affordable housing in the city and the pressure on local government to house the homeless, it is not certain that political pressures would permit NYCHA to maintain such a preference. The Quality Housing and Work Resposibility Act of 1998 also establishes minimum rents of up to $50 and authorizes public housing authorities to charge ceiling (or maximum) rents to maintain working families. These changes to rent-setting will have little impact in New York since there are virtually no NYCHA tenants who pay less than $50 a month, and the Authority has already instituted ceiling rents.

Congress has also debated creating an exemption from the Davis-Bacon Act for housing authorities that would permit NYCHA to pay less than "prevailing" wages for nonunionized employees such as NYCHA residents. This change would create a major opening for the employment of NYCHA residents on modernization projects. As noted earlier, relatively few residents currently work on the billions of dollars in NYCHA modernization projects. At a minimum, eliminating the requirement to pay workers prevailing wages would offer NYCHA strong leverage to negotiate with the construction trades for developing training programs for NYCHA residents, as well as for opening up the unions for NYCHA residents.

Congress is also likely to create programs that would allow NYCHA and hundreds of other housing authorities to combine several different funding sources to create employment initiatives. Some housing advocates are concerned that NYCHA might use its discretion under the program to move out poor families and entice middle-income families (Thrush 1996). However, NYCHA could also use this new flexibility to provide needed social services to troubled developments—such as preparing tenants to work on NYCHA modernization projects—which they are now restricted from doing. Such a program would also allow NYCHA to retain revenues from its commercial properties. All such revenues now revert to HUD. NYCHA would have incentives to increase its commercial revenues, such as by leasing roof space for commercial antennae or renting advertising space. The revenues might offset ongoing budget reductions in public housing.

The 1998 housing legislation also extended President Clinton's "one-strike you're out" policy and make it difficult for residents convicted of drug felonies to live in public housing. The crux of the question in public housing, however, is "out to what?" Do evicted residents move into homeless shelters, at considerably more expense to the city? Do they move into city-owned *in rem* housing? Also, where are they to enroll in drug programs when there is typically a waiting list for these services? Without answers to these questions, it is unclear how these changes would be enforced.

Congress also permitted housing authorities to voluntarily convert housing developments into "tenant-based" or "choice-based" housing, provided that it is cheaper than continuing to maintain them as public housing. Also, distressed housing developments may qualify for involuntary voucherization at the discretion of the HUD secretary. Voucherization is intended to allow public housing residents to move out of public housing, should they so desire, and thus to force housing authorities to be competitive with market alternatives. However, such a policy raises many unanswered questions. For example, if public housing residents were to use vouchers to move into housing that then became more expensive, how would the vouchers be financed? (U.S. General Accounting Office 1995a). In addition, should NYCHA use its scarce modernization dollars to subsidize units in locations that could be rented at market levels, thereby generating surplus income for use at subsidized units? If so, wouldn't there be an increase in racial and economic isolation—the opposite of what voucherization is declared to accomplish?

As already set forth in Table 5.1, more than one-fifth of NYCHA's developments are located in majority white census tracts; yet as Table 5.7 indicates, overall its white population is less than 10 percent. This indicates that public housing in New York actually contributes to racial

TABLE 5.7
Racial/Ethnic Composition of New York City Public Housing, 1985–1995

Racial/Ethnic Status of Household	1985	1990	1995
White	13.3%	10.3%	8.0%
Black	56.0%	54.5%	54.2%
Puerto Rican	26.7%	28.5%	29.5%
All Others[1]	4.7%	6.7%	8.3%

Source: New York City Housing Authority.
1. In 1995, the category "All Others" consisted of Other Hispanic (6.0%), Asian/Pacific Islanders (2.1%), and American Indian/Other (0.2%).

TABLE 5.8
Average Number of Years Families Lived in New York City Public Housing,
1985–1995

Program	1985	1990	1995
Federal	13.4	15.2	16.8
State	12.2	14.7	16.4
City	13.1	15.3	15.3
All Programs	13.2	15.2	16.7

Source: New York City Housing Authority.

integration in many communities. In any event there is reason to believe that few tenants would utilize vouchers to move away from public housing. Table 5.8 shows the average length of stay for public housing families. The length of stay has increased since 1985, no doubt because vacancy rates for affordable housing (less than $500 per month) are less than 2 percent in the city (Blackburn 1995).

CONCLUSION

Many public housing authorities throughout the nation have increasingly become deeply troubled as a result of poor design, inadequate funding, extraordinarily high levels of concentrated poverty, the absence of social services, high crime rates, and managerial problems. Until recently, the New York City Housing Authority appeared immune from these problems and maintained a reputation as one of the finest housing authorities in the nation. As we approach the twenty-first century, NYCHA is facing a series of challenges that will determine whether it will continue to lead the nation or follow the fate of many other large city authorities.

The City of New York, in general, and NYCHA, in particular, must determine what role public housing should play in solving the city's long-standing housing crisis. Now that Congress has given the Authority the power to screen out tenants with criminal records and the ability to reserve a substantial proportion of its units for working families, much thought must be given to what will happen to the city's welfare-dependent population, which cannot afford private market housing. On the one hand, families at the economic margins might encounter additional hardship if they were less able to obtain public housing. On the other hand, if NYCHA were to become a warehouse for troubled homeless families unable to cope in the private market, an invaluable housing resource would soon be wasted.

NOTES

1. HUD considers housing authorities "troubled" if they score less than sixty out of one hundred points against HUD's "PHMAP" assessment indicators.

2. See Nenno (1996, 104). Nenno divides public housing into three periods: the early "economic focus" period in which public housing provided temporary housing for unemployed and low-wage workers during the Depression; the World War II period in which public housing housed defense workers; and the post–World War II period, which she says "laid the seeds of today's public housing program" (102).

3. In 1991, 62 percent of Forest Hills residents were still white. By comparison, 7.5 of all NYCHA residents were white at that time.

4. Building public housing in segregated ghettos such as Harlem and Chicago's South Side was seldom cheaper than building in white neighborhoods. Because of de facto segregation, landlords in black ghettos had a captive market and were thus able to charge exorbitant rents—which drove up land prices. See Marcuse (n.d.).

5. Comments made in the hearing before the Subcommittee on Housing and Community Development of the Committee on Banking, Finance and Urban Affairs, House of Representatives, June 7, 1995, 29.

6. Adam Glantz, a HUD spokesperson, quoted in Sengupta (1994).

7. For data on declining wages, see Danziger and Gottschalk (1995).

8. Data is compiled from NYCHA's 1995 "Guide to Projects."

9. NYCHA, like most public housing authorities, is inadequately funded for housing management or poverty management. According to NYCHA's general manager, their unmet modernization (facility repair and replacement) needs total $6 billion.

10. Data is compiled from NYCHA's 1995 "Guide to Projects."

11. See Marcuse (n.d.) for a discussion of how mayors have appointed NYCHA Board members to fulfill campaign promises or shift NYCHA resources to other City priorities.

REFERENCES

Blackburn, Anthony. 1995. *Housing New York: 1993*. New York: City of New York Department of Housing Preservation and Development, June, 169.

Danziger, Sheldon, and Peter Gottschalk. 1995. *American Unequal*. New York: Russell Sage Foundation.

Gray, Christopher. 1995. "Street Scapes/Public Housing; In the Beginning, New York Created First Houses." *New York Times*, September 24.

Graziano, Paul. 1996. "Housing and Community Development in the Changing Fiscal Environment: New Direction for New York City." Presentation at New York University School of Law Center for Real Estate and Urban Policy, March 28.

Hicks, Jonathan. 1995. "Housing Police Folded into Citywide Force." *New York Times*, May 1.

Houppert, Karen. 1996. "Danger at the Door: Tenisha Smith Was Raped Twice in a City-Owned Apartment Building That Didn't Have Any Outside Locks. Now She's Suing the Housing Authority for Negligence." *Village Voice*, January 30.

Marcuse, Peter. n.d. "Public Housing in New York City: History of a Program." Unpublished manuscript.

Mariano, Ann. 1994. "House Panel Halts Plan to Move Poor Families." *Washington Post*, September 3, A1, cited in Pollack (1996).

Marzulli, John. 1996. "City Eyes Plan to Shift Cops." *Daily News*, March 18.

Massey, Douglas S., and Nancy A. Denton. 1993. *American Apartheid: Segregation and the Making of the Underclass*. Cambridge: Harvard University Press.

Massey, Douglas S., and Shawn M. Kanaiaupuni. 1993. "Public Housing and the Concentration of Poverty." *Social Science Quarterly* 74, no. 1 (March).

Meehan, Eugene J. 1975. *Public Housing Policy: Convention vs. Reality*. New Brunswick, N.J.: Center for Urban Policy Research, Rutgers University.

Moses, Paul. 1996. "Paint Removal to Cost $150 Million." *Newsday*, March 5.

Nenno, Mary K., ed. 1996. *Ending the Stalemate: Moving Housing and Urban Development into the Mainstream of America's Future*. New York: University Press of America.

Pollack, Harold. 1996. "Don't They Want to Go?: Section 8 and Efforts to Relocate Residents of Poor Neighborhoods." Presentation for the Brookings Institute Conference on Social Networks and Urban Poverty, New York City, March 2, p. 2.

Rosenbaum, James. 1993. "Closing the Gap: Does Residential Integration Improve the Employment and Education of Low-Income Blacks?" In *Affordable Housing and Public Policy: Strategies for Metropolitan Chicago*, ed. Lawrence Joseph. Chicago: Center for Urban Research and Policy Studies.

Sampson, Robert J. 1994. "Concentrated Poverty and Crime: A Synopsis of Prior Community Level Research." Background memorandum prepared for the Social Science Research Council Policy Conference on Persistent Urban Poverty, Washington, D.C.

Sengupta, Somini. 1994. "Program Hopes to Place City Poor in Long Island Housing." *Newsday*, March 24.

Shuldiner, Joseph. 1994. *Statement before the Senate Subcommittee on Housing and Urban Affairs*. Washington, D.C.: U.S. Department of Housing and Urban Development, May 5, 49.

Stone, Michael E. 1993. *Shelter Poverty*. Philadelphia: Temple University Press.

Swarns, Rachel. 1995. "Sixty Years Later and Still a Success." *New York Times*, December 18.

Tein, Michael. 1992. "The Devaluation of Nonwhite Community in Remedies for Subsidized Housing Discrimination." *University of Pennsylvania Law Review*, 1463–1503.

Thompson, Phillip. 1993. "The Clinton Agenda: What's in It for Us? Here's How Henry Cisneros Can Help Out." *Newsday*, February 2.

Thrush, Glenn. 1996. "Public Housing Stealth Attack." *City Limits* (June/July): 6.

U.S. Department of Housing and Urban Development. 1992. *Evaluation of Resident Management in Public Housing*. Washington, D.C.: HUD (December).

United States, General Accounting Office. 1995a. "Public Housing: Converting to Housing Certificates Raises Major Questions about Cost." Letter Report, June 20, 1995, GAO/RCED-95-195.

U.S. General Accounting Office. 1995b. "Public Housing: Status of HUD's Takeover of the Chicago Housing Authority." Testimony before the Subcommittee on Human Resources and Intergovernmental Relations, Committee on Governmental Reform and Oversight, U.S. House of Representatives (September 5).

Wilson, William J. 1987. *The Truly Disadvantaged: The Inner City, the Underclass, and Public Policy*. Chicago: University of Chicago Press.

CHAPTER 6

THE FUTURE OF HUD-SUBSIDIZED HOUSING: THE NEW YORK CITY CASE

Victor Bach

After more than three decades, the partnership between the federal government and the private sector in the development and provision of low-income housing has reached a crossroads. New York City, like other large cities with a short supply of affordable housing and a persistent problem of homelessness, has benefited from enormous public investment in privately developed multifamily rental housing targeted for use by lower-income tenants in an otherwise taut, high-cost rental market.

Among the threats to this stock, the future of federal subsidy commitments is a central issue. The subsidy arrangements that produced and sustain this housing are time-limited. They are reaching expiration in crescendo over the next decade, during a period of tightened federal social spending. Increasingly, both partners—the owner and the U.S. Department of Housing and Urban Development (HUD)—will come to a point at which either one can reassess the relationship and decide whether or not to continue. For current HUD tenants whose homes are at risk, for low-income families who seek decent affordable housing, and for New York and other tight-market cities, these public and private decisions are critical.

New York City has a great deal at stake, perhaps more than most cities. HUD subsidies have produced about 500 private assisted developments, on the order of 92,000 units across its five boroughs. This housing constitutes a major share of all HUD-stimulated housing development, about one out of sixteen subsidized units produced nation-

---

This chapter is dedicated to Tamara Reed, tenant leader and activist with Manhattan Plaza Tenants Association, who had to leave us before the work was done.

ally (Wallace 1995). A significant loss of these units to low-income use will exacerbate the acute shortage of low-rent housing in a city where the capacity of the private rental market to absorb new households—with or without vouchers—is virtually nonexistent.

Preserving these HUD-assisted low-income housing resources depends largely on government commitments to sustain the housing federal subsidies built. Washington's current reconstruction and reinvention of housing policy poses serious risks. Continuing federal withdrawal from its investment in assisted low-income housing, coupled with pull-outs by private owners who can profit from market conversion, means that large cities like New York, and its HUD tenant constituencies, face difficult losses and a problematic future.

THE PRIVATE HUD-ASSISTED HOUSING PROGRAMS

Origins

The private sector housing subsidy programs were not always a feature of federal policy. They first emerged in 1959 with a small program for financing nonprofit development of elderly housing at below-market interest rates.[1] In a major policy shift that continued through the 1980s, private initiative took on a growing role in the federal housing agenda.

Before 1959 federal housing policy was essentially bifurcated. The Federal Housing Administration (FHA) insured private mortgage lending in housing for mainstream middle- or modest-income families. Housing constructed under these programs was largely single-family homeownership and some rental housing, mostly in the suburbs. The Public Housing Administration (PHA) was the locus of low-income housing initiative, providing deep, long-term capital subsidies to locally created housing authorities. This housing typically accommodated poor families in rental housing, under public auspices, largely in major urban centers. Although not conceived as complementary strategies, FHA and PHA effectively segregated public and private sector development activity by incomes served, by housing benefits—tenure and type—and by location.

The shift toward private development under federal subsidies was propelled by multiple forces. In public housing, controversies surrounding local governmental approval, together with vacillating commitments from the Eisenhower Administration, had produced a "dreary deadlock," acknowledged by ardent advocates of public housing. A growing and increasingly vocal critique of urban renewal, as a "federal bulldozer" that uprooted minority inner-city families, provoked a call for new, more expedient ways to produce housing for "displaced families," using nonprofit entities and limited-dividend, profit-motivated corporations, as well as public agencies. The idea of subsidizing low-income families to live in private, rather than public, housing was not without great controversy, as illustrated by the congressional debates surrounding legislation of the rent supplement program in the 1965 Housing Act (Feagin et al. 1972).

A deepening recognition of the "urban crisis"—harshly visible in wholesale neighborhood abandonment in some cities—and of the role of housing as a major discontent in the inner-city disorders of the mid-1960s (Kerner Commission 1968) led to the milestone 1968 Housing Act at the end of the Johnson Administration. This legislation set unprecedented national goals for volume production of six million low-income housing units over the next decade. The sensed urgency of a full-scale response with all private hands needed—a call for a General Motors for housing—underlay the creation of the National Housing Partnership "for the purpose of securing the participation of private investors in programs and projects to provide housing for low- and moderate-income families." The private real estate and construction industries, generally opposed to government intrusion into local housing markets, were in the midst of a cyclical recession and became advocates for an expanded federal-private role in low-income housing (Hartman 1975).

The Programs

Beginning in 1961, a succession of three major federal subsidy programs were used to stimulate private development of low-income housing:[2]

- the Section 221(d)(3) below-market-interest-rate (BMIR) program (from 1961 to 1968)
- the Section 236 program (from 1968 to 1974)
- the Section 8 new construction or substantial rehabilitation program (from 1974 on)

Known by their section numbers in the 1937 Housing Act, the three programs are variants of the "supply-side" model in federal housing policy, which links assistance with expanded housing supply. Subsidies are "project based," that is, they are tied to designated, federally approved "brick-and-mortar" housing developments produced through new construction or substantial rehabilitation. Assistance extends to all units in the development.

As the private programs evolved, a number of different subsidy mechanisms were put into practice and a growing infrastructure of regulations circumscribed their use. To assure the targeting of housing benefits, federal use restrictions limited occupancy of vacant units to targeted lower-income groups. Rent regulations determined what "affordable" rents could be charged and tied rent increases to cost changes or to adjusted market trends.[3] HUD oversight included periodic inspections among other accountability mechanisms. The major differences among the project-based subsidy programs are summarized in the appendix to this chapter.

Program Interrelationships

Program differences and interrelationships are best understood in terms of the form each subsidy takes. Section 221BMIR and Section 236 are *mortgage interest subsidy* programs: FHA insurance underwrites long-term, forty-year mortgages, and HUD provides direct federal subsidies to reduce mortgage interest rates. Affordability is the product of lowered debt service costs; resulting rents determine the range of income levels that can be reached. In the mortgage subsidy programs, profit-motivated owners can prepay the mortgage after twenty years, thereby terminating use and rent restrictions and any other federal regulation. Nonprofit developers are "locked in" for the full forty-year term.

In contrast, project-based Section 8 is a *rent subsidy* program. Housing Assistance Payment (HAP) agreements commit HUD rent subsidies to cover the gap between the tenant's rent contribution (at 30 percent of income) and the Fair Market Rent (FMR) set by HUD for that particular project and unit, depending on construction and projected operating costs. At the start of the Section 8 program in 1974, it was assumed that most private financing would not be federally insured; the federal commitment was the time-limited HAP contract, providing project-based subsidies for fifteen to twenty years—for substantial rehabilitation and new construction, respectively—and on rare occasions for as long as forty years.[4] Owner options for terminating subsidies vary, depending on the year the commitment was made and the type of development.[5] It is striking that, during the program's early years, profit-motivated owners could opt out of HAP agreements and terminate subsidies after a period as short as five years, and every five years thereafter. Nonprofits were "locked in" for the full term of the HAP commitment.

Despite the original conception that the two types would not be used in conjunction, mortgage subsidies and rent subsidies were often used in combination. Many Section 221 and 236 developments experienced serious operating deficits, particularly during the OPEC inflation of the 1970s. The shortfalls were remedied by adding a deep layer of project-based rent assistance to the mortgage subsidy, to increase rent streams from low-income tenants. Rent assistance took one of two forms: rent supplements or the later Section 8 Loan Management Set Aside (LMSA) program.

Federal rent supplements (under the 1965 Housing Act) provided project-based rent assistance tied to designated units with very low-income tenants, usually only a portion of the units in the development. These commitments span forty years, during which the owner is locked into federal use and rent restrictions. When LMSA rent subsidies were made available to underbudgeted Section 221 and 236 properties, they provided fifteen-year commitments of project-based rent subsidies to all units in the project, available to all income-eligible households, with tenant rent contributions set at 30 percent of income. Under LMSA, owners can opt out of subsidy agreements every five years. For obvious reasons, many owners used the opportunity to convert rent supplement arrangements to LMSA agreements.

THE HOUSING THAT HUD SUBSIDIES BUILT

New York is, in a sense, a special case for HUD-assisted housing. The Mitchell-Lama experience,[6] combined with the city's historical housing activism—including the active role unions played in developing affordable, unsubsidized cooperative and rental housing for members—and the city's positive "forerunner" record with public housing had generated a robust, experienced development sector ready to make good use of federal subsidies becoming available for private low-income housing.[7]

Throughout the 1970s this sector grew and diversified. In addition to profit-motivated developers, an increasingly sophisticated nonprofit industry—both citywide and community-based housing development organizations—gained skills in attracting investors, in financial packaging, in marketing and tenant selection, in design and development, and in property management. The Settlement Housing Fund was founded in 1969 and became a leading citywide nonprofit among several others. Community-based nonprofit housing development groups multiplied, in large part as a response to neighborhood housing abandonment; they now own and manage over 45,000 apartments across the city, using a wide range of local and federal subsidy programs (Turetsky 1993). In general, private sector involvement has generated new forms of low-income rental housing, run by a changing, varied group of owners and managers, in a range of locations somewhat different from prevailing local patterns of public housing.

The Stock and the Subsidy Programs

The 500 HUD-subsidized projects developed in New York City—containing about 92,000 units—derive from the broad range of evolving federal and state/local subsidy mechanisms.[8] (See Table 6.1.) Among them, the eighty-three Mitchell-Lama developments account for only one out of six projects, but, because of their scale, they comprise close to half of HUD-assisted units; they include projects financed by the state, the city, or the Urban Development Corporation (UDC). Project-based Section 8 new construction and substantial rehabilitation projects are in the majority, but they are smaller in scale and represent only one-third of the units produced.

TABLE 6.1
HUD-Subsidized Projects and Units in New York City,
by Development Program

		Projects	Units	Mean Units per Project
Section 221(d)(3)BMIR		**63**	**8,400**	**133**
	HUD	61	8,100	133
	City M-L	2	300	150
Section 236		**161**	**49,900**	**310**
	HUD	81	11,000	136
	UDC M-L	29	13,800	476
	State M-L	12	9,800	817
	City M-L	39	15,200	390
Section 8NC/SR		**277**	**33,600**	**121**
	HUD	275	31,700	115
	State M-L	1	240	240
	City M-L	1	1,680	1,680
Totals		**501**	**91,900**	**183**
	HUD	417	50,800	122
	UDC M-L	29	13,800	480
	State M-L	13	10,100	777
	City M-L	42	17,200	410

Note: M-L is an abbreviation for Mitchell-Lama Program

The use of project-based LMSA rent assistance to deepen subsidies for the Section 221 and 236 developments is widespread, reaching more than half of the 224 mortgage-subsidized projects. Over the thirty-year period of private sector subsidies, Section 8 rent assistance has become the dominant subsidy stream—four out of five subsidized developments receive project-based Section 8 assistance. The experience confirms current policy wisdom, for public as well as assisted housing, that mortgage subsidies or capital grants, by themselves, are no longer sufficient to reach families of limited income.

Location of HUD-Subsidized Projects

HUD-subsidized developments exhibit two dominant patterns of location. The stock is widely dispersed across the five boroughs and most of the city's fifty-nine community districts. At the same time, there are large concentrations in lower-income, minority districts, such as Central and East Harlem in Manhattan; Bedford-Stuyvesant, East New York, and Ocean Hill-Brownsville in Brooklyn; and the South-Central Bronx.

The distribution by borough has an even spread across Manhattan (166 projects, 28,800 units), the Bronx (153 projects, 26,300 units), and Brooklyn (149 projects, 26,100 units), but assisted housing is sparser in the two low-density boroughs of Queens (17 projects, 6,100 units) and Staten Island (17 projects, 4,200 units). Within the Bronx every community district has subsidized projects, but the lowest-income districts in South-Central Bronx account for nearly all projects (93 percent) and units (88 percent) in the borough. In Brooklyn, the pattern is similar, with high concentrations in Bedford-Stuyvesant, East New York (including the 5,600-unit Starrett City development), Crown Heights, and Ocean Hill/Brownsville.

In Manhattan, there is a strikingly different pattern, with projects dispersed across districts with very different submarket profiles. While close to half of the projects are located in Central Harlem and East Harlem, there are substantial, if lesser concentrations in districts with more robust "upscale" submarkets: in the Lower East Side, the Chelsea-Clinton district, the Upper West Side, and the East Side. The pattern reflects the character and scale of Manhattan development, in contrast with the other boroughs, where large-scale redevelopment took place in many now marketable areas that originally were designated for urban renewal. The bulk of the housing located in the East Side is in the Phipps Houses complex, the north building of the Waterside development along the East River, and the Roosevelt Island complex. On the West Side, there is a large cluster of developments in the gentrifying Clinton neighborhood, including the impressive Manhattan Plaza complex, and another cluster of striking Mitchell-Lama developments in the Struyker's Bay urban renewal area, alongside a new span of luxury housing developments.

In Queens and Staten Island, the development pattern is much more uneven. Large concentrations occur in only one or two community districts, in the Rockaways, in Queens, and in the Stapleton neighborhood of Staten Island.

The federal premise was that with private initiative it would be possible to site low-income housing in a wider range of neighborhoods, without the controversy attending local approval of public housing. In New York, public housing was not the heated issue it was elsewhere.[9] Nevertheless, the pattern of assisted housing development shows a great deal of locational variation, rather than one that consistently reinforces segregation by income, race, or ethnicity. In Manhattan, below 96th Street, the development pattern in economically and racially diverse neighborhoods could serve as a model for the nation's fair housing goals. Unfortunately, the current risks of subsidy termination are high in these upscale markets, with strong incentives for owners to convert to market at the first opportunity. The fair housing issue is a key question for preservation policy—whether it can sustain low-income housing in diverse, better-off areas, given the conflict between social location objectives and private equity considerations.

Occupancy and Conditions

Taken as a whole, the HUD-assisted stock can be characterized as high-rise multifamily development; most households (63 percent) are in buildings of one hundred or more units, a density consistent with rental housing across the city. Over three-quarters of the units (77 percent) are one- or two-bedroom apartments. The proportion of units suitable for large families with three or more bedrooms is 14 percent, somewhat less than is found in the city's public housing (24 percent).[10]

Median contract rents in 1993 (exclusive of rent subsidies) were $425 a month, about 15 percent more affordable than the city median rent of $501, but twice as high as median public housing rents of $203. Close to half (45 percent) of tenants in assisted housing had annual incomes of less than $10,000, more than two-thirds (69 percent) incomes of less than $25,000. However, median incomes were higher than those for public or city-owned housing. Median gross rent-income ratios in 1993 were similar in assisted housing (30 percent) and public housing (29 percent), but assisted housing placed a larger rent burden on poverty-level households (49 percent) than public housing (34 percent).

Both assisted and public housing are far more affordable than market rate housing for poor families; the citywide median rent-income ratio for poverty-level rental households in 1993 was 72 percent.

As a whole, the city's HUD-assisted stock houses a diverse tenant population. African American households are the largest subgroup (43 percent), followed by white households (32 percent), Hispanic households (21 percent), and Asian households (3 percent). This pattern over-represents white and African American households, whose citywide household poverty rates are 24 and 31 percent, respectively, and under-represents Hispanic households, among which 39 percent are poor. In comparison, public and city-owned housing have occupancy patterns that also consistently overrepresent African Americans and underrepresent Hispanics, but occupancy by white households is less than 10 percent. Factors underlying the racial/ethnic distribution of assisted housing opportunities are unclear; biases in tenant selection, to the extent they played a role, might be compounded by the influences of project location and sponsor purpose. As already noted, there are high concentrations of assisted housing in predominantly African American neighborhoods, such as Central Harlem and Central Brooklyn. Some Section 8 developments were targeted to the elderly, which may explain why close to one-third of tenants (32 percent) in assisted housing are elderly households, a larger share than is found in either public or city-owned housing.

Aggregate indicators of condition suggest that the HUD-subsidized stock is in relatively sound shape. According to data from the 1993 Housing and Vacancy Survey, overcrowding (more than one person per room) occurs at a relatively low rate (5 percent), compared to public housing (9 percent), city-owned housing (15 percent), and rentals citywide (10 percent). The incidence of units with one or more condition defects is also low (4 percent) compared with public housing (10 percent), city-owned housing (47 percent), and citywide rentals (11 percent).

Although there are a number of distressed subsidized projects with seriously deteriorated conditions or that defaulted on their mortgages, there has been no systematic assessment of New York's assisted housing inventory. Among American cities, New York contains the largest portfolio of HUD-subsidized properties, yet its overall record appears to be one of relatively high performance on several counts: First, the incidence of deficiencies is below that for public housing despite the acknowledged national reputation for high performance of the city's housing authority. Second, to the extent that imminent FHA foreclosure for mortgage default indicates distress, New York, despite its large inventory, has few at-risk assisted developments, compared to many other large cities, such as Dallas, St. Louis, and Atlanta.[11]

HUD now has possession of the mortgage or outright ownership of 39 developments in the city. Several other developments have intact mortgages but serious condition problems. Approximately forty-three developments containing about 8,000 units appear to be at risk, constituting about 9 percent of the city's portfolio. This level of distress is considerably lower than the national estimate of 20 percent.

MAJOR THREATS TO NEW YORK'S FEDERALLY ASSISTED HOUSING

"Threats" to the assisted stock are defined here as either displacement pressures on current low-income HUD tenants—through unaffordable rents, poor conditions, or actual forced moves—or potential losses in "brick-and-mortar" units available to future generations of low-income apartment seekers (the virtual waiting list). A development that survives by shifting to a wider income mix is a threatened development, in that it represents a loss in available low-income housing resources. Major threats to the assisted stock are divided into three categories: subsidy expiration, distressed housing, and the current thrust of Washington policy.

Subsidy Expiration

Private Incentives and Public Purpose. That subsidies would someday end was an integral part of the legislative conception of the HUD-assisted programs, but this underlying premise needs to be critically reexamined in light of recent experience. Its precedent is in the New York State Mitchell-Lama legislation, under which a profit-motivated owner was permitted, after the twentieth anniversary, to "buy out" of the mortgage through prepayment, thereby terminating rent and income restrictions. A signal victory for New York's development community, the time limit was rationalized as a necessary incentive to gain private participation. It was also assumed that "bought-out" housing would be replaced, over time, by a continuing pipeline of new government-financed projects, without any net reduction in the assisted inventory. These perceptions of the long-term politics of housing development were carried into the federal legislation.

The federal mortgage subsidy programs—under Sections 221 and 236 of the Housing Act—incorporated "expiring use restrictions," allowing profit-motivated owners to prepay mortgages after twenty years, while locking in nonprofits for the full forty-year term. Under the subsequent project-based Section 8 programs, the "escape hatches" were even earlier: Generally, owners received fifteen- to twenty-year HAP rental assistance commitments, but they could exercise an "opt-out" option every five years.

Under the pressure of securing private sector participation in low-income housing development, the cost-benefit calculus of expiring subsidies was never fully explored by policymakers. The programs made possible large infusions of public subsidies for investment in a durable capital good with a theoretical useful life of fifty years—in actuality, often much more—in which limited-income tenants were to live. Nevertheless, ownership of the capital asset remained in private hands; it could be obtained with only a small initial equity investment and it yielded an assured rate of return and substantial tax shelter benefits, often with federal mortgage insurance to eliminate any risks to private lenders. If the property happened to be located in an appreciating market, there would come a point—after five, ten, fifteen, or twenty years—when the owner could terminate subsidy arrangements and extract full equity value, effectively wiping out the cumulative public investment in the property and its original public purpose with a stroke of the pen.

By the mid-1980s the first crop of mortgage prepayments threatened tenant disruption and displacement in California and Massachusetts, states that were also large, early users of the subsidy programs. The well-publicized conflicts, and a national expectation of large numbers of prepayments looming ahead, led to pressure for federal legislation.

Emergence of Federal Preservation Policy. The preservation paradigm incorporated in the ensuing legislation—enacted as the Emergency Low-income Housing Preservation Act (ELIHPA) in 1987 and Low-income Preservation and Resident Homeownership Act (LIHPRHA) (Title VI) in 1990[12]—represented what has been called a "grand compromise" between private interest and public purpose: Owner prepayment and subsidy termination were made conditional: Owners were required to give at least a year's notice to tenants, HUD, and state and local governments of their intent to prepay. HUD procedures required an open window—a period of from one to two years—during which prepaying owners were asked to consider selling the property (at appraised market prices) to residents, nonprofits, and other "preserving purchasers." Federal funds were made available, either to underwrite such preservation sales or to provide owners who had accrued substantial equity with "incentives to stay in" (extensions). In the latter case, HUD arrangements allowed owners to extract their equity, provided they agreed to retain subsidies and use restrictions for the remaining useful life of the property. In either case, owners were assured full equity return, based on appraised market values. If federal procedures and safeguards failed to turn up a preserving purchaser within the LIHPRHA processing period (from one to two years), owners could prepay and tenants would be given a three-year transitional period of rent protections to defer displacement pressures.

The legislation passed by Congress was a federal landmark in assisted housing policy, but it provided no guarantee of preservation. It extended only to properties whose owners met a threshold per-unit equity, not to distressed or less marketable projects. Appropriations for LIHPRHA were limited, considering national preservation needs; once HUD exceeded them, owners were entitled to prepay upon notification. Moreover, high-value projects exceeding federal cost limits—set at a preservation value based on rents at 130 percent of FMR—were not eligible and could fall through the LIHPRHA safety net.

Since 1995, due to deficit reduction pressures and waning housing priorities, the scope of Washington's preservation agenda has narrowed. Recent legislative changes have restored the owners' right to prepay, effectively making LIHPRHA voluntary. To avert tenant displacement when owners prepay and raise rents, in-place low-income tenants receive one-year "sticky vouchers" to meet rents in excess of 30 percent of income; the voucher sticks to that unit as long as the original tenant stays, then it vanishes. Even that safety net may be pulled back; pending legislative proposals would maintain the "sticky vouchers" in "low-vacancy areas," but in looser markets would restrict them to elderly or disabled tenants. Since HUD's operational definition of "low-vacancy area" is a local rental market with a vacancy rate of no more than 6 percent, in New York City the displacement of low-income tenants is not likely to be an issue as long as "sticky vouchers" are renewed annually. Over the long run, the more critical issue is the loss of housing resources targeted to low-income use.

Congressional attempts to defund LIHPRHA have been increasingly successful. Until 1997, organized tenant and owner constituencies managed to gain limited funding support, even in a tight HUD budget, to address the existing pipeline of HUD-assisted projects where owners had already filed notice and obtained HUD approval of plans. Capital grants have increasingly been used to finance LIHPRHA sales, instead of Section 8 rent assistance, because of lowered costs and uncertainties about long-term Section 8 commitments. In allocating funds, HUD has accorded priority to sales to residents and to nonprofit organizations; for owners interested in extending ownership through "incentives to stay," funding has been difficult to obtain. In fiscal year 1998, LIHPRHA was defunded and processing has been suspended for projects without HUD-approved plans, effectively moving toward a sunset of the preservation program.

New York Experience with Mortgage Prepayment. Despite its large stock of assisted housing, New York City's experience with mortgage prepayment has not yet been traumatic. This is due, in part, to the suppressed citywide real estate market of the late 1980s and early 1990s. In the dominant submarket locations—large clusters of assisted housing in low-income, minority neighborhoods—property values have not appreciated substantially. Since owners can prepay at any point after the twentieth year, some owners may be waiting for values to rise before exercising their rights to terminate participation in the program. In addition, more than one-third of the mortgage-subsidized projects are locked in for forty years: Nonprofits played a prominent role in assisted housing—in one out of five (46 out of 210) mortgage-subsidized developments. Another 28 profit-motivated developments are locked in by rent supplements; these are state and city Mitchell-Lama projects developed in the mid-1970s.

The most compelling reason for the slow pace of prepayments and LIHPRHA filings in New York may be rent regulation, which dampens owner incentives to terminate subsidies. Under the Rent Stabilization laws, rental properties that transit out of government rent regulation—whether by HUD or by state/local Mitchell-Lama authorities—automatically fall under local rent stabilization, provided that they were developed prior to 1974. More than three out of five for-profit developments potentially eligible for prepayment—83 out of 136 projects—had been developed by 1973.

As a result, any owner prepayments occurring before 1987, when Congress first required notification, may have gone unnoticed in New York City. Indeed, in one case, when the owner of a seventeen-unit building in the Chelsea neighborhood of Manhattan prepaid its mortgage loan and sold its building, the only change tenants noted was the new address to send the same rent checks. The presence of rent regulation has also produced substantial federal savings in preservation costs. In the case of Tower West—a 217-unit, Section 236 Mitchell-Lama building on the Upper West Side (the City's first LIHPRHA graduate)—early appraisals by HUD and the owner agreed on a preservation value of $39 million. When tenants and advocates realized both appraisals were based on prevailing unregulated rents, an unprecedented third appraisal was conducted by HUD, which reduced preservation value to $20 million, with a 50 percent federal saving. HUD subsequently suspended LIHPRHA processing in the city for about eighteen months, until rent regulation could be taken into account, a factor that has slowed processing for New York City projects.

Of housing developments potentially eligible for prepayment, all 136 developments reached their twentieth year by 1997. To date, however, only eighteen developments had owner notices of intent filed with HUD. The list includes a wide range of submarket locations: Six projects are located in Manhattan; all but one of these Mitchell-Lama projects are in the Upper West and East Sides, where there has been strong market escalation. Surprisingly, six developments are located in Staten Island and four in Queens, locations where the market has gained steadily in strength.

The fact that most owners filing notice under LIHPRHA were interested in "incentives to stay" rather than sales is notable, but not unique to New York. Within the national pipeline of about 225 unfunded projects filed under LIHPRHA, only twenty-five are for sale. But, in the course of processing, owners can switch from incentives to sales. The emphasis could shift to sales if, as is likely, LIHPRHA reduces or eliminates stay-in incentives.

In that sense, Washington's disappearing commitment to preservation has ominous implications for the city's assisted housing. Since ten of the city's twelve remaining "incentive" requests are subject to local rent regulation, how many will switch to sales or ultimately prepay remains an open question. Because LIHPRHA has been scaled back, Congress recently passed a special "carve-out" provision to compensate for the eighteen-month hiatus in HUD processing due to the rent regulation issues raised by Tower West; its intent is to extend LIHPRHA eligibility in New York. To date, this measure affects only two developments—one in Staten Island, one in Queens—where owners filed the earliest requests for stay-in incentives. Because HUD is according priority in its pipeline to funding resident and nonprofit sales, and attempting to distribute limited funds across the fifty states, the "carve-out" may not be in time to preserve the majority of New York projects that have filed notice for incentives. These developments may be at risk of mortgage prepayment and loss to the city's assisted stock.

Section 8 Expirations. The problem of looming Section 8 expirations—inherent in the program from its inception in 1975—has been addressed by Congress only in recent years. Automatic renewals of expiring Section 8 new construction and substantial rehabilitation contracts call for a national outlay of about $60 billion by the end of the decade.[13] The irony is that these escalating costs occur during a singular period of severe federal budget constraints on social spending.

Under federal budget scoring, the full Section 8 subsidy commitment must be obligated in its first year, regardless of its duration. To help reduce the budget impact of Section 8 extensions, Congress has adopted an incremental policy of one-year renewals upon expiration, at current rent levels. This poses uncertainties for tenants: federal law requires that owners give tenants a one-year notice of possible subsidy termination; tenants now automatically receive notice each year with their lease renewals. It also presents problems for owners, whose operating budgets may be strained at fixed rents, or who will have difficulty refinancing under short-term, year-to-year subsidy commitments.

The more critical preservation problem concerns those project-based Section 8 developments that may be at high risk of loss—those projects located in appreciating, high-rent districts, where owners have strong incentives to opt out at contract expiration and terminate subsidies. Current safeguards against tenant displacement include "super-vouchers" that enable in-place tenants to meet increased rents for another year, but there is no assurance of ongoing rent subsidies at those levels. For the community and for the city, the real loss is in low-income housing resources—in "brick and mortar" units available to low-income households once original in-place tenants are gone. In localities with tight rental markets, owner opt-outs, along with mortgage prepayments, will shrink the affordable housing supply and intensify the difficulty low-income households have in obtaining decent housing.

In New York City, expirations for Section 8 developments began in 1996, peaking to about 5,000 units per year by 2002 and dropping off by 2007.[14] It is unclear how many developments in the city are at risk of owner opt-out. HUD estimates that nationwide about 20 percent of assisted housing developments are in advantageous market contexts that make owner termination likely (U.S. Department of Housing and Urban Development 1993). Although the policy impact of year-to-year Section 8 renewals, and of tenant-based subsidies in opt-out contexts, is unclear, it is certainly not positive. If HUD national estimates are valid for New York City, close to 7,000 units in about fifty developments will lose project-based Section 8 assistance as a result of owner opt-outs.

As for expirations of Section 8 loan management set asides, the 104th Congress has revoked the requirement, under the McKinney Act of 1988, that HUD offer a five-year renewal when the original fifteen-year commitment expires. Present policy is one of "attrition," under which Section 8 LMSA is no longer project based, but renewed only for those units with in-place assisted tenants, one year at a time at current

rent levels. To make matters worse, Congress is considering a more extreme measure to terminate LMSA contracts at expiration and shift rent assistance to tenant-based vouchers.

In New York, some developments with early expirations have already received five-year renewals; for those now expiring, LMSA attrition could have substantial negative impacts. Tied to the older Section 221 and 236 developments, these expirations precede those for the younger Section 8 developments. More than half of the 210 older assisted developments—114 projects with an estimated 17,000 units—receive LMSA, the bulk of them expiring by 1998. While it is unclear what proportion of HUD tenants actually receive rent benefits, the attrition will withdraw project-based funding and put vacant unsubsidized units out of reach to low-income users. It can also exert a destabilizing effect on an otherwise viable development if assisted tenants move out in significant numbers and are not replaced by tenants who can afford economic rents. LMSA projects tend to be located in the city's poorer neighborhoods, where the demand for apartments is primarily from low- and very low-income tenants. Ironically, the destabilization of the older projects will have a telling impact on just those communities HUD should be seeking to revitalize. Destabilization will take the form of vacancies, declining rent rolls, operating shortfalls, and increasing pressures on owners to disinvest in communities already hard hit by private disinvestment and abandonment.

Distressed Housing

The Incidence of Distress. Washington's image of the failure of the low-income housing programs is exaggerated, particularly from a New York City perspective. National studies indicate that about 20 percent of assisted developments are seriously distressed, in deteriorated condition with continued financial or social viability in question. Another 27 percent of developments are in good condition, located in strong markets where they are prime candidates for owner termination of subsidies at the earliest opportunity. The mainstream majority (about 53 percent) are relatively stable projects in at least reparable condition, where subsidized rents are consistent with surrounding market rents, making opt-outs unlikely and continuing subsidy necessary to sustain the current tenant profile.[15]

In the summer of 1994, HUD Secretary Henry Cisneros testified to pending failures in the FHA multifamily portfolio, a potential loss of $12 billion over the next three to five years to cover owner defaults and mortgage foreclosures. These figures need to be put into perspective.

The costs associated with high risks in the assisted housing programs—as much as a 25 percent projected loss rate—were expected from the start when Congress initiated the private subsidy programs. Indeed, the Government National Mortgage Administration (Ginnie Mae) was created as the secondary market for Sections 235 and 236 mortgages, in order to shield Fannie Mae (Federal National Mortgage Administration), and its "blue chip" FHA holdings since the New Deal, from the potential risk.

Washington studies of the status of the assisted stock are based on broad national samples of subsidized projects; there are no comparable studies of the city's inventory and it is difficult to extrapolate from the national picture. Although New York's assisted housing inventory is lower on the distress scale than the national figures suggest, the existence of severely distressed projects in the city's assisted inventory needs to be acknowledged. Typically, owners receive large infusions of federal assistance— mortgage subsidies compounded with Section 8 LMSA—ample enough to enable them to provide minimally decent housing conditions. In the case of distressed housing, where buildings undergo consistent neglect and mismanagement, owners are realizing sustained profits at tenant and public expense.

Among the 43 developments identified as distressed, nearly all have experienced both long-term neglect and mortgage failure, with HUD already in possession of the mortgage. By and large these developments cluster in the city's poorest neighborhoods: the South Bronx, Central Brooklyn, Central and East Harlem. Examples are not hard to find in the local media: at Elva McZeal Apartments in the East New York section of Brooklyn, tenants have succeeded, after years of serious deterioration and mismanagement, in pressing HUD to intervene; a receiver has been installed to collect rents and restore services, while plans are developed to transfer the project to resident ownership. Less successful but more well-known instances of distress include Parkhill Apartments in Staten Island, the Gates Avenue corridor and Willard Price Apartments in the Bedford-Stuyvesant neighborhood, the Noble Drew Ali complex in East New York, and the large José de Diego Beekman complex in the South Bronx.

HUD's Changing Role in Distressed Housing. Even if instances of this kind of abuse are not pervasive and misrepresent the large majority of developments, the central question is how HUD, charged with oversight of the subsidized multifamily inventory, allowed them to continue for so long, particularly after voluble, repeated tenant protests made to HUD. Federal regulations call for periodic federal inspections by HUD field offices; in the older Section 221 and 236 developments, where distress is more likely, inspections are required to help justify owner requests for annual rent increases based on needed improvements. Tenants frequently report that year-to-year rent increases were approved by HUD, based on the same scope of work, left undone since the previous year. Asked to intervene by tenant advocates, the typical HUD response was of the order: "Do you want us to cut off the subsidies? What would happen to tenants?"

Problems in FHA/HUD administration were evident from the start of the subsidized programs and many have been inherited by succeeding administrations. In the early Section 221 and 236 programs, construction costs had to be kept within bounds to bring rents within reach of federally targeted low- and moderate-income levels. In some instances, corners were cut, conventional construction standards were bypassed, and operating costs tended to be underestimated. HUD, newly formed in 1965, was soon charged with volume production under the ambitious housing goals of the 1968 Act, the numbers to be incorporated in the president's annual housing message. Moreover, FHA's expertise was in underwriting development, typically not in inner-city settings; it had less experience in the oversight of housing management called for in the lower-income rental programs.

The Section 8 development programs, initiated during the Ford Administration in the mid-1970s, benefited from HUD's prior experience with the mortgage subsidy programs. Nevertheless, the HUD scandals uncovered by HUD Secretary Jack Kemp in the Bush Administration confirmed that the agency had been weakly administered and vulnerable to patronage and corruption during the Reagan years.[16] Apart from the waxing and waning of administrative capacity and its commitment to the subsidy programs, there is the existential question of bureaucratic bias: whether administrators—given their class identity and natural self-interest—are more likely to develop alliances with owners or with tenants.

During the Kemp administration of HUD, there were earnest attempts to deal with the earlier scandals and reform the agency's oversight of its portfolio. The emergence of the National Alliance of HUD Tenants—spurred by Assisted Housing Network of the National Low-income Housing Coalition and by the Boston HUD Tenants Alliance— opened up, for the first time, an ongoing dialogue between tenants and the agency. To deal with distressed housing, Kemp developed the Comprehensive Multifamily Servicing Program, which widened the range of HUD responses to distress to include receivership arrangements and HUD takeover (U.S. Department of Housing and Urban Development 1991). The program was never implemented, but its momentum was accelerated under the Cisneros Administration, through a HUD task force to develop strategies to address distressed housing. "SWAT" teams were centrally dispatched by HUD to conduct field assessments of troubled developments.

Congressional resistance to support of HUD budget requests, based on concerns about deep-seated problems in the HUD inventory, has intensified external pressure on the agency to correct the problems. Under Secretary Andrew Cuomo, HUD has moved more aggressively to place mismanaged projects in the hands of court-appointed receivers to collect rents, conduct repairs, and restore services. In March, 1997, Cuomo announced a "get tough" initiative and began enforcement action against negligent landlords. In New York City, HUD took possession of a 114-unit South Bronx development, initiated foreclosure, and turned over management to a private firm, Arco Management. Arco now manages 14 developments in the city, including three in the Gates Avenue Corridor in Bedford-Stuyvesant, eight in the Jose de Diego-Beekman complex in the South Bronx, and two in Central Harlem. HUD holds the mortgage as the mortgagee-in-possession for each of these developments except for the Willard Price Apartments in Bedford-Stuyvesant, where it has initiated a court action for appointment of Arco as receiver.

But enforcement is not the equivalent of preservation; key policy questions concerning treatment of the distressed stock remain to be resolved. The central question is the extent to which the agency will commit resources to promote the sale and transfer of distressed properties to responsible owners—particularly resident associations or community-based nonprofits with a stake in preserving an affordable community housing resource. This preservation strategy also assumes the agency will commit scarce up-front capital to enable preserving owners to finance and carry out necessary repairs. At the other extreme, HUD could simply choose to divest itself from otherwise unmarketable properties by providing tenants with vouchers and having the properties vacated and disposed of as expeditiously as possible. In its ongoing struggle with Congress over budget and appropriate legislation, HUD continues to press for wider powers to "voucher out," while acknowledging that such strategies are unworkable in low-vacancy areas.

In New York City, vouchering out the distressed stock poses major problems because of the limited capacity of the city's tight rental market to absorb households with vouchers. As a result, the fate of the distressed stock now under receivership will depend on HUD's willingness to negotiate and facilitate sale to preserving owners and commit the necessary upfront capital to assure the property is transferred in sound condition from the start.

Despite recent progress, in light of recent and projected staff cutbacks, HUD has reason to be daunted by the labor-intensive, administrative burden of overseeing a large portfolio of federally assisted housing. To the extent that this housing is preserved, the problem is not only how much capital and rent subsidies will cost. There are tough questions of administrative capacity and resources when dealing with a large portfolio of aging housing with many inherited problems.

The Current Thrust of Washington Policy

The Budget Squeeze. Federal budget balancing began in earnest in early 1995, with projected HUD cuts of 20 to 30 percent that could not have been more ill timed for the agency. The budget issues, calling for HUD and other agencies to be downsized, should be viewed as a politically imposed constraint, not a resource constraint. At the same time, defense appropriations were increased. In addition, nothing was done to stem over $80 billion in annual federal tax revenue losses due to homeowner mortgage and property tax deductions.[17]

In 1994, still reeling from radical surgery during the Reagan/Bush years—which left it at 60 percent of its 1980 budget in constant dollars—HUD faced $12 billion in insurance losses in its multifamily portfolio and a wave of $60 billion in Section 8 renewals by the year 2000, which, alone, would absorb close to 75 percent of the agency's budget. The metaphor in currency is an unstoppable train barreling down the tracks toward HUD—the agency needed to get off the track, the sooner the better. After rumblings in late 1994 that the White House—along with several key Congressmembers—was considering dismantling HUD, the agency quickly responded to an increasingly hostile environment by getting off the track with its first Reinvention Blueprint (U.S. Department of Housing and Urban Development 1995a).

The Reinvention of Federal Housing Policy. Budgetary realities are always grim, but HUD's blueprint forwarded a set of revisions that rationalized federal withdrawal as a conceptual advancement in policy. In its approach to housing, the blueprint signaled a major retreat from the supply-side development model that has dominated federal policy for sixty years; it set the stage for full HUD disengagement from its current investments—and from the inherent risks—in its national multibillion-dollar housing portfolio.

The reinvention narrative formed a self-critique of HUD's past housing programs and a dramatic shift toward market-based solutions. The radical proposal to "voucher out" public and assisted housing called for ultimate deregulation of all HUD-funded projects and conversion from project-based subsidies tied to designated developments to portable tenant-based subsidies that offered tenants a wider range of choices. Under a new "market discipline," the deregulated, formerly assisted housing would be forced to compete for tenants—with or without vouchers. Deficient owners could no longer stake a claim to ongoing streams of project-based subsidies. Vouchered tenants, no longer dependent on specified developments for housing assistance, could move to wherever opportunity presented itself. Further aping market realities, HUD proposed removing the good cause for eviction provision; at lease termination a tenant could be evicted at the owner's pleasure. The view of supply-side, project-based subsidies as promoting a "toxic" or "addictive" dependency among owners and tenants alike was a subtext running through the blueprint.[18] Interestingly, the second version of the blueprint empathizes with long-term tenants frustrated at not being able to purchase homes by referring to them as "lifers" (Cisneros 1996).

Although HUD has lost the debate over universal voucherization to opposition from HUD tenant and industry advocates, in New York—a city with a large proportion of renter households and a tight market—the afterimages of the blueprint were intense. In a March 1995 appearance in the city, Secretary Cisneros admitted that the voucher approach was unworkable in New York.[19] Even with vouchers, it is unlikely that HUD tenants in stable developments would move in large numbers, but those who remained would lose HUD as a recourse when they tried to deal with deficient management and conditions, with arbitrary evictions upon lease termination, or with unaffordable rent increases.[20] Subsequent policy developments have lessened concerns about forced displacement; the use of enhanced "super" or "sticky" vouchers for in-place tenants facing unaffordable rent increases and recent HUD proposals to prohibit vouchering-out in low-vacancy areas are key examples.

The Mark-to-Market Model/Portfolio Restructuring. One of the factors underlying the high cost projected for renewal of expiring project-based Section 8 contracts was the relatively high per-unit cost of the subsidy, particularly in a substantial portion of developments where subsidized rents exceed market rents. The rents for Section 8 developments tend to be high for several reasons: high interest rates during the 1970s and 1980s inflated debt servicing, and deeper rent subsidies were also needed to successfully target low- and very low-income tenants. Over time, the high initial FMRs set for each development were automatically increased by HUD through annual adjustments based on market trends. As a result, Section 8 rents have escalated to well in excess of comparable submarket "street" rents in about 25 percent of projects nationally (U.S. Department of Housing and Urban Development 1993). The disparity between Section 8 rents and unsubsidized rents may, in some instances, also be justified by the higher quality of Section 8 housing compared to nearby private rentals.

In its 1995 blueprint, HUD proposed to reduce the cost of the Section 8 program by implementing a "mark-to-market model." Under budgetary pressure to reduce its exposure to insurance risks and above-market subsidy costs, HUD's target was the entire stock of federally insured housing receiving project-based Section 8, including the older mortgage-subsidy projects under LMSA. Under the original proposal, the insurance fund would be used to write down debt to bring rents within area FMRs; federal insurance would be withdrawn, as would regulations governing rent, use restrictions, and conditions; project-based subsidies would be discontinued and tenants would be given portable vouchers to support rent payments. To counter displacement impacts, special protections were included for elderly and disabled tenants.

In New York City, the toll would have been great: 366 (out of 501) assisted developments would have been subject to mark-to-market restructuring. Existing tenants would be protected by their housing vouchers, but once they moved away, died, or no longer qualified for the program, their former apartments would no longer qualify for assistance. Although it was originally envisioned that Section 8 developments would use "pure" uninsured private financing, nearly all of the city's Section 8 NC/SR projects—252 out of 288 developments—have federally insured mortgages. Another 114 developments with rents subsidized under LMSA have FHA-insured mortgages. In a memorandum on mark-to-market displacement, HUD claimed that "local regulations—such as rent control or local use restrictions—in tight markets like New York City, will avert or substantially slow displacement stemming from market conversion" (U.S. Department of Housing and Urban Development 1995b). In fact, four out of five of the projects targeted by HUD for market conversion were developed after 1973 and therefore would not qualify for city rent protections.

Against HUD pressure for immediate, full-scale implementation to all applicable projects, the "one size fits all" mark-to-market model stimulated the same type of intense resistance that had formed against voucherization. The resulting debate narrowed the scope of HUD's original blanket proposal to a more limited, flexible approach that came to be called "portfolio restructuring."

Under restructuring, the emphasis shifted from blanket deregulation and voucherization to a more flexible, strategic attempt to reduce

HUD costs in over-subsidized developments, while retaining project-based funding—at lower subsidy levels—where feasible. Refinanced projects that retained project-based funding would shift away from automatic adjustments to a "budget-based" system for determining future subsidy levels. The older mortgage subsidy projects—where rents are generally below area FMR and would increase at market levels—are not included. Only Section 8 developments where rents exceed 120 percent of FMR are subject to restructuring.

Although the housing industry acknowledged the savings in subsidy costs that restructuring would realize, a 1996 voluntary mark-to-market demonstration passed by Congress has not recruited many interested owners to date. Requiring refinancing at low current interest rates is sound and, of course, has not met with opposition. However, investors are concerned about the negative tax consequences that would occur as HUD wrote down debt on their buildings. Proposals from both tenant and industry advocates called for continued project-based funding at budget-based levels and for exit tax relief through mortgage bifurcation, using a "soft", deferred second mortgage. Despite HUD opposition, the provisions were enacted in late 1997 in the Multifamily Assisted Housing Reform and Affordability Act (MAHRAA). The Internal Revenue Service has recently ruled, in response to owner requests, that participating owners will not incur tax liability. Concerns remain, however, with respect to HUD's preference for vouchering out restructured projects in feasible market areas and for inclusion of private intermediaries to administer restructuring, despite the preference in the law for state or local housing finance agencies.

In New York City, about 71 developments—totaling about 10,000 units—have rents that exceed 120 percent of FMR and will be subject to portfolio restructuring, with most contracts (58 developments) reaching expiration in years 1999 to 2001.[21] Under current proposals to reform the Section 8 program, upon expiration owners could either choose to opt-out or restructure. There is no provision for incentives to preserve higher-value properties where owners are likely to opt out. Although assisted tenants would receive vouchers, there is no requirement that the opting-out owner accept vouchers; nor is the level of assistance increased to help prevent excessive rent burdens and displacement. Restructuring plans require that owners commit to project-based assistance for up to twenty years, but use and affordability restrictions would be determined by the administrator, enabling the development to accommodate a wider range of income levels, and a changing tenant profile over the future (National Housing Law Project 1997).

The potential threats raised by restructuring include tenant displacement from high-value projects, where owners will likely opt out rather than restructure. For stable developments located in sound sub-markets, owners and restructuring intermediaries will have room to negotiate Section 8 extensions and affordability and use restrictions that preserve project viability while minimizing ongoing subsidy commitments. However, there may be a net loss of units available to the lowest-income households as income targets widen. In marginally viable developments that cannot operate within restructured rents close to market levels, the projects may be lost through vouchering out and disposition.

The submarket location of the seventy-eight New York City developments subject to restructuring provides some indication of the likely outcome of the Section 8 restructuring. Most are located in low- or modest-rent districts of the city, with twenty-eight in the South-Central Bronx, ten in Central Brooklyn, and thirteen in the Harlem districts. There is some doubt about whether those developments could affect the economies intended by restructuring and continue operations at rent levels consistent with the prevailing submarket in which they are located. At the other extreme, there are five developments located in the gentrifying Chelsea-Clinton district of Manhattan that are candidates for restructuring by the end of the decade; if market conditions continue, owners faced with the choice of restructuring or opting out would probably take the latter option.

Welfare Reform. An estimated two out of five tenants (39 percent) living in New York's assisted housing rely on public assistance as a source of income.[22] New York's present public assistance grant structure is bifurcated into a basic needs grant and a shelter allowance grant, the latter intended to meet housing-related costs, at a maximum of $286 a month for the city's typical three-person TANF household. Although shelter allowance maximums have lagged behind actual rental costs, for the city alone the public assistance rent stream amounts to $1.4 billion annually (Community Service Society of New York 1997; Citizens Housing and Planning Council 1997). Extrapolated for 36,000 public assistance households in assisted housing, the welfare rent stream to the federally subsidized stock amounts to about $120 million annually. The stability of this rent stream, and the resultant housing subsidy levels that are required to support in-place tenants on public assistance, depends on a federal welfare system undergoing radical reform and devolution (U.S. Department of Housing and Urban Development 1996).

Under federal welfare reform—the Personal Responsibility Act of 1996—each state is free to restructure assistance under an annual block grant. The law establishes a five-year time limit on a family's receipt of federal assistance; it cuts off food stamps and SSI to some legal immigrants; and its guidelines call for a 50 percent reduction in the rolls by 2002 through welfare-to-work transitions. The most immediate housing threats are likely to result from state decisions to cut benefit levels—in New York, the governor originally recommended a phased reduction in benefits, from 10 percent after eighteen months to 45 percent after four years. These changes would have had an enormous, immediate impact on the rent-paying ability of publicly assisted households, even before federal time limits were reached. Because of the opposition of the state legislature to the Governor's proposals, it appears that benefit levels will remain stable for the time being. However, reductions in benefits to legal immigrants, as well as state changes in Home Relief for adults, will strain family budgets and place greater burdens on federal housing subsidies to meet prevailing rents, effectively transferring reductions in federal welfare spending to a wrenchingly strained federal housing budget.

Public assistance households whose rent is subsidized under the Section 8 program are less likely to feel the strain because federal subsidies cover the rent gap above 30 percent of income. However, within the city's assisted stock, about 110 of the older, mortgage-subsidized developments—with an estimated 41,000 units—do not receive project-based Section 8. The extent of public assistance within this stock is not known, nor is the degree to which households receive tenant-based assistance, through Section 8 or rent supplements. If close to 39 percent of households are public assisted, then the deepening effects of welfare withdrawal over time may have serious consequences for the viability and affordability of a substantial portion of the assisted stock.

Expected Impacts in New York City. In the midst of a sea change in federal policy—both in housing and social policy—the future of New York City's HUD-assisted housing stock is fraught with uncertainties. It is certain that under the prevailing policy climate there will be significant net losses in current low-income housing resources and adverse consequences for households that are or would be HUD tenants.

The dominant thrust of policy is toward devolution of federal responsibility and minimal resource commitments to housing priorities. The consequences will include a downsized HUD, with its primary role to dispense funds to lower levels of government and intermediaries; greater reliance on local intermediaries to oversee and restructure the federal multifamily housing portfolio; and withdrawal of the preservation safety net, freeing owners to terminate subsidies at expiration and move to top market rents, while tenants cope with displacement pressures and try to suffice with vouchers. To minimize federal subsidy costs in the remaining assisted stock, affordability and use restrictions will be loosened, opening this housing to a wider range of income levels, even as tenants who continue to rely on public assistance experience reductions in their incomes and rent-paying ability.

On the positive side, HUD has moved to "get tough" and tighten its enforcement efforts to deal with negligent owners and its distressed properties. This increased vigilance will prevent the neglect and loss of deteriorated stock and protect against further tenant hardship, provided that capital is available to restore the buildings and transfer them to preserving owners—particularly to resident or nonprofit ownership. Otherwise, loss and displacement will not be averted.

There is also growing recognition in emerging federal policies of the real limitations of tenant-based vouchers in cities, like New York, with tight rental markets. Constraints on vouchering-out in low-vacancy areas and the use of enhanced vouchers in mortgage prepayments and Section 8 opt-outs will provide some stability to in-place tenants who would otherwise face displacement pressures.

The critical issue for New York City is the extent to which scarce "brick and mortar" low-income housing resources can be maintained within a changing federal policy environment. The waning federal commitment to housing preservation could result in major net losses in housing available for low-income use, roughly estimated at 30 percent of the stock—about 30,000 units—and possibly more. Consistent with national estimates, the city can expect to lose about 20 percent of its assisted housing to buy-outs and opt-outs by owners who can profit from market conversion (U.S. Department of Housing and Urban Development 1993). About 2,500 units are in the LIHPRHA pipeline for stay-in incentives that may not be realized and could switch to prepayment and sales, with others to follow. Section 8 expirations will peak in five years, with unknown consequences.

At the bottom end of the inventory, the fate of marginal and distressed projects depends on whether projects can survive LMSA attrition or portfolio restructuring intact, and whether the responsible intermediaries intervene to turn this stock into viable, self-sustaining housing, without loss of use and affordability restrictions. The city may lose some portion of its marginal distressed stock to HUD terminations and vouchers, but how much is uncertain. National figures suggest that as much as 20 percent of assisted housing, particularly in the older programs, is at risk.

The retention of project-based subsidies is essential for the preservation of the stable majority of developments in the city that are economically viable and in reasonable condition, but not at imminent risk of owner exit. But, to the extent that federal resources thin out, asset managers will be tempted to flex use restrictions, move toward a wider, higher mix of incomes to cover expenses, and increase and/or deregulate rents to make the existing stock more self-supporting. It is conceivable that the losses through internal rearrangements of rents and tenant income mix will outweigh those from owner or HUD terminations.

The new flexibility may leave buildings that continue to stand, function, and run at a comfortable return, with less federal exposure. But there will be a net loss of housing resources for low-income households. Considering the sheer arithmetic of such housing losses against an emergency shortage of affordable housing, there will be greater pressures on the city to deal with the adverse social and fiscal consequences.

SURVIVAL OF THE FEDERAL-PRIVATE PARTNERSHIP

The resolution of federal housing preservation issues will involve a good deal of negotiation and compromise among interested parties: current tenants, owners, and the federal government. Although debates over assisted housing continue, our recent experience with federally assisted, private housing also provides important lessons for the creation of new housing programs in the future.

Assuming that the supply-side development model survives in some form—at the least, in tight-market cities where market-based vouchers are unworkable—the policy question for the future is whether private initiative can be harnessed in a way that represents the best of the thirty-year experience with subsidized housing, but at lesser public and social costs and risks. In short, what have we learned from the past about how to do it in the future?

The central issue is the public purpose–private equity question that threatens some of the most successful housing—namely, the costs that subsidy expiration extracts in wiping out long-term public investments in housing and in displacing tenants. How much of a private incentive is necessary to participation at lower public and social costs?

Among the alternatives, longer-term private commitments should be explored, as in the case of locked-in nonprofits now participating in the subsidy programs. The capacity of the nonprofit sector—committed to long-term ownership at lesser costs—to bear a larger share of the development load needs to be given serious consideration and priority.

As for the profit-motivated sector, consideration should be given to "shared equity" arrangements, under which the public retains a share of the equity in property—say half—should the owner opt to terminate time-limited subsidy arrangements. Shared equity may not prevent subsidy termination, but it would reduce incentives to owners and lessen the public costs of preservation strategies, like LIHPRHA, that promote transfers to preserving owners.

Finally, the "public utility" model should be explored, under which qualified private providers are designated or franchised to provide a public service, with a guarantee of reasonable returns for the foreseeable future, without expiration limits. Oversight of providers would be necessary, as would ongoing adjustments to costs and rates of return, and provisions for replacement of deficient providers. The model suggests it might be possible to combine private initiative in the development of public infrastructure, without the risks of housing loss and tenant displacement inherent in the present repertoire of private subsidy programs.

APPENDIX: THE MAJOR HUD SUBSIDY PROGRAMS AT RISK

Section 221(d)(3)BMIR

Subsidy incentives: Mortgage insurance underwrote long-term (forty-year) below-market private/government financing; interest-rate subsidies brought rates down to 3 percent; for-profit ownership of rental housing could be achieved with low equity requirements at an assured profit margin. Investor incentives included depreciation allowances and tax shelter benefits.

Use restrictions: Vacant units were restricted to "low- and moderate-income" households, defined as up to median city household income.

Rent-setting: Affordability was achieved by lowering debt servicing costs, through below-market interest rates and forty-year mortgage terms. Rents are "budget-based," covering costs and allowable profit margins, with increases subject to HUD oversight and approval. Household rents are set at these levels, unless they can afford more within 30 percent of income, in which case a household can be charged up to the full economic (unsubsidized) rent for the unit.

Expiration: Nonprofit and public developers (as well as HUD) are "locked in" for the full forty-year mortgage term. However, profit-motivated owners are permitted to prepay the mortgage after twenty years, thereby terminating restrictions and regulations, making it possible to raise rents to market levels.

Section 236

Section 236 is similar to 221BMIR, with the following exceptions:

Subsidy incentives: Interest-rate reduction subsidies reduce rates down to 1 percent.

Use restrictions: Initial occupancy is targeted more narrowly to "lower-income" levels, defined as up to 135 percent of the maximum income for local entry into public housing.

Section 8 New Construction and Substantial Rehabilitation

Subsidy incentives: HUD and the owner agree to a Fair Market Rent (FMR) level for each unit in the development, depending on production costs, debt service, and projected operating costs. Federal mortgage insurance to facilitate private financing may or may not be provided. A Housing Assistance Payment (HAP) agreement assures the owner that HUD will provide rent subsidies to cover the gap between the FMR and tenant rent payments set at 30 percent of income. Equity requirements and investor risks are low; investor incentives include the use of (accelerated) depreciation as tax shelter. Full Section 8 rent subsidies (70 percent of FMR) are set aside at inception for the life of the HAP agreement.

Use restrictions: Vacant units are targeted only to low- and very low-income households, at 80 and 50 percent of area median respectively, with most units to be rented to very low-income households.

Rent-setting: Tenant rents are regulated by HUD and set at 30 percent of income. Aggregate rents paid to the owner are set through annual adjustments in the FMR made by HUD on the basis of market trends. In that sense, the FMR is not budget-based; it is driven by market trends.

Expiration: It is difficult to generalize about Section 8 expirations; commitments will depend on the year the project was developed, whether it was rehabilitated or newly constructed, and whether state tax-exempt financing was used (see tables). In general, HAP agreements for new construction tend to be for at least twenty years, up to forty years in some cases. For substantial rehabilitation, the HAP agreement is usually fifteen years in duration. Many HAP agreements prior to 1980 provided owners an "opt-out" point at five-year intervals, at which the owner had the option to terminate subsidies.

NOTES

1. New York had innovated the private subsidy model in the state Mitchell-Lama Program in 1955, which used below-market financing (usually state and municipal tax exempt bonds) to promote affordable housing development for low- and moderate-income households.

2. Section 202 housing for the elderly and disabled is also a private, project-based subsidy program. But it is omitted here because it is available only to nonprofit corporations, which are "locked" into subsidy arrangements for the full forty-year mortgage term. As a result, this housing is not currently at risk of subsidy expiration.

3. In the case of federally subsidized Mitchell-Lama developments, rents are overseen and regulated by state or local agencies rather than directly by HUD.

4. For a New York example, see Schur (1977).

5. These differences are summarized in three useful tables in State of California (1987).

6. The Mitchell-Lama Program generally refers to the New York State housing program (begun in 1955), which created thousands of below-market rental and mutual apartments for persons of middle income. These developments were constructed pursuant to the provisions of Article 2 of the Private Housing Finance Law. Below-market state and municipal construction financing in conjunction with municipal tax exemptions resulted in substantially lower rentals than would have been possible through the private sector alone. As a condition for the financial aid, the developments have submitted to public supervision and monitoring to ensure that their operation is conducted efficiently and economically and that the middle-income population intended to be benefited by the program receives good housing with adequate services (excerpted from *Housing Programs of New York State* 1986).

7. For an interesting glimpse of the period, see Husock (1990).

8. The term *project*, as used here, is a building or set of buildings considered by HUD as a unitary development for the purpose of transacting federal insurance, mortgage subsidy agreements, or Section 8 HAP agreements.

9. One exception is the Forest Hills proposal during the Lindsay Administration.

10. The figures in this section are those cited for "other regulated housing" contained in Blackburn (1995). No such data is disaggregated for HUD-subsidized units, as defined here, which comprise only two-thirds of the "other regulated" category that also includes Section 8 elderly housing and

Mitchell-Lama developments that are not federally subsidized. Care should be taken in viewing these data as supporting more than broad inferences.

11. See, for instance, HUD lists of pending foreclosures in the assisted housing stock, prepared in 1994 in support of HUD Secretary Henry Cisneros's testimony before Congress.

12. ELIHPA was an interim measure, followed by LIHPRHA in Title VI of the 1990 Housing Act.

13. The figure is based on 1995 congressional estimates of annual unit costs of $7,400 for Section 8 NC/SR and $3,351 for LMSA—in 1996 dollars—using budget scoring of 17.5-year renewals for NC/SR and five-year renewals for LMSA.

14. Figures cited here are estimates prepared by New York City Housing Development Corporation (1996).

15. See U.S. Department of Housing and Urban Development (1993, exhibit 3.1), among others, and House Republican Budget Committee (1995).

16. For a concise description of HUD management deficiencies, see U.S. General Accounting Office (1995) and Dyckman (1997).

17. Sensible proposals to cap tax benefits for luxury and second homes could generate an estimated $15 billion annual contribution to a federal housing trust fund.

18. The adjectives *toxic* and *addictive* to describe Section 8 and public housing were used by the former HUD Housing Commissioner, Austin Fitts, until recently a prominent consultant to HUD, at a meeting of Women in Housing and Finance, New York City, September 1995.

19. Among seventeen large cities, success rates for Section 8 voucher and certificate recipients were found to be lowest in New York (34 and 32 percent, respectively); the next lowest was Boston (47 and 48 percent), and the others were over 60 percent successful. See U.S. Department of Housing and Urban Development (1990). In 1989, the New York City Housing Authority estimated that about 71 percent of certificates were turned back at the end of the four-month period in which they can be used (Oser 1989). Most certificates are used by in-place tenants, rather than movers, most of them for elderly or small adult households. See also Cisneros (1996). A recent report by the Citizens Housing and Planning Council (1998), however, reports that success rates have risen in recent years.

20. Section 8 voucher assistance is also diminishing in value. FMRs were reset in 1995 from the 45th percentile to the 40th percentile of area market rent. Proposals to raise tenant contributions to more than 30 percent of income

have been considered, for which the proposed repeal of the Brooke amendment may be a prelude.

21. Figures are derived from a listing titled Portfolio Engineering Data, prepared in 1996 by the National Housing Trust, based on presently available
HUD data, without independent verification.

22. This estimate is based on an extrapolation. About 51 percent of households
in public housing are publicly assisted. Since the proportion of public housing households earning less than $10,000 is 58.5 percent, compared with 45.4
percent for "other regulated" housing, the public assistance figure for the
latter was proportionally reduced. See Blackburn (1995, 111 and 292).

REFERENCES

Blackburn, Anthony J. 1995. *Housing New York City, 1993*. City of New York, Department of Housing Preservation and Development, June.

Cisneros, Henry G. 1996. *Renewing America's Communities from the Ground Up:
The Plan to Continue the Transformation of HUD*. Washington, D.C.: HUD,
February, 2.

Citizens Housing and Planning Council, 1998. *Paying the Rent: An Evaluation of
the Section 8 Existing Housing Program in New York City*. New York: Author.

Citizens Housing and Planning Council. 1997. *An Analysis of the Housing Impacts
of Governor Pataki's Welfare Proposals*. Committee on Welfare and Housing.

Community Service Society of New York. 1997. "Housing and Welfare Reform:
Issues for New York City." *Urban Agenda Issue Brief*, no. 3 (March).

Dyckman, Lawrence J. 1997. *HUD's Management Deficiencies, Progress on Reforms
and Issues for Its Future*. Statement, March 6.

Feagin, Joe R., Charles Tilly, and Constance W. Williams. 1972. *Subsidizing the
Poor: A Boston Housing Experiment*. Lexington, Mass.: D. C. Heath, chapter 3.

Hartman, Charles W. 1975. *Housing and Social Policy*. Englewood Cliffs, N.J.:
Prentice Hall, chapter 5.

House Republican Budget Committee. 1995. "Mark-to-Market Budget/Analy-
sis Assumptions" (draft). U.S. House of Representatives, April 25, 13.

Housing Programs of New York State. 1986. Prepared by William B. Eimecke, Director of Housing, New York State.

Husock, Howard. 1990. "Occupancy Controls and Racial Integration at Starrett
City." *Case Study Program (C16-90-962.0)*, 1–4, Kennedy School of Government.

Kerner Commission Report. 1968. *Report of the National Advisory Commission on Civil Disorders*. New York: E. P. Dutton.

National Housing Law Project. 1997. "Not-So-New Proposals for Section 8 Program Restructuring." *Housing Law Bulletin* (May): 71–74.

New York City Housing Development Corporation. 1996. *Section 8 Mark-to-Market Strategy: A Closer Look at the Impact on New York City*. January, 12.

Oser, Alan S. 1989. "Rent Supplement Review Nears." *New York Times*, March 12.

Schur, Robert. 1977. "Old-Style Ripoffs Are Still Alive and Well." *City Limits*, nos. 2 and 3 (February and March).

State of California. 1987. *Housing Alert: Estimates of Low-income Rental Units Subject to Termination of Rent and/or Mortgage Subsidies, 1988–2008*. Sacramento: Senate Office of Research, December.

Turetsky, Doug. 1993. *We Are the Landlords Now: A Report on Community-Based Housing Management*. New York: Community Service Society, 2.

U.S. Department of Housing and Urban Development. 1996. *The Impacts of Federal Welfare Reform on HUD Public and Assisted Housing: An Initial Assessment*. Office of Policy Development, October.

———. 1995a. *HUD Reinvention: From Blueprint to Action*. Washington, D.C., March.

———. 1995b. *Mark-to-Market Displacement Issues: The Size of the Problem and Solutions* (Memorandum, undated).

———. 1993. *Assessment of the HUD-Insured Multifamily Housing Stock, Final Report*, vol. 1, chapter 2. Washington, D.C.: HUD Office of Policy Development and Research, September.

———. 1991. *Notice to Regional Administrators: Comprehensive Multifamily Servicing Program*, H 91-22, March 11.

———. 1990. *Final Comprehensive Report of the Freestanding Housing Voucher Demonstration*, vol. 2, Table G.22. Washington, D.C., May.

U.S. General Accounting Office. 1995. *Housing and Urban Development, Reforms at HUD and Issues for Its Future*. Testimony of Judy A. England-Joseph, February 22.

Wallace, James E. 1995. "Financing Affordable Housing in the United States." *Housing Policy Debate* 6, 4:785–814.

CHAPTER 7

THE HOUSING COURT'S ROLE IN MAINTAINING AFFORDABLE HOUSING

Paula Galowitz

INTRODUCTION

Any discussion of housing and community development in New York City would be incomplete without an examination of the New York City Housing Court. The court was specifically created by the New York State Legislature as a mechanism for providing safe, decent, and habitable housing (New York City Civil Court Act § 110). Given the court's central role in overseeing housing conditions and the huge number of litigants who pass through its doors, the court plays a major role in shaping housing patterns in New York City.

Yet, the Housing Court is widely regarded as an ineffective institution that has not fulfilled its mandate of preserving the city's housing stock. The court has had little influence on the enforcement of the housing maintenance code, a task that the court was specifically designed to accomplish. Furthermore, the court has failed to serve as an effective forum for adjudicating landlord and tenant disputes.

This chapter will examine the reasons for the Housing Court's shortcomings and consider whether the court can be reformed to enable it to play a more effective part in community preservation and development. The discussion first will describe the Legislature's goals in creating the court. The discussion then will examine the systemic pressures that stand in the way of an activist, effective housing court, and will consider some of the current proposals for reforming the court. The chapter will conclude by suggesting structural changes for the Housing Court.

THE AMBITIOUS ASPIRATIONS OF THE COURT'S CREATORS

The New York City Housing Court (formally called the Housing Part of the Civil Court of the City of New York) was established by the New York State Legislature in 1972 and began operations the following year. The Legislature created the court in order to remedy a jurisdictional gap that stymied enforcement of the housing maintenance code. The Civil Court had jurisdiction over housing eviction cases but lacked the authority to enforce the housing maintenance code. Because violations of the code gave rise to criminal sanctions, they were under the jurisdiction of the Criminal Court.

The new Housing Court combined jurisdiction over violations of the housing maintenance code and the Civil Court's traditional caseload of eviction cases (Kramer 1995). Other jurisdictions, such as Pittsburgh and Boston, created specialized housing courts around the same time as New York. The impetus for these specialized courts was a dissatisfaction with the manner in which the existing courts handled serious housing issues and a desire to create courts with expertise in housing matters. "[S]everal jurisdictions, hoping to improve housing court administrations, began to establish specialized housing courts typically characterized by their flexibility and innovative powers" (Scott 1979).

In New York, at the time that the Housing Court was created, there was widespread abandonment of residential buildings; the court was created to "retard the deterioration and subsequent abandonment of residential buildings" and encourage critically needed housing investment (Cohen 1979). As the New York State Legislature explained in the statute creating the Housing Court:

> A part of the [Civil] court shall be devoted to actions and proceedings involving the enforcement of state and local laws for the establishment and maintenance of housing standards, including, but not limited to, the multiple dwelling law and the housing maintenance code, building code and health code of the administrative code of the City of New York. (New York City Civil Court Act § 110[a])

In the legislative findings and policy statement underlying the enabling legislation, the Legislature articulated the purposes of the court:

> The legislature finds that the effective enforcement of state and local laws for the establishment and maintenance of proper housing standards is essential to the health, safety, welfare and reasonable

comfort of the citizens of the state. . . . The legislature finds that the
effective enforcement of proper housing standards in the City of
New York will be greatly advanced by the creation of a housing
part of the civil court of the City of New York with jurisdiction of
sufficient scope (i) to consolidate all actions related to effective
building maintenance and operation, (ii) to recommend or employ
any and all of the remedies, programs, procedures and sanctions
authorized by federal, state or local laws for the enforcement of
housing standards, regardless of the relief originally sought by the
plaintiff, if it believes that such other or additional remedies, programs, procedures or sanctions will be more effective to accomplish and protect and promote the public interest and compliance,
and (iii) to retain continuing jurisdiction of any action or proceeding relating to a building until all violations of state or local laws
for the establishment and maintenance of proper housing standards have been removed and until it is satisfied that their immediate recurrence is not likely.

The primary mandate of the new court was to address maintenance and
repair issues and to create a more flexible mechanism to preserve the
city's declining housing stock.

THE CURRENT STATE OF THE HOUSING COURT

In the two and one-half decades that the Housing Court has been
in existence, it has become a profoundly important institution. The decisions of the Housing Court directly affect millions of New York City
tenants and landlords. If a New Yorker has contact with the court system, that contact is more likely to be with the Housing Court than any
other court, whether city, state, or federal.

New York City is not the only jurisdiction that has created a court
that focuses solely on landlord-tenant disputes and on matters relating
to housing. Other cities, such as Boston, Philadelphia, Pittsburgh,
Chicago, Detroit, Cleveland, Toledo, Washington, D.C., St. Louis, and
Minneapolis–St. Paul, have created specialized housing courts. In other
jurisdictions, housing matters are heard in the general municipal courts,
small claims courts, or divided among several courts.

However, the Housing Court's impact on New York City is greater
than that of equivalent courts in other cities because of its high percentage of rental housing. In most large cities, the majority of housing is not
rental. In New York City, the "housing stock was (and still is) comprised
two-thirds of rental housing and one-third of owner-occupied housing,

nearly the reverse proportion of any other large city" (see Braconi, chapter 4 in this volume).

As a result, the number of cases processed each year in Housing Court in New York City is extremely high. In 1995, approximately 300,000 new cases were filed in the clerk's offices. The most common type of action filed was a "nonpayment case," in which a landlord sues a tenant to collect overdue rent in a residential apartment; in 1995, there were 266,259 nonpayment cases, which is approximately 90 percent of the cases in Housing Court.[1] There were also 20,641 cases, or approximately 7 percent, in which a landlord sued a tenant in a holdover action, a proceeding in which a landlord attempts to evict a tenant for reasons other than a failure to pay rent (such as violating the lease, subletting the apartment without the landlord's permission, committing a nuisance). During this same year, final judgments were entered in 198,120 cases in residential apartments (of which 148,351 involved an appearance by a tenant prior to the court entering a judgment for the landlord). Warrants of eviction (which allow a marshal to evict a tenant) were issued in 96,795 cases.

In addition to the nonpayment and holdover cases in Housing Court, there were approximately 9,675 cases started in 1995 by the New York City Department of Housing Preservation and Development (HPD) and by tenants to enforce housing maintenance standards. Of these 9,675 cases (approximately 3 percent of the court's caseload), 1,121 cases (or approximately 12 percent) were initiated by HPD and the balance by individual litigants (Belzaguy 1996). Tenants can initiate such HP (Housing Part) Actions to require landlords to repair housing conditions, restore essential services such as heat and hot water, and correct violations found in the common areas of the building. Tenants can also complain about the inadequate housing conditions in the context of a nonpayment action by asserting the defense of a breach of the warranty of habitability. This defense is based on the Warranty of Habitability statute (Real Property Law § 235-b), which provides that in every agreement to lease residential property the landlord warrants that the apartment and the common areas are fit for human habitation, for all reasonable uses intended by the landlord and the tenant, and that there are no conditions that are dangerous to life, health, or safety. If there has been a breach of the warranty of habitability, the tenant is entitled to a rent reduction and an order for the landlord to repair the conditions. Unfortunately, there are no available statistics on the frequency in which breach of the warranty of habitability is asserted as a defense in nonpayment actions.

The small number of cases brought to enforce the housing maintenance standards is surprising, given that Housing Court was specifically created as a mechanism for providing safe, decent, and habitable housing. The Housing Court has become, in practice, a forum for collecting rent (Association of the Bar 1988). Approximately 90 percent of the cases are nonpayment actions while only 3 percent are brought to enforce the housing maintenance code.

As a result of the huge caseload and as a consequence of the eviction actions, Housing Court has become one of the most significant courts in the state. As explained in the narrative part of the 1996–97 Budget Request for the Housing Court of the New York State Office of Court Administration:

> Over time, the Housing Part of the New York City Civil Court has developed into one of the most important courts in the State. In 1978, 74,248 summary landlord and tenant proceedings were added to the calendar in the housing part, last year that number stood at 158,970 and 183,304 were disposed of. Those dispositions included, among other things, thousands of evictions of individuals and families who must face a New York City real estate market with a low vacancy rate of apartments, many of which are unaffordable to low and middle-income families. These evictions are a principal source of homelessness in New York City. Additionally, through its power to enforce corrections of housing code violations, the Housing Court is increasingly responsible for preservation of New York City's diminishing stock of affordable housing. (State of New York Court System Budget for 1996–97)

The actual nature of Housing Court adjudication becomes apparent when one looks beyond raw caseload numbers and considers the number of judges who sit in the court. At present, there are only thirty-five judges in this part of the city's judicial system. As a result, each judge has an average caseload of almost 7,000 cases each year, which is significantly higher than judges in the Civil Court.[2] Needless to say, the judges are reduced to rushing through their huge daily calendars. Litigants generally receive fewer than five minutes of attention from a Housing Court judge (Fund for Modern Courts 1994). Compounding the gargantuan caseload are the woefully inadequate numbers of court attorneys, *pro se* attorneys (court attorneys in the clerk's office whose job is to assist litigants who are not represented by attorneys), housing inspectors, translators, and other personnel to handle the caseload of the court.

Justice would be difficult enough to dispense under these conditions if both sides were adequately represented and the judges could rely on lawyers to frame the issues and to explain procedures and rulings to the litigants. Yet, one of the two sides in Housing Court—the tenant—is routinely unrepresented. According to a relatively recent survey, 97.5 percent of the landlords who appear in Housing Court are represented by counsel but only 11.9 percent of tenants have legal representation (Community Training and Resource Center 1993). These statistics, which were gathered before the recent budgetary cuts in legal services, substantially understate the number of tenants who will go unrepresented once the full impact of the budget cuts is felt.

When a court system has as high a caseload and as few resources as New York City's Housing Court, there is too little time for too many cases. The inevitable result is a court system in which stipulations to settle cases are agreed to in the hallways outside the courtroom without adequate judicial supervision. This pressure to settle, characteristic of all cases in Housing Court, including nonpayment cases, emanates from the huge caseloads as well as from the encouragement of court attorneys (the attorney for the individual Housing Court judges) and Housing Court judges. *Pro se* litigants (those who appear on their own behalf and are not represented by an attorney) are particularly susceptible to these pressures. If the litigants cannot resolve the case, they may have to wait most of the day before seeing a judge. In addition, *pro se* litigants may not know their rights and may fail to realize that they are entitled to a trial and do not have to settle. Some monitors for the Fund for Modern Courts recently observed Housing Court and expressed concern about "negotiations between landlords or landlords' attorneys that occur in the chaotic atmosphere of the courthouse hallways." The monitors commented that "tenants are frequently approached by attorneys before going into the courtrooms and are asked to agree to stipulations . . . [and] that [t]enants may not always understand the implications of what they are asked to agree to, but may feel undue pressure to sign" (Fund for Modern Courts 1994). Thus, the system is characterized by immense pressures to settle, lack of judicial involvement, and cursory examination of the claims of both parties, including claims or defenses that may not be articulated by *pro se* litigants.

The physical conditions of the Housing Court mirror—and exacerbate—the general misery and hopelessness of many of the litigants who appear there. The facilities have been repeatedly condemned as inadequate. They are variously described as "deplorable," "chaotic," and "grossly inadequate" (Fund for Modern Courts 1994). The inadequacy of some of the facilities make it feel like it is not a "real" court. Moreover, the small courtrooms in most of Housing Court mean that litigants, particularly those that are *pro se*, must wait in the crowded hallways and are unable to observe the proceedings in the courtroom and learn from watching other cases. This shortage of space, concomitant noise, and lack of adequate personnel to answer questions contribute to the confusion that permeates the court.

These systemic obstacles are exacerbated by a rancorous atmosphere, in which the two sides—both of which generally feel like they are being mistreated—routinely express their anger and resentment. While one can readily understand why tenants feel powerless, given the imbalance of attorney resources, landlords also claim that the process is slanted against them. From the perspective of many landlords, there is an institutional pro-tenant bias in Housing Court. Some landlords believe that a disproportionate number of former legal services and housing agency attorneys have become Housing Court judges (Allen 1994). In a lawsuit filed in 1989, an organization of landlords brought a suit in federal court, alleging that Housing Court discriminates against landlords in favor of tenants (*Miller v. Silbermann* 1989). The plaintiffs claimed systemic bias, alleging that the policies and practices of the defendants (the administrative judges who supervise Housing Court, various judges, and court personnel) included:

> systematically (a) processing, hearing and determining the law in a biased, coercive, and intimidating fashion against plaintiffs, (b) delaying the issuance of warrants, (c) refusing to enforce the provisions of RPAPL § 745 requiring the deposit of rent, (d) refusing to enforce the provisions of RPAPL § 747 (1) requiring the award of costs to a prevailing owner, (e) refusing to enforce lease provisions requiring the award of attorneys' fees to an owner, and (f) refusing property owners permission to establish owners' information tables. (*Miller v. Silbermann*, Complaint, ¶ 150)

The essence of plaintiffs' allegations was that the judges and court personnel, through "policies, customs, patterns, and practices, in applying the law and their own rules and regulations have transformed the Housing Part of the New York Civil Court into a biased tribunal . . . effectively tak[ing] the tenant's side in contested housing disputes" (ibid., ¶ 5). The plaintiffs requested that the court appoint a special master to supervise the Housing Court's operation.

In 1991, a temporary settlement was reached in the case by the parties, which resulted in some changes in the operation of Housing Court (such as the right of owners to establish an information table in the lobby of the court, the availability of a court reporter to record proceedings at a particular time each day, a memorandum issued by the administrative judge detailing the rent deposit requirements of RPAPL § 745 [2]). That settlement also provided that the case could be restored to the calendar within three years. The following year, in November 1992, the plaintiffs moved to restore the case to the calendar and amend the complaint, claiming that the systemic bias against landlords (and in favor of tenants) continued; subsequently, various tenant advocacy groups and legal representatives were permitted to intervene in the action (*Miller v. Silbermann* 1993). After hearing oral arguments on the defendants' motion to dismiss the lawsuit in May 1996, the judge appointed a special master, former Congressperson S. William Green, to help spur settlement talks between the parties. The special master, whose role was that of a mediator, was not asked to investigate or issue a report on the plaintiff's allegations (Goldstein 1996). Subsequently, the court dismissed the lawsuit, determining that the plaintiffs lacked standing because they alleged injury that was only speculative in nature. The court also concluded that the federal courts should abstain because the relief the plaintiffs sought would require "continuous supervision of and interference in Housing Court proceedings" (*Miller v. Silbermann* 1997).

While landlord and tenant activists do not agree on many things, they do agree that Housing Court is not functioning as it should (Kramer 1995; Hoffman 1994). The overwhelming caseload, combined with the severe lack of resources and personnel and the inadequate physical conditions of the court, inevitably results in an institution that cannot possibly function as it should. While there are no available studies on the impact of huge caseloads on the fairness of the process, it can be assumed that they have a detrimental effect. Certainly, monitors observing Housing Court have criticized its functioning. As noted in the Citizen Court Monitors' Report on the New York City Housing Court of the Fund for Modern Courts:

> Throughout the four branches of the Housing Court that were observed, monitors found a chaotic atmosphere in which judges and court personnel try to serve the public amid grossly inadequate physical facilities and overwhelming caseloads and where case after case goes before a judge to receive less than five minutes of attention. (Fund for Modern Courts 1994)[3]

Unfortunately, the problems in Housing Court are not unique to New York City. In other jurisdictions, both tenants and landlords are dissatisfied with the overwhelming number of cases in the Housing Court forum as well as the lack of time spent by the judge on each case (Nasatir 1995).[4] In addition, landlords were much more likely to be represented by counsel than tenants. Dissatisfaction with the functioning of the Housing Court appears to be endemic.

CURRENT PROPOSALS TO IMPROVE THE HOUSING COURT: THE PIECEMEAL APPROACH TO REFORM

Over the years, there have been a variety of proposals for reforming the Housing Court. Generally, these proposals have been directed at a discrete problem rather than the underlying dysfunctions of the court. To provide an illustration of this phenomenon of piecemeal reform, this section will examine two approaches to reform: "specialized parts" and "mandatory rent deposits."

Specialized Parts

One of the existing proposals for reforming the Housing Court is to create specialized courtrooms or "parts" to increase the efficiency of judges' handling of the cases. In one permutation of this plan, one judge would preside over all the cases from a particular type of landlord. Special parts in the Housing Court for cases involving the City of New York Department of Housing Preservation and Development and New York City Housing Authority currently exist. In 1998, pursuant to a plan created by the Chief Judge of the New York State Court of Appeals, a separate cooperative/condominium part was established.

Proponents of this approach contend that special parts are necessary since disputes between the boards of directors of cooperatives and the shareholders of the cooperatives (the owners of the apartments) differ from traditional landlord-tenant disputes, and judges often are not "well-versed in the nuances of state laws that pertain to co-op buildings" (Goldstein 1995). Critics of the plan warn that it will unnecessarily strain the court's resources. It will further divert the court's focus and reduce resources for the preservation of the existing housing stock. Critics also point out that the appropriate remedy for an uninformed judiciary is better training, not restructuring of the court system to funnel cases (Goldstein 1995). While there are some differences in the applicable laws, the better solution would be better training for the judges, particularly given the potential drain on the court's already overburdened resources attributable to the creation of another special part.

The second permutation of the proposal for specialized courts is to create neighborhood parts, in which a single judge would hear all the cases from a particular geographical area. The rationale for this plan is that the judge would become familiar with the housing stock of that neighborhood and thereby acquire a better basis for evaluating and dealing with building-wide complaints and for steering parties to appropriate community resources. As one proponent of the plan puts it, the judge's greater awareness of community-based "economic resources" and "supportive human resources" could be "critical to find[ing] the right contractor or enabling tenants to retain their shelter and owners to be paid" (Gould 1996).

Although the "neighborhood part" proposal has much to recommend it, the viability of the plan would depend on the adequacy of the planning process. In particular, careful thought would have to be given to the identification of goals and the criteria for evaluating whether the goals have been achieved. Moreover, if a neighborhood part is to effectively serve a particular community, representatives of that community should be consulted and, ideally, should play an integral role in the planning process. Finally, the planning process would have to take into account the need for specialized resources, such as pro se attorneys, interpreters, and court employees to interact with community groups.

Mandatory Rent Deposits

For years, landlords' representatives have proposed "mandatory rent deposits" as a remedy for systemic delays that, they assert, unfairly prejudice landlords in nonpayment cases. The basis of the complaint is that in some nonpayment cases, in which a case may continue for six months or longer, a landlord who ultimately prevails may not recover the rent for the months that the case lingered in court. In 1997, as part of the New York State Legislature's overhaul of the state's rent regulation laws, mandatory rent deposits were required in certain circumstances. Subject to certain exceptions, the legislation requires tenants to deposit with the Housing Court all rent that has accrued since the date the case commenced if the tenant requests a second adjournment. A tenant must also deposit rent after thirty days have passed since the parties first appeared in court, not counting any periods of time attributable to adjournments requested by the landlord. If the tenant fails to deposit the claimed rent, the court would be required to dismiss the tenant's defenses and counterclaims and to enter an immediate judgment for the landlord.

The 1997 legislation, which has been challenged on constitutional grounds, is problematic on a number of fronts. First, it rests upon a flawed conception of the nature of the difficulty. It simplistically assumes that the fault for a delay should be attributed to the tenant whenever the tenant files a pretrial motion that requires consideration by the court for more than thirty days. But often, in these situations, delay is more properly attributable to the enormous caseload of the court and its grossly inadequate number of judges and other court personnel. Moreover, in some of these situations, the source of the delay is some action or failing on the part of the landlord. For example, if the landlord's papers failed to state a cause of action and the tenant moves to dismiss on that ground, delays occasioned by the adjudication of the motion are more fairly attributable to the landlord than the tenant. As to the situations where the tenant requests a second adjournment, there are many reasons why the tenant might justifiably need the second adjournment. For example, although the statute limits the first adjournment to ten days unless the landlord agrees to a longer adjournment (Real Property Actions and Proceedings Law § 745 [1]), it may take longer than ten days for the tenant to obtain counsel.

Second, there is no support for the legislation's underlying assumption that the length of a proceeding affects a landlord's ability to collect unpaid rent.[5] A 1995 study prepared for a landlords' organization, the Rent Stabilization Association of New York, Inc., asserted in a conclusory fashion that "experience shows that rent loss is more likely in those cases that drag on longer" (de Seve 1995). But the study offered no empirical evidence to support this assertion. The study, entitled "The Need for Mandatory Rent Deposits in New York City Housing Court," analyzed computer records of all Housing Court cases for a specific time period in 1993 and 1994; the tables, graphs, and summary data in the report were "derived from the Housing Court database, informal surveys of property owners, discussions with property owner/tenant lawyers, data on the rent registration database maintained by the Rent Stabilization Association, and eviction data from the marshal's office" (de Seve, 7). However, there is no support for some of the more critical conclusions. For example, the report concludes that rent is lost in 40,912 cases (de Seve, 12–13); of those cases, approximately 62 percent are from what is labeled as "evaded," but there is no explanation for what is meant by "evasion" and no identification of the source of these figures. Indeed, the statistical data gathered by the study would seem to refute its final conclusion. The study showed that the cases that drag on for the longest periods of time tend to be those that involve above-average rent (the above-average rent is defined by the study as $528 monthly), not the low-rent cases (de Seve 1995). Since the above-average rent cases typically involve tenants who are financially solvent, landlords should be able to obtain and enforce monetary judgments even if the tenant moves without paying the rent while the case is pending. (Of course, the landlord may incur the additional costs of locating a tenant who has moved and collecting on the judgment.) However, some lost revenue in an undetermined number of cases and undetermined amount should not have resulted in the overbroad remedy of mandatory rent deposit, with the severe sanction of immediate judgment for the landlord if the tenant does not deposit all of the claimed rent.

Finally, the automatic imposition of the draconian remedy of dismissal ignores the equitable and public policy considerations that often exist in Housing Court cases. The legislation deprives tenants of their day in court and their opportunity to be heard even in situations in which the amount of rent being sought is illegal or in which there are breach of warranty defenses. A tenant would be evicted without any determination by a court or even counsel (if, as typically occurs, the tenant is unrepresented) that there should be a judgment for the landlord, simply because the tenant requested a second adjournment or the court takes more than thirty days from the date the parties first appeared to complete a trial on the matter. Moreover, the court would be required to issue an order authorizing the eviction of a tenant even if he or she had meritorious claims or defenses simply because the tenant lacked sufficient funds to post monies prior to trial (perhaps because the tenant used the monies to make essential repairs to the apartment that the landlord unlawfully refused to make). To the extent that a judge believes that a tenant is delaying the proceeding, the court already has the power under existing law to condition a second adjournment on the deposit of current rent with the court (Real Property Actions and Proceedings Law § 745 (2))[6] failure to deposit the rent would result in an immediate trial.

Ultimately, however, the greatest flaw of the mandatory deposit requirements contained in the 1997 legislation is that it accepts the status quo rather than trying to improve the system. The legislation assumed that delay is an incurable feature of Housing Court and tried to ameliorate the asserted consequences of the delay for one side of the proceedings, the landlords. In this regard, the legislation is a perfect illustration of the piecemeal approach to Housing Court reform. The next section will explore some structural reforms that could remedy a number of the problems that currently afflict Housing Court.

STRUCTURAL CHANGES: AN AGENDA FOR REFORM

Counsel for Unrepresented Litigants

As explained earlier, landlords are represented by counsel in virtually all Housing Court cases, but tenants appear with counsel in only 12 percent of the cases (a number likely to diminish in the wake of recent legal services budget cuts). Although there have been attempts to establish a right to counsel in Housing Court, these efforts have thus far proven unsuccessful. In the late 1980s, a class action was filed on behalf of low-income tenants, seeking a declaratory judgment that the federal and state constitutions and a state statute require provision of court-assigned counsel to tenants in eviction proceedings (*Donaldson v. State of New York* 1989). However, when the request for class certification was denied and the claims of the named plaintiffs became moot, the litigation was not pursued.

Around the time of the *Donaldson* litigation, the City's Human Resources Administration (HRA) began providing funding for legal representation of families with children that are on public assistance and facing eviction. The results readily demonstrate the importance of counsel. The Legal Aid Society's Homelessness Prevention Legal Services Program for Families with Children, one of the organizations that receives HRA funding, reports a success rate of over 90 percent in preventing evictions (The Legal Aid Society 1996). In the vast majority of cases the tenants were able to keep their apartments; in a few of the cases, the tenant and his or her family were able to obtain time or other assistance to relocate to another apartment. For example, in the Brooklyn office of the The Legal Aid Society, of the 1,162 cases that were closed in 1995, 1,063 families retained their apartments (approximately 91 percent), 73 families were given time or other assistance to find another apartment (approximately 6 percent), and only five families of the 1,162 (approximately .004 percent) were evicted. (In the balance of the cases, legal representation was not completed.) The success rate is particularly significant given that, in approximately 30 percent of the cases, the tenant came to The Legal Aid Society after the tenant already had a judgment entered against him or her or had signed a stipulation (agreement) in the case. In these cases in which tenants came to The Legal Aid Society after having had judgments of eviction entered, approximately nine out of ten retained their apartments, 7 percent were given time or other assistance to find another apartment, and 1 percent were evicted.

Unfortunately, statistics comparing the success rate of the homelessness prevention project with unrepresented tenants are not available. However, there are figures available for warrants of possession issued by the court (the document that allows the landlord to get a marshal to evict the tenant) and the numbers of evictions that take place. In 1995, Housing Court judges issued 96,795 warrants of possession (L&T Clerk's Office 1996) and there were 24,995 evictions (Hevesi 1996). Thus, 26 percent of the tenants were evicted by a marshal. This figure actually understates the numbers of tenants who were unsuccessful in court since some significant percentage of tenants will leave their apartments prior to actual eviction by the marshal. While these numbers do not indicate what proportion of these tenants were unrepresented by counsel, only approximately 11.9 percent of tenants have legal representation (Community Training and Resource Center 1993). It is reasonable to assume that less than 11.9 percent of the tenants evicted by a marshal had legal representation. Thus, The Legal Aid Society's eviction rate of .004 percent compares quite favorably with the overall numbers of tenants who are evicted. Unfortunately, only a small proportion of low-income tenants are represented by the various antieviction programs.

The argument for providing counsel to unrepresented low-income tenants can be made on equitable, legal, and public policy grounds. First, the Housing Court cannot function effectively as an adversary system if one side is always represented and the other is virtually never represented.[7] The imbalance of attorney resources means that legal issues will tend to be framed in a one-sided way and the court will often not be apprised of the arguments and authorities for ruling in the tenant's favor. Indeed, the high success rate of the HRA-funded homelessness prevention representation program graphically demonstrates how differently the system functions when both sides have legal assistance.

Second, the complex web of substantive and procedural protections for tenants—designed by the Legislature to prevent or ameliorate housing code violations such as breaches of the warranty of habitability—depend on the availability of counsel to make use of the procedures and to assert substantive rights. *Pro se* litigants have little hope of learning what they need to know in order to advocate effectively on their own behalf. As stated by the Association of the Bar of the City of New York (1988), "no tenant can defend and protect his or her rights adequately in the Housing Court without the assistance of counsel." It has also been noted that tenants have a particular need for counsel in jurisdictions with extensive procedural and substantive protections, since "the risk of error for a tenant who appears unrepresented is much greater than in jurisdictions with fewer rights" (Scherer 1988). The provision of counsel to tenants has resulted in needed repairs of dwellings, reductions in rent overcharges, and the receipt of rent subsidies (Liebman and Kirschenbaum 1994).

Third, when the litigant is a low-income tenant, an adverse ruling in Housing Court and consequent eviction can result in homelessness—at great cost not only to the tenant but also the city. According to statistics compiled by the New York City Department of Investigation, the number of evictions has been increasing: in 1993, there were 21,937 evictions; that number rose to 23,970 in 1994, and to 24,995 in 1995 (Hevesi

1996). Studies documenting the connection between eviction and homelessness in New York City have shown that substantial numbers of
homeless families lost their permanent housing due to an eviction (Association of the Bar 1989; Dehavenon and Boone 1991). The population
that appears in Housing Court is the poorest of the city's housed population; almost 50 percent of this group have incomes below $10,000
(Community Training and Resource Center 1993). When tenants at this
level of poverty are evicted, their options are severely limited, since
they live in a city that continues to experience a crisis in affordable
housing. According to a recently published vacancy survey for New
York City, there is a vacancy rate of 1.1 percent for apartments renting
for $500 a month or less and a vacancy rate of .58 percent for apartments
renting for under $300 a month (Blackburn 1995).

By providing counsel to low-income tenants and preventing im-
proper evictions, the city could avoid the needless expenditure of funds
for shelter. Indeed, studies have found that every dollar spent on anti-
eviction legal services for low-income tenants in Housing Court could
save four dollars in shelter costs for those families that would otherwise
have been evicted (New York State Department of Social Services 1991).
One organization that studied the issue concluded that there would be
a "total cost savings in public dollars realized by providing counsel to
all low-income tenants who face eviction" (Community Training and
Resource Center 1993).[8] Although provision of counsel would not prevent all evictions, it would substantially decrease the number of im-
proper evictions. Thus, a right to counsel would benefit litigants, the
court, the city, and society's interests in providing a more just system
and maintaining people in habitable housing.

Inadequacy of Monies Available to Pay Rent

Some of the most significant difficulties in Housing Court can be
traced back to a central systemic problem in housing: the fact that, in
large numbers of cases, rent levels exceed the tenant's ability to pay.[9] As
Schill and Scafidi have explained, "a substantial proportion of low- and
moderate-income residents . . . pay rents that are beyond their means"
(see chapter 1 in this volume). Of the 525, 736 households that pay more
than half of their incomes in rent, 94.5% were composed of households
earning less than half the city's median income. Almost nine out of ten
households that experience one or more severe housing problems are
those in which the individuals or families earn very low incomes (see
Schill and Scafidi, chapter 1 in this volume). It is a result of "the gap between what New Yorkers can pay and the housing that is available

[that] has caused many New Yorkers to live in shelters or on the street" (see Schill and Scafidi, chapter 1 in this volume).

While the unbalanced relationship between income and rent is true for working-class tenants, it is even more so for public assistance recipients. It has been demonstrated that the shelter levels for rent are woefully inadequate. The shelter portion of the public assistance grant, which is $286 for a family of three, is close to $100 less than what the Rent Guidelines Board has determined to be the average cost of operating a rent stabilized apartment in New York City (Braconi, chapter 4 in this volume). Over 77 percent of public assistance households currently pay rents that are either at or above the shelter allowance, with the average family paying rent of $180 each month over the shelter allowance (Citizens Housing and Planning Council 1996). As one commentator has observed, "Given the enormous gap between economic rents and the shelter allowance, the mystery is not why 5 percent of the city's welfare families become homeless each year, but why the rest do not" (Braconi, chapter 4 in this volume).

In recent years, the magnitude of the problem has been ameliorated to a certain extent by court rulings in *Jiggetts v. Grinker*, a class action brought in the New York State courts by recipients of AFDC (Aid to Families with Dependent Children). The *Jiggetts* plaintiffs argued that they were entitled to grant levels adequate to pay the rents actually charged and that the New York State Department of Social Services (the state agency responsible for administering public assistance) had violated this entitlement by failing to increase the shelter allowance to keep pace with increased shelter costs (*Jiggetts v. Grinker* 1988).

The case ultimately reached the New York Court of Appeals on the defendants' appeal of the trial court's denial of a motion to dismiss. The trial court had rejected the defendants' argument that the state had no statutory obligation to provide shelter allowances equal to the rents being charged public assistance recipients. Upholding the trial court's ruling that the case presented a justiciable controversy, the Court of Appeals stated that the relevant state statute "imposes a statutory duty on the State Commissioner of Social Services to establish shelter allowances that bear a reasonable relation to the cost of housing in New York City" (*Jiggetts v. Grinker* 1990). The case was remanded for a trial on the adequacy of the shelter grant. While the case was pending, an administrative procedure was implemented pursuant to *Jiggetts* that allows AFDC recipients to receive shelter costs in excess of the shelter grant. After a lengthy trial, the trial court determined, in a decision dated April 16, 1997, that the shelter allowances did not bear a reasonable relationship to the cost of housing in New York City. The court ordered the Commissioner of the New York State Department of Social Services to promulgate a reasonable shelter allowance schedule (*Jiggetts v. Dowling 1997*). At the present time, over 25,000 families in New York City receive supplemental shelter allowances under this program; the average amount of these rent payments is $234 each month (Citizens Housing and Planning Council 1996).

These *Jiggetts* payments are more important than ever, given the recent cutbacks and changes in public assistance. The Emergency Home Relief (EHR) program—a cost-effective program that helped the working poor keep their housing by providing emergency assistance for shelter arrears for those households with gross income that did not exceed 125 percent of the federal poverty level—has now been virtually eliminated in New York City. Moreover, it is likely that the welfare "reform" legislation recently enacted by Congress, which imposes time limits and stringent restrictions on eligibility, will further exacerbate the crisis of inadequate income to pay rent and will result in the denial of public assistance to many who would qualify under current guidelines.

In this era of declining federal and state assistance, it is in the interest of both landlords and tenants for *Jiggetts* supplemental rent payments to continue, since they increase the amount tenants can pay for rent and the monies available to landlords for maintenance of their buildings. "Federal and state policy changes involving public assistance and rent subsidy will invariably cause rent rolls to decline in thousands of buildings housing low-income families. Building owners—both nonprofit and for profit—will need to search out new ways of controlling their operating costs" (Schwartz and Vidal, chapter 9 in this volume). Yet, the Pataki Administration has proposed changes in the public assistance program that would not only reduce the shelter grant allowances but would attempt to undercut the *Jiggetts* supplemental rent payment program. The governor has proposed reducing the public assistance grant by approximately 25 percent and combining the shelter grant with the basic grant, so that there would be a single grant of a reduced amount. "Welfare reform will impair the ability of recipient households to pay their rents, causing rent arrears to increase and making it increasingly difficult for building owners to maintain their buildings and pay their property taxes. Furthermore, over time, decreased rent collection can be expected to reduce the value of many rental properties" (Schwartz and Vidal, chapter 9 in this volume).

One question that arises is the extent to which Housing Court can hope to solve the structural problems of the inadequacy of income for rent and, in some buildings, the insufficiency of the rent rolls to run the building. Housing Court obviously cannot rectify the insufficiency of the public assistance grant. However, one of the ways for housing reformers to solve the perennial problems of Housing Court is to attack them at their source by ensuring that there is an adequate shelter allowance or shelter subsidy for those on public assistance and the working poor.[10] Although such a remedy would require substantial expenditure of funds, and may encounter budgetary or political constraints, it would have an enormous positive impact on landlords, the court system, the city, and society as a whole. If tenants were to have adequate income for shelter, then the landlords would have increased resources to maintain their buildings; if there were adequate income, then there would likely be fewer defaults by owners, more monies for city real estate taxes, and myriad other ripple effects that would benefit the city's coffers. Finally, there would eventually be a dramatic improvement in Housing Court, in that the caseloads would decline and judges would finally be able to attend properly to the cases that come before them.

CHANGING THE FOCUS AND TONE OF HOUSING COURT LITIGATION

The last sections of this part of the chapter focus on structural reforms that would dramatically change the nature of the Housing Court's docket and the ways in which cases are litigated. There are also more minor changes that could be made to help the Housing Court accomplish its original objective to ensure a sufficient supply of adequate and safe housing for the people of New York City.

The first of these is to change the current imbalance of eviction actions over repair actions. Only approximately 3 percent of the court's cases are tenant-initiated actions for repairs (Kirschenbaum 1994). This caseload does not reflect the intentions of the creators of the court. "[A]ltering the balance of cases in the Housing Court so that there are fewer eviction cases and more cases involving maintaining housing standards would bring the Housing Court closer to the mission it was created to perform, enforcing State and local laws for establishing and maintaining housing standards" (Fund for Modern Courts 1994). There should be a greater effort to disseminate information about the availability of tenant-initiated lawsuits for repairs. Moreover, judges should give more serious consideration to tenant defenses of breach of warranty of habitability to ensure that repairs are completed and orders of repairs are enforced.

It has been suggested by some that aggressive enforcement of the housing code could result in more housing abandonment or increases in the rent (Komesar 1973; Meyers 1975), while others believe these regulations can be used to increase the supply of safe and decent housing without substantial negative consequences (Ackerman 1971; Kennedy 1987). The debate over the likely effects of active code enforcement has been ongoing for more than two decades. As noted by one commentator, "[l]egal academics have debated the utility of code enforcement as an element of housing policy for more than twenty years. . . . [but] none of the theorists to date have been able to establish conclusively that code enforcement will precipitate unaffordable rent increases or landlord abandonment of properties" (Kinning 1993). On the current state of the record, there is no legitimate basis for concluding that the Housing Court should refrain from using all the powers at its disposal, including aggressive enforcement of the housing code, to maintain adequate and safe housing.

Second, judges can advise *pro se* litigants of their statutorily granted substantive and procedural remedies. With such a large percentage of the tenants unrepresented, the role of the court and that of the judge must, of necessity, be different than in other courts. If the *pro se* litigant does not understand the proceedings, he or she is effectively silenced. It has been suggested that *pro se* litigants, in general, are silenced by the judicial system and that our system rejects the narrative way in which *pro se* litigants communicate (Bezdek 1992). Moreover, *pro se* litigants are silenced in the hallways, not just in the courtrooms. Litigants must be allowed to have a voice. The judge should be more of a translator and protector of the rights of the unrepresented. Judges should be given training, guidelines, and peer support for alternative methodologies that give support to *pro se* litigants. The court also should have more user-friendly methods and processes, such as plain language documents and informational pamphlets that explain the court process and the basic elements of various defenses.

These changes would require additional Housing Court judges. It is widely agreed that the current number of Housing Court judges is inadequate to handle the current caseload; the Office of Court Administration has previously acknowledged in its budget request that, based on caseload analyses, the number of judges should be increased to fifty from the current thirty-five (State of New York Court System Budget for 1996–97). More judges than the fifty recommended by the Office of Court Administration would be required to fulfill the additional roles of giving more serious consideration to breach-of-warranty defenses and a more active role in advising *pro se* litigants of their rights and available remedies.

CONCLUSION

The arguments for creating specialized housing courts in New York City and other jurisdictions remain as valid today as they were when these courts were first created. In various municipalities throughout the country, there continues to be a compelling need for forums with expertise in housing matters, as well as flexible and innovative powers. Indeed, it could be said that the need for such a mechanism is more pressing than ever, given the decline in affordable housing over the course of the past two decades and the cutbacks in public assistance that are presently taking place.

Unfortunately, Housing Court, which is a fundamental and critical part of the answer for the preservation of the housing stock, has not fulfilled its mandate. Housing Court can, and must, prevent reductions in the supply of low-income housing by enforcing housing maintenance codes and serving as an effective forum for the adjudication of landlord-tenant disputes. There are some who would suggest that more energetic code enforcement might harm tenants in the long run since it might cause landlords to abandon their buildings rather than operate them at a loss (where the monies recovered from rents fail to cover the operating expenses for the building). However, tenants are not advantaged by having to live in apartments that fall below minimum housing maintenance standards; nor is the public served by a system that produces unlivable housing. Moreover, to the extent that landlords are in financial distress, there should be strategies to save buildings in jeopardy without requiring tenants to live in uninhabitable apartments.[11]

As the foregoing discussion has suggested, there are reforms that could be adopted to enable the court to accomplish its original objectives. These proposed reforms could also be implemented in other jurisdictions. With the right kinds of changes, the Housing Court could become precisely what the Legislature intended: a powerful force for the "maintenance of proper housing standards . . . essential to the health, safety, welfare and reasonable comfort of the citizens of the state" (N.Y. Civ. Court Act § 110[a], statement of policy).

NOTES

1. The statistics for Housing Court include proceedings in residential apartments and commercial property. Approximately 5 percent of the caseload is commercial cases. The total statistics for Housing Court for 1995 includ-

ing the commercial cases are: 303,897 cases; final judgments for the landlord were entered in 209,730 cases (including 54,139 cases in which the
judgment was entered after a default by the tenant); and warrants of possession were issued in 103,619 cases (Report of Landlord and Tenant
Clerk's Office 1996).

2. In 1995 there were approximately 28,000 new cases initiated in Civil Court,
   where there are about fifty sitting judges (Belzaguy 1996). However, the nature of the practice is completely different from Housing Court (for example, there is more complicated and lengthy motion practice, discovery, and
   trials in Civil Court), so that it is difficult to compare based solely on the
   volume of the respective caseloads.

3. The Fund for Modern Courts, Inc., is a "nonpartisan, nonprofit, statewide
   court reform organization . . . concerned with the quality and administration of justice in New York State" (Fund for Modern Courts 1994).

4. The conclusion is not based on empirical data but rather anecdotal information obtained from interviews of attorneys representing landlords and
   tenants in Philadelphia, Boston, Chicago, Dallas, and Los Angeles. (Only
   Philadelphia, Boston, and Chicago have specialized housing courts.) The
   paper was completed for a course in Real Estate Transactions at the University of Pennsylvania Law School.

5. In some situations, a delay benefits the landlord since it gives the tenant
   time to obtain the rent from public assistance.

6. Pursuant to the statute, a request by a tenant for an adjournment to obtain
   legal counsel does not count toward the rent deposit rule; the court can also
   waive the deposit requirement for good cause shown (Real Property Actions and Proceedings Law § 745 [2]. If there are immediately hazardous violations of record as defined in the city's housing maintenance code, the
   court cannot require a rent deposit (Real Property Actions and Proceedings
   Law § 745 [2][e]).

7. Suggestions of alternative dispute resolution mechanisms, such as mediation, will not solve the problem of the unequal bargaining powers of the
   landlord and the tenant. (For a discussion of the critique of mediation, see
   Gunning [1995].)

8. One issue with comparing the costs of providing anti-eviction assistance
   with the costs of providing shelter to the homeless is the source of the
   funding. Prior to the Personal Responsibility and Work Opportunity Rec-
   onciliation Act of 1996 (the Welfare Reform Act), the costs of the city's
   Human Resources Administration funding for anti-eviction legal representation, as well as funding for shelters for homeless families, was paid
   by the federal government (50 percent), the state (25 percent), and the city
   (25 percent). The Personal Responsibility and Work Opportunity Recon-

ciliation Act changes the funding formulas for all of these programs since the money from the federal government will now be given in block grants to the states. It is unclear what the percentage allocation will be between the state and the city. However, since the state receives all of the monies previously funded by the federal government in a block grant, the state and the city now have more freedom to allocate the same amount of monies. They could therefore use the monies to provide counsel to low-income tenants.

9. The Fair Market Rents set by the U.S. Department of Housing and Urban Development for Section 8 units that it administers far exceed the public assistance shelter grants; those proposed rents for New York City for fiscal year 1997 are $662 monthly for a zero-bedroom apartment, $738 monthly for a one-bedroom apartment, $838 monthly for a two-bedroom apartment, $1,048 monthly for a three-bedroom apartment, and $1,174 for a four-bedroom apartment (Federal Register 1996).

10. It has been suggested that some form of the SCRIE (Senior Citizen Rent Increase Exemption) program could be extended to the working poor (Scherer 1996). Under SCRIE, eligible low-income senior citizens are exempted from rent increases if their rent exceeds one-third of the disposable household income. The landlord receives the rent monies that he or she would have received from the tenant in the form of a reduction of the building's property taxes.

11. A study by the Community Service Society and the Rockefeller Brothers Fund determined that a number of privately owned buildings in New York City were in financial distress; the study recommended that the city establish a task force to develop a strategy to save buildings that were at risk (Kennedy 1993).

REFERENCES

Ackerman, Bruce. 1973. "More on Slum Housing and Redistribution Policy: A Reply to Professor Komesar." *Yale Law Journal* 82:1194.

———. 1971. "Regulating Slum Housing Markets on Behalf of the Poor: Of Housing Codes, Housing Subsidies and Income Redistribution Policy." *Yale Law Journal* 80:1093.

Allen, Charlotte. 1994. "Let the Landlord Beware." *City Journal* (summer).

Association of the Bar of the City of New York. 1989. *Preventing Homelessness through Representation of Tenants Faced with Eviction*. Record of the Association of the Bar of the City of New York.

————. 1988. *Housing Court Pro Bono Project*. Committee on Legal Assistance.

Belzaguy, Ernesto. 1996. Deputy Chief Clerk, Housing Court, Civil Court of the City of New York. Telephone interview.

Bezdek, Barbara. 1992. "Silence in the Court: Participation and Subordination of Poor Tenants' Voices in Legal Process." *Hofstra Law Review* 20:533.

Blackburn, Anthony, J. 1995. *Housing New York City: 1993*. New York: Department of Housing Preservation and Development.

Citizens Housing and Planning Council. 1996. *Pataki Welfare Plan Rattles Housing* 2, 1:1–4.

Cohen, Leonard N. 1979. "The New York City Housing Court—An Evaluation." *Urban Law Annual* 17:27.

Community Training and Resource Center and City-Wide Task Force on Housing Court, Inc. 1993. *Housing Court, Evictions and Homelessness: The Costs and Benefits of Establishing a Right to Counsel*.

Dehavenon, Ann Lou, and Margaret Boone. 1991. *No Room at the Inn: An Interim Report with Recommendations on Homeless Families with Children Requesting Shelter at New York City's Emergency Assistance Unit in 1991*.

de Seve, Charles W. 1995. *The Need for Mandatory Rent Deposits in New York City Housing Court*. American Economics Group for the Rent Stabilization Association of New York.

Donaldson v. State of New York. 1989. 156 App. Div. 2d 290, 548 N.Y.S.2d 676 (1st Dept.).

Federal Register. 1996. 61 Fed. Reg. 20982, 20986 (May 8).

Fund for Modern Courts. 1994. *Citizen Court Monitors' Report on the New York City Housing Court*.

Goldstein, Matthew. 1996. "Ex-Congressman Named to Mediate Housing Case." *New York Law Journal* (June 19).

————. 1995. "Court Studies Need to Create Co-op/Tenant Parts." *New York Law Journal* (December 29).

Gould, Bruce J. 1996. *Housing Court: Reality and Vision*. Citizens Housing and Planning Council of New York (May).

Gunning, Isabelle. 1995. "Diversity Issues in Mediation: Controlling Negative Cultural Myths." *Journal of Dispute Resolution* 55.

Hevesi, Dennis. 1996. "Landlord vs. Tenant: City Eviction Wars." *New York Times*, August 4, sec. 9, 1.

Hoffman, Jan. 1994. "Chaos Presides in New York Housing Courts." *New York Times*, December 28, col. 2, 1.

Jiggetts v. Grinker. 1988. 139 Misc.2d 476, 528 N.Y.S.2d 462 (Sup. Ct., New York Co. 1988), rev'd, 148 A.D.2d 1, 543 N.Y.S.2d 414 (1st Dept. 1989), *rev'd*, 75 N.Y.2d 411, 554 N.Y.S.2d 92 (1990); excerpts from trial court's decision (*Jiggetts v. Dowling*) reported in *New York Law Journal*, April 22, 1997.

Kennedy, Duncan. 1987. "The Effect of the Warranty of Habitability on Low-Income Housing: Milking and Class Violence." *Florida State University Law Review* 15:485.

Kennedy, Shawn G. 1993. "Study Sees Rising Distress for Landlords." *New York Times*, March 31, col. 5, B-1.

Kinning, Robin Powers. 1993. "Selective Housing Code Enforcement and Low-Income Housing Policy: Minneapolis Case Study." *Fordham Urban Law Journal* 21:159, 160.

Kirschenbaum, Jill. 1994. "On the Road to Nowhere." *City Limits* (April).

Komesar, Neil. 1973. "Return to Slumville: A Critique of the Ackerman Analysis of Housing Code Enforcement and the Poor." *Yale Law Journal* 82:1175.

Kramer, Rita. 1995. "Housing Court's Rough Justice." *City Journal* (autumn).

Legal Aid Society. 1996. *Status Report on the Work of the Legal Aid Society's Homelessness Prevention Legal Services Program for Families with Children, Results and Analysis, April 2, 1991–December 31, 1995*. New York: The Legal Aid Society.

Liebman, Hanna, and Jill Kirschenbaum. 1994. "Balancing the Scales." *City Limits* (June/July).

Meyers, Charles. 1975. "The Covenant of Habitability and the American Law Institute." *Stanford Law Review* 27:879.

Miller v. Silbermann. 1989. 89 Civ. 3573 [S.D.N.Y.]); motion granting intervention is reported at 832 F. Supp. 663 (S.D.N.Y. 1993); motion dismissing the action is reported at 951 F.Supp. 485 (S.D.N.Y. 1997).

Nasatir, David. 1995. *Housing Courts or Not?: Different Approaches to Handling Landlord and Tenant Litigation*. Unpublished paper.

New York State Assembly. 1996. A. 8704.

New York State Department of Social Services. 1991. *The Homelessness Prevention Program: Outcomes and Effectiveness*.

New York State Senate. 1995. S. 5019-A.

Report of Landlord and Tenant (L and T) Clerk's Office. 1996.

Scherer, Andrew. 1988. "Gideon's Shelter: The Need to Recognize a Right to Counsel for Indigent Defendants in Eviction Proceedings." *Harvard Civil Rights-Civil Liberties Law Review* 23:557, 588.

Scherer, Andrew. 1996. Legal Services for New York. Telephone interview.

Scott, Randall W. 1979. *Housing Courts and Housing Justice: An Overview*. Urban Law Annual, 17:3.

State of New York Unified Court System Budget for the Fiscal Year 1996–97.

CHAPTER 8

HOMELESSNESS AND PUBLIC SHELTER PROVISION IN NEW YORK CITY

Dennis P. Culhane, Stephen Metraux, and Susan M. Wachter

New York City, faced since the 1970s with growing numbers of homeless individuals and families and aggressive litigation on their behalf, has built the largest public shelter system in the United States as the centerpiece of its response to homelessness. The size of this system—both its average daily census of 24,472 in 1995 and its annual expenditures of $500 million—is far beyond the scope of any other city's efforts against homelessness. Yet despite the scale of these measures the shelter system has faced crises and controversies through three mayoral administrations and their varied approaches to reducing the need for this system. This chapter assesses homelessness policy in New York City through analyzing empirical data collected from the shelter system. A variety of approaches produce a set of shelter utilization patterns and trends that, taken together, form a unique and grounded perspective from which to evaluate key components of this policy.

HOMELESSNESS POLICY IN NEW YORK CITY: A REVIEW

New York City's current public shelter system took shape as the result of a 1979 class action suit filed on behalf of the growing number of homeless men on New York City's streets and in response to an inadequate city shelter system, then a patchwork of welfare hotels and rooming houses. The suit, *Callahan v. Carey*, argued that, based on the New York State Constitution and other lesser statutes, the city's home-

This research was supported by a grant from the Edna McConnell Clark Foundation, Program for New York Neighborhoods.

less men had the right to shelter that met certain minimum standards of decency. In 1981 the parties settled and, in the resulting consent decree, the city of New York agreed to provide shelter to any homeless man (a) who met the need standard for the home relief program in New York State, or (b) who by reason of physical, mental, or social dysfunction was in need of temporary shelter. Similarly, in two 1983 suits, *McCain v. Koch* and *Eldredge v. Koch*, the court set standards for safe and suitable shelter for homeless families and homeless women, respectively (Demers 1995; Hopper and Cox 1986).

Following *Callahan*, the city set up a network of temporary accommodations in a reluctant response to what it perceived as a passing crisis. For single adults, large buildings previously used as armories, schools, and hospitals were converted to provide rudimentary overnight accommodations. With few demands placed upon the shelter users and few services available, these shelters became notorious for violence and drug use, with critics pointing out their function as human warehouses (Grunberg and Eagle 1990). Homeless families were sheltered in a separate set of facilities, initially consisting of either squalid yet expensive welfare hotels (Kozol 1988) or dormitory-type facilities, both of which homeless advocates decried as being particularly unsuitable for children.

As the 1980s progressed it became clear that homelessness was not a temporary phenomenon. Demand for both the single adult and the family shelters steadily increased, and there also emerged a group of chronic shelter users for whom these facilities became a *de facto* residence. Along with this increased utilization came increased costs, from $50 million in 1982 to almost $300 million in 1988 (New York City Commission on the Homeless 1992). Continued court actions by homeless advocates led both to rulings mandating that the city stop using barracks-style shelters and welfare hotels for families, and to political pressure calling for alternatives to the large single adult shelters. At the same time, in an effort to reduce the shelter system census, city officials examined ways to increase social services and housing opportunities.

In 1988, toward the end of his administration, Mayor Ed Koch acknowledged the need to come up with long-term responses to homelessness and initiated a series of proposals aimed at revamping the shelter system. This included building new "Tier II" shelters for homeless families that provided private quarters resembling efficiency apartments, and smaller shelters that provided housing and services to specific groups of single adults, such as the mentally ill or employed persons. The Koch Administration also announced plans to make more housing available for families through three measures: accelerating the renovation of the large supply of foreclosed, city-owned housing; arranging more priority placements through the New York City Housing Authority; and instituting the Emergency Assistance Rehousing Program (EARP) that provided city subsidies to supplement federal Section 8 rental assistance vouchers as an incentive for landlords to accept homeless families as tenants. Finally, the city planned to create 5,000 single-room occupancy units for homeless single adults through a partnership with New York State (Blau 1992).

Politically, these measures came too late to effectively counteract David Dinkins's emphasis on homelessness in his successful 1989 mayoral campaign, featuring his slogan "a shelter is not a home." Upon taking office, however, Dinkins found the shelter system to be not a home but a political quagmire, and his promises to address homelessness through more permanent housing never translated into coherent policy. Under Dinkins, the shelter system met fierce opposition from communities opposed to locating new shelters in their neighborhoods; met stubborn resistance from many homeless single adults who avoided shelters in favor of the streets; and, in contrast, met criticism for being too comfortable for families, many of whom supposedly declared themselves homeless solely to obtain city shelter and a quick subsidized housing placement (Ellickson 1990; Filer 1990). Circumstances supported this argument as the demand for family shelter soared during the Dinkins regime despite (or because of) the city's having both made available 27,000 housing units for homeless households (single adults and families) and expanded Tier II shelters to accommodate over 3,200 homeless families on a given night (Dugger 1991).

The Dinkins Administration was sharply divided in the face of this vexing set of conditions. On one hand, Dinkins went ahead with the plans laid out by the Koch administration to expand both shelter capacity and housing. But on the other hand, these actions received criticism from the commission Dinkins hand-picked to study homelessness. Led by Andrew Cuomo, the governor's son and director of a large, nonprofit housing venture for homeless families, the commission noted that the New York City shelter system poorly served the city's homeless population. The commission's report (New York City Commission on the Homeless 1992) portrayed the homeless population as beset by drug abuse, mental illness, educational and vocational deficiencies, and family dysfunction; conditions that were exacerbated by the lack of demands made on the sheltered population and that resulted in a "revolving door" system where housing placements often only led to repeat shelter stays. The commission recommended that the city fund nonprofit agencies to not only run its shelters but also to provide intensive services to address these individual deficits. Dinkins was now caught between the commission's recommendations stressing services, aides who favored continued priority on housing, and a budget that allowed scant funding for either initiative. In response, he took from each approach, eventually implementing several measures proposed by the Cuomo report, but also continuing to fund housing programs and solidifying the shelter system's niche in the municipal bureaucracy through creation of the Department of Homeless Services (DHS).

This policy toward homelessness appeared to be driven more by a shelter system in a constant state of crisis than by any unified vision. The city scrambled to meet the demand for family shelter by increasing placements to welfare hotels and barracks shelters—two practices it had pledged to discontinue in the face of court orders. The city further raised the ire of homeless advocates and flouted a third set of court rulings with its practice of having homeless families stay for days or weeks in central intake offices, known as Emergency Assistance Units (EAUs), before placing them in a shelter. By 1992 the city was again facing contempt of court charges, was running out of suitable apartment buildings for subsequent placements (Dugger 1992), and had fewer public housing vacancies reserved for homeless families. In response the city attempted to create restrictions on both shelter entries and exits by adopting two measures proposed in the Cuomo report. The first of these measures set up a process for turning away families applying for shelter who had other housing options, and the second required homeless households to participate in appropriate social services, such as drug treatment, as a precondition to receiving housing placement. This represented the city's first moves to modify the universal shelter-on-demand policy implemented in the *Callahan* consent decree and toward what city officials called a "new social contract" (Finder 1993). But neither measure stanched the flow of entries into the family shelter system, for the screening procedures failed to turn away many families, and the services requirement appeared to be more a symbolic gesture than a policy change. For, in the face of the upcoming mayoral election, much of the funding for services was shifted toward developing more permanent housing (Dugger 1993a). And DHS, in centralizing the city's homeless programs, also provided New Yorkers of all political persuasions a focus toward which they could vent their increasing frustration over the city's response to homelessness.

In contrast to a beleaguered family shelter system, the demand on the single adults shelter system reportedly declined 10 percent from 1989 to 1993 (Dugger 1993b). Along with, and perhaps partly responsible for, these encouraging statistics came the successful implementation of the SRO housing construction first proposed under Koch in a joint state and city venture. By 1995 this initiative created 7,500 units of housing with supportive services for single adults, most of whom came from shelters and who had physical disabilities, mental illness, or substance abuse problems. After construction expenses, this housing cost half of the $18,000 to $21,000 needed annually to provide a shelter bed (Kennedy 1995; *Economist* 1996a). Community response to these SRO buildings was also much more accommodating than it was toward Dinkins's attempt to implement another Koch proposal to build smaller, service-oriented shelters throughout the city. The acrimonious community opposition over the prospect of locating shelters in so many neighborhoods left the city continuing to rely on the notorious larger shelters and deprived it of any effective means to entice homeless persons from the streets to enter shelters. As a result homeless persons still seemed to maintain a ubiquitous presence in the city's public spaces, a presence that Dinkins then sought to reduce through force (Roberts 1991). The bulldozing of a homeless encampment at Tompkins Square Park was the best known of these coercive measures, an incident that served as a symbol for many as to how far Dinkins's policies had come from his campaign stance as a compassionate champion of the homeless.

As Dinkins had done with Koch, in 1993 Rudolph Giuliani won the mayoral election in a campaign where he criticized the Dinkins Administration for its homelessness policies. While Dinkins had projected a more compassionate alternative to Koch, Mayor Giuliani's posture against Dinkins now was one of toughness. Mayor Giuliani proposed to drastically alter city homeless policy—with campaign pledges to limit shelter stays to ninety days; to mount a legal challenge to the *Callahan* consent decree; to end housing placements for homeless families; and to give shelter users the options either to pay lodging fees or to participate in social service programs. This tone would also be echoed on the state level a year later as newly elected governor George Pataki quickly ordered that all state shelter aid would be tied to the provision of supportive services to shelter residents and proposed limitations on both welfare aid to families and "home relief" general assistance for childless adults.

Mayor Giuliani's policy changes have proven to be more moderate than his campaign rhetoric suggested (Dugger 1994), yet he seems to move in a consistent direction of reducing both the extent and the responsiveness of city-funded homeless services. He has yet to launch a major offensive against the *Callahan* consent decree, but he has chipped away at it by following up on Dinkins's and Cuomo's original proposals to link shelter to services and to implement a more rigorous prescreening process for homeless households seeking shelter. Mayor Giuliani has cut housing placements available to homeless persons from 5,466 in 1993 to less than 3,000 in the 1996–97 fiscal year through cutting back EARP, and through scaling back SRO housing construction (*Economist* 1996b)—the primary housing programs left from past administrations. DHS has continued to rely on EAU offices to double as sleeping areas, and the Giuliani Administration has chosen to pay the court-imposed fines, $4 million by May 1995 (Demers 1995), instead of remedying the situation. The prospect of staying in a shelter has become less attractive under Mayor Giuliani (Goldberg 1996), but so has staying on the streets as police crackdowns regularly roust persons who panhandle or sleep in public places, part of Mayor Giuliani's "quality of life" initiatives aimed at improving the aesthetic quality of public spaces (Krauss 1994). Predictably, Mayor Giuliani has come under fire for making the shelter system less responsive to the needs of the city's homeless, but, unlike Dinkins, these actions are consistent with campaign rhetoric that made few overtures to those favoring an expanded municipal response to homelessness.

The history of New York City homeless policy over the last two decades offers numerous issues that merit further consideration and debate. Questions concerning the role of the courts in dictating homeless policy to city government (Demers 1995); the political dynamics that led to the nation's largest shelter system (Kirchheimer 1990); the role of New York City's shelter system in the context of the larger political economy (Blau 1992); and the shelter as a reincarnation of the poorhouse (Culhane 1992; Hopper 1990) are but some of the topics that contribute to the multifaceted dialogue on this subject. More practical questions, however, also arise out of this examination of city homelessness policy. Specifically, how will the most recent changes in shelter policy, when combined with an array of service and entitlement cuts, impact New York City's poor population; and what can be taken from the past eighteen years since the *Callahan* decree to develop a more effective shelter system?

AGGREGATE TRENDS IN SHELTER UTILIZATION

The remainder of this chapter focuses on shelter utilization data and the particular implications the data contain for the debate on New York City's homeless policy. Applying a range of methods produces findings that offer some empirical evidence pertaining to the relative merits of providing a sheltered population with social, medical, and mental health services on one hand and with housing and rental assistance on the other hand. In related issues, the data also offer some insight on the effectiveness of the shelter system in providing a temporary, as opposed to long-term or chronic housing respite, and on the rates of repeat shelter episodes. And finally, this chapter also uses the shelter utilization data as a basis for taking the dialogue on homelessness out of the shelters and into the neighborhoods where homelessness originates. Contrary to much of the debate on these issues that has involved ideology more than empirical evidence, the purpose here is to take the turbulent experience of the past two decades as a basis for future homeless policy.

One byproduct of the centralized nature of the New York City shelter system is the comprehensive records it maintains on persons and families who stay in its shelters, offering a rich database from which to explore trends, dynamics, and determinants of public shelter utilization. Although many cities have more recently followed its lead, no other city in the United States has amassed as significant an archival source of information regarding the use of public shelters over time as has New York City. While the data miss periods of homelessness outside of city-run shelters, either on the streets or in the modest network of shelters not receiving municipal assistance, the data nonetheless provide an extraordinary opportunity for understanding the role of public shelters in New York City.[1]

SHELTER UTILIZATION OVER TIME

Counts of the number of persons utilizing the shelter system have an enormous influence on homeless policy, yet there has been little attention given to the dynamics of these numbers, and resulting trends, over time. Part of the reason for this has been the lack of available longitudinal data. Estimates of the size of the homeless population were frequently of a "point prevalent" nature (Burt and Cohen 1989; Wright and Devine 1992; Rossi et al. 1987), and their methodology was akin to taking a "snapshot" of the homeless population size on a particular day. Any longer-term counts then were derived by manipulating this point-prevalent figure. Within the shelter system, the point-prevalent count is known as the daily shelter census, which gives the numbers of either persons or families staying in the shelter on a given night.

The daily census is the statistic that is of the most immediate concern to the city's homeless services, as it largely dictates the resources

allocated to the shelter system. The daily census can be loosely translated as the level of demand on the shelter system at any one time.
When, for example, the number of families requesting shelter on a
given night exceeds the capacity of the available facilities, the city must
place them all, but typically will resort to increased use of either EAUs
or welfare hotels as makeshift shelter accommodations. Similarly, an increased single-adult census may lead to the opening of another armory
building to shelter the overflow demand (Krauss 1994). Much of city
homeless policy has focused on how to reduce the daily census, and solutions have sought to either limit entry into the shelters, such as by
screening shelter applicants; to increase exits, such as by increasing the
rate of housing placements; or, in Mayor Giuliani's campaign proposal,
by setting a limit on the length of shelter stays.

Daily census figures can quickly gauge the size of a population,
but they must also be interpreted carefully. Well-known seasonal
trends cause daily census numbers to fluctuate, with the daily family
shelter census peaking in the summer months while the daily adult
shelter census peaks in the winter months. Daily census counts also
give no information on the day-to-day turnover among the sheltered
population. There is no way of knowing how many people from one
census day are also staying in the shelter system on another census
day. A higher rate of turnover, with a steady average daily census, will
mean a larger group of people are using the shelter system and that
homelessness will affect a greater proportion of the overall population. Culhane et al. (1994), using the New York City shelter data and
less extensive data on the Philadelphia shelter system, found that the
number of people who become homeless over long periods of time is
considerably higher than the numbers who are homeless on any one
night. In contrast to the 0.11 to 0.25 percent of the population that
point-prevalent estimates attribute as homeless on a given night, Culhane et al. found that about 1 percent of both New York City's and
Philadelphia's populations had spent time in a homeless shelter some-
time in 1992, with this number of New York City shelter users approaching 3 percent of the 1990 population in the five-year period of
1988 to 1992.[2]

Tables 8.1 and 8.2 show, along with the daily census, several alternative ways to gauge the size of New York City's sheltered homeless
population since 1987. The difference between the average daily census,[3] as a point in time count, and the "prevalence" rates, which indicate
the number of persons or families who have stayed in a shelter over the
course of a year, is analogous to the difference between a snapshot and
a documentary film. Calculating the relative proportion of these two

TABLE 8.1
Shelter Utilization Rates in the New York City Family Shelter System,
1987–1995

	Incidence (new cases)			Prevalence (total cases)			Avg. Daily Census		Turnover
Year	Families	Adults	Children	Families	Adults	Children	Families	Persons	Rate (fam.)
1987	7,885	9,931	14,093	11,177	14,490	21,852	3,764.9	13,523.6	2.97
1988	6,721	8,490	10,977	12,870	16,800	23,932	4,900.5	17,385.9	2.63
1989	6,198	8,021	10,069	12,751	17,114	23,282	4,133.9	14,208.5	3.08
1990	7,276	9,223	12,119	13,434	17,729	23,333	3,619.6	12,018.3	3.71
1991	7,260	9,395	11,694	13,656	18,175	23,464	4,577.7	15,089.7	2.98
1992	7,302	9,384	11,542	14,898	19,984	25,542	5,267.2	17,176.8	2.83
1993	6,391	8,173	10,033	14,578	19,515	24,856	5,667.3	18,282.7	2.57
1994	6,665	8,426	10,316	14,659	19,563	24,979	5,678.2	18,076.0	2.58
1995	5,399	6,825	8,637	13,302	17,682	23,180	5,676.9	18,142.9	2.34
Total[1]	64,389	82,427	107,239				4,809.6	17,100.5	13.56

1. Totals reflect unduplicated number of families, adults, and children who experienced a stay in the New York City family shelter system over 1987–1995. The total turnover rate reflects the turnover during the course of this eight-year time period.

TABLE 8.2
Shelter Utilization Rates in the New York City Single-Adult Shelter System,
1987–1995

Year	Incidence (new cases)	Prevalence (total cases)	Avg. Daily Census	Turnover Rate
1987	31,956	40,884	7,116.5	5.74
1988	21,624	42,401	9,039.4	4.69
1989	18,237	42,218	9,458.2	4.46
1990	13,256	34,822	8,703.3	4.00
1991	11,989	32,156	7,792.5	4.13
1992	10,633	29,211	7,068.2	4.13
1993	9,294	26,959	6,283.3	4.29
1994	8,988	27,004	5,973.4	4.52
1995	8,911	24,153	6,329.2	3.82
Total[1]		143,816	8,470.45	16.98

1. Totals reflect unduplicated number of single adults who experienced a stay in the New York City single-adult shelter system over 1987–1995. The total turnover rate reflects the turnover during the course of this eight-year time period.

statistics produces the "turnover rate" shown in the tables, which can be intuitively understood as the number of persons who slept in a hypothetical shelter bed over the course of a year. Finally, the incidence column reflects the persons and families who entered a public shelter for the first time that year, with the sum of the first year's prevalence rate and the subsequent years' incidence rates reflecting the total number of persons and families who spent time in a shelter during the study period.

Summarizing the tables for the nine-year period beginning January 1, 1987, and ending December 31, 1995, 333,482 people (unduplicated) stayed in public shelters for one day or more in New York City, representing 4.6 percent of the city's 1990 population.[4] The majority, or 57 percent, were members of families, including 35 percent who were children. The remaining 43 percent were single-adult households, unaccompanied by children. As shown in Table 8.1, after a 15 percent jump in 1988, the annual prevalence of public shelter use by family households increased at a much more modest 2.3 percent average rate from 1989 through 1994, and then dropped 9 percent in 1995. In contrast, Table 8.2 confirms newspaper reports that show a declining single adult shelter population. The annual prevalence for the single-adult shelter system, after peaking in 1988 and 1989, subsequently plummeted by 18 percent in 1990 and then sustained a protracted but more modest average decline of 6 percent from 1991 through 1995.

Incidence rates, when compared to prevalence rates, give a rough idea of the extent to which the shelter population consists of persons experiencing initial shelter episodes. Starting with the 1988 annual rates,[5] the proportion of new families to total families has fluctuated in the range of 41 percent to 54 percent. The numbers of new families annually fluctuate and are not significantly correlated with the corresponding annual prevalence rates.[6] The incidence rates for the single-adult shelter system again suggest a different story, however. There is a consistently lower proportion of incidence to prevalence in the single-adult shelters from 1988 to 1994, with the proportion declining each year from about one-half in 1988 to about one-third in 1994, and then rising slightly to 37 percent in 1995. This trend suggests that those left among this declining shelter population are increasingly the repeat stayers, but the drop in incidence has been smaller than the drop in prevalence, indicating that the declining shelter utilization cannot be due solely to the drop in new persons entering the shelter.

Looking at the effects that prevalence and turnover each have on the average daily census, it is possible to associate these three statistics with homeless policy during this time. From 1989 to 1990, the average daily family shelter census decreased despite a rising demand for shelter (that is, prevalence). This was due to more families leaving the system than entering, and is indicated by increasing turnover rates. Although it is risky to attribute reasons for this without further data, the timing of this increase in turnover rates, which started in 1989, is consistent with when housing, from the programs started under the Koch Administration, started becoming widely available to sheltered families[7] and exits to housing became more widely available. The subsequent increase in both prevalence and incidence, starting in 1990, came about a year after the increase in turnover and could conceivably be attributed to the time it took for word to spread about the increased housing opportunities.

In 1991, however, falling turnover rates, with unchanging incidence and prevalence rates, indicate a slowdown in the number of families exiting the system—and a bottled-up shelter system and a host of problems for the Dinkins Administration. In 1991 and 1992 the city was running out of buildings to renovate (Dugger 1992) as the average daily census increased by 46 percent. The city, in response, increased its use of welfare hotels and dormitory shelters and had families staying in EAUs. Nonetheless, the demand for shelter kept increasing, with incidence going up during this time even though by then shelters had become more difficult to navigate successfully to a housing placement. The first significant drop in prevalence occurred in 1995, with the number of families using the shelter system that year dropping 9 percent, yet the average daily census remained unchanged. This suggests that the families in the shelter system are staying longer, and that achieving a reduction in the demand for shelter will, by itself, not decrease the size of the shelter system.

Housing placements, until recently, appear to have had the effect of reducing demand on the single-adult shelter system. In 1990, the first year of declining incidence and prevalence rates, 5,000 units of SRO housing, from the city-state partnership program, started to become available. It was also in this period that the city created the Division for AIDS Services, which provides housing to all persons with AIDS who request it. These two alternate housing streams could have absorbed many of the persons who previously would have been in shelters. In housing persons with disabilities, this housing would have served those who presumably were among the heaviest shelter users. While the decline in single-adult shelter utilization is likely to come from a combination of many reasons, the juxtaposition of this decline with supported housing availability is one more indicator of the success of this program, which has been favorably received but cut back under Mayor Giuliani. Statistics from 1995, while showing a further decline in prevalence, also show an end to five years of declining shelter system size, as the average daily census increased by 6 percent. As with the 1995 family shelter statistics, this decline indicates that people in the shelter system are staying longer.

PATTERNS OF SHELTER USE

Another question that this shelter utilization data can address is how sheltered households make use of the shelter system. Using survival analysis techniques allows for an idea of how long people stay in shelters[8] and how many of these households, upon leaving, will return to the shelter system. Survival curves use the shelter stay data to graphically show the probability of either a shelter exit (Figure 8.1) or a shelter readmission (Figure 8.2) occurring to a homeless household at or after a specific time (Allison 1995). From day zero, when all households start their shelter stay, Figure 8.1 shows that for single adults many shelter stays end quickly, as half of all shelter stays are over in less than twenty-nine days. By day ninety, 75 percent of single adult stays will end, and in seven months' time 90 percent of all shelter stays are over. This curve is flatter for families, as families have considerably longer stays per household than do single adults. For comparison, Figure 8.1 also shows that half of all family stays end by day 46; 75 percent end by

FIGURE 8.1
Homeless Shelter Stay Survival Curves

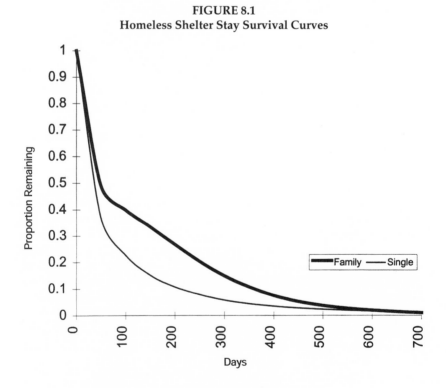

FIGURE 8.2
Survival Curves of Homeless Shelter Return Rates

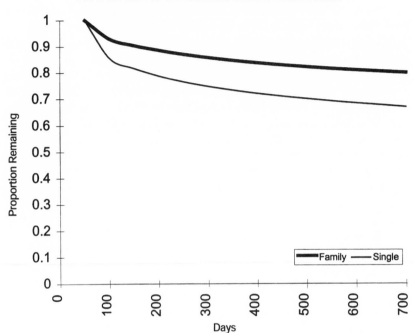

day 212; and that it takes 360 days, almost one year, for 90 percent of the stays to end.

According to Figure 8.1, the majority of all shelter stays last less than three months—but how many of these households experience repeat shelter stays? Figure 8.2 shows the survival curves whereby households, family and single, avoid repeat shelter stays in the two years following first shelter admission.[9] Among families, only 20 percent will return to shelter, while among single adults, 35 percent do so.[10] A higher proportion of single-adult households compared to family households return to shelter, but the rate of reentry among those who do return follows a similar pattern for both types of household. Among the households in both shelter systems that do return to shelter, half of them will do so within six months of exit, and only 15 percent of single household readmissions and 18 percent of family household readmissions will occur after one year of exit. Taken together, these figures show something that is not often noted about the New York City shelter system: most households use it for emergency shelter—a one-time stay of less than ninety days.

DETERMINANTS OF SHELTER EXIT AMONG SINGLE ADULTS

Two studies of shelter use by single adults (Culhane and Kuhn 1998; Kuhn and Culhane 1998) offer insight as to who is at higher risk for long-term shelter stays and for repeat shelter stays, and to what extent shelter days are consumed disproportionately by the long-term stayers. The New York City shelter database, in addition to information on shelter stays, also offers information on the persons using the shelters, based on intake interviews with clients upon their admission to the shelter system. This data include demographics, as well as "indicators" for a mental health problem, medical conditions, and substance abuse problems. While these indicators have an uncertain rate of reliability, they nonetheless produce results that are consistent with what might be expected, that the presence of increased age, mental illness, medical conditions, and substance abuse all contribute to a decreased likelihood of shelter exit or, in other words, to longer shelter stays (Culhane and Kuhn 1998).

Using cluster analysis, Kuhn and Culhane (1998) use the frequency of shelter admission and length of stay to group single adults into three distinct groups. In Table 8.3, the first and largest group, the transitionally homeless, are characterized by stays that are relatively brief and short in number. The second group, the episodically homeless, also stays relatively briefly but, because it has a high average number of shelter admissions, persons in this group accumulate, on average, 4.5 times as many total shelter days as the transitionally homeless. Persons in the third group, the chronically homeless, have, on average, relatively few shelter admissions but when they stay it tends to be for a long time—2.4 times as many shelter days as the episodically homeless and 11 times as many days as the transitionally homeless.

Each cluster also is distinct from the other two in terms of demographic characteristics and presence of disability indicators (also in Table 8.3). The transitional cluster is relatively young and is the least likely to have a mental illness indicator, a medical condition, or a substance abuse indicator, although the levels of disability and substance abuse are still quite high. The episodic cluster is similar to the transitional in terms of age, but is half as likely to be white and has nearly twice the rate of a mental illness indicator, as well as a nearly 50 percent higher rate of medical conditions. Of the episodic group, 40 percent also received a positive substance abuse indicator. The chronic group, in comparison, is the oldest, with twice the proportion of persons over fifty than the episodic group as well as the highest rates of both a mental illness indicator and a medical problem, and a high substance abuse indicator rate. Both the episodic and the chronic appear to be, as a

TABLE 8.3
Cluster Statistics, Demographics, and Treatment Variables in Model for
New York City Single-Adult Shelter System Users

	Transitional	Episodic	Chronic	Total
Summary Statistics				
Number of Clients	59,367	6,700	7,196	73,263
Avg. # of Episodes	1.36	4.85	2.27	1.77
Avg. # of Days	57.8	263.8	637.8	133.6
Avg. Days per Episode	42.4	54.4	280.9	75.4
% of Client Days Used	35.1	18.1	46.9	100
% of Clients	81.0	9.1	9.8	100
Ratio (%Days / %Clients)	0.43	1.97	4.77	1
Demographics				
% White	11.9	6.1	9.5	11.1
% Male	81.5	81.8	82.3	81.6
% under 30	36.1	37.7	23.2	35
% over 50	8.3	6.3	13.9	8.7
Treatment Variables				
Mental Illness	6.5%	11.8%	15.1%	7.8%
Medical	14.2%	19.8%	24.0%	15.7%
Substance Abuse	28.2%	40.0%	37.9%	30.2%
Any of the Three	38.4%	52.6%	55.4%	41.4%
All Three	1.3%	3.0%	3.3%	1.7%

Source: Table adapted from Kuhn and Culhane (1998).

group, very disabled, as over half of each group has at least one of the three indicators.

The results of this cluster analysis point to the need for service targeting strategies. Broadly speaking, the chronic group are the long-term shelter users, and for whom shelters represent extended housing arrangements rather than emergency accommodations. This group, 10 percent of the sheltered single-adult population, appears deceptively large in point in time counts because as a group it consumes a disproportionate 47 percent of all shelter days. This would likely be the proper population to target with long-term, supported housing programs, including subsidized apartments, structured living arrangements, and, in some cases, long-term care programs. Reducing the size of this population is likely to have a large effect on the average daily census.

The episodic group, on the other hand, would not seem to be the proper target for such programs, at least in the short term. This would appear to be the group that spends time in shelters between stints in jails, hospitals, or living on the streets and would include those homeless persons who avoid shelters in all but the coldest or most extreme circumstances. This group, however, representing 9 percent of the shelter population, also uses a disproportionate 18 percent of the total shelter days. This group could benefit from structured and service-intensive programs intended to stabilize them before assisting them in locating long-term housing, and thus stand to benefit most from transitional housing programs.

Diverting these groups to more appropriate housing and services would promise a reduced shelter system while only having to target expensive housing and service programs to 19 percent of the shelter population. The remaining 81 percent of single adults who use shelters, the transitionally homeless, collectively use only 35 percent of the system days. This group appears to have more in common with the housed poor than with long-term homeless persons, and they may benefit best from community-based programs that do not exclusively target homeless persons or persons in shelters. Many in this group could undoubtedly benefit from access to treatment programs and social services, but these services need not be linked to shelters. Indeed, they may be more effectively located in community-based programs, if goals include preventing homelessness or more quickly reintegrating this population into the community.

DETERMINANTS OF SHELTER EXIT AND REENTRY AMONG FAMILIES

Among families, fewer background variables are available for determining the characteristics associated with patterns of shelter use.[11] However, the New York data on families do include information on the cause of homelessness and type of shelter discharge, and this information, together with basic demographic variables, is useful for examining predictors of shelter exit and reentry. Homeless families have, on average, longer stays than do homeless single adults, largely because stays in the family system are drawn out by long waits to gain placement in subsidized housing programs. Families in public shelters are faced with a multifaceted housing dilemma that involves choosing between this option of waiting in shelters for subsidized housing, searching for private housing with typically unaffordable rents, or moving into an alternative arrangement, when available, where housing stability is likely to be highly volatile (Metraux 1996).

Wong, Culhane, and Kuhn (1997) examined these three types of exit from family shelter and the relationship between the types of exit and the timing of the exit. Figure 8.3 shows competing hazard rates,

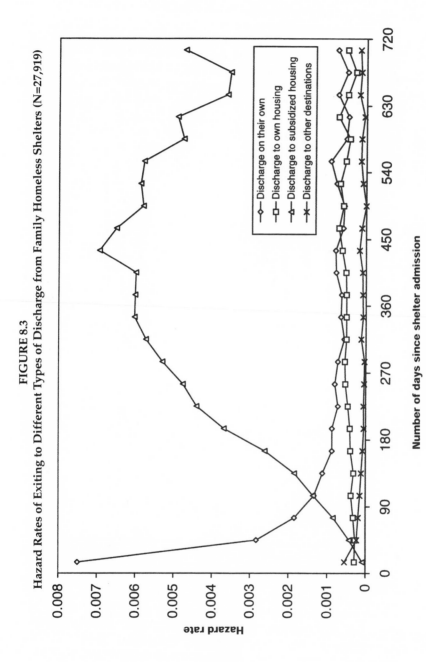

FIGURE 8.3

Hazard Rates of Exiting to Different Types of Discharge from Family Homeless Shelters (N=27,919)

Source: Wong, Culhane and Kuhn (1997)

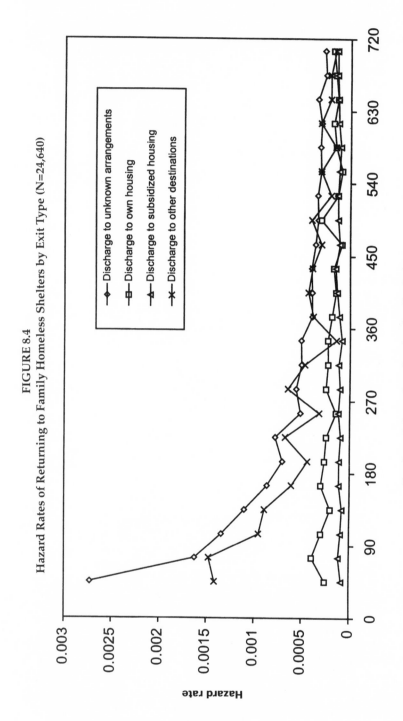

FIGURE 8.4
Hazard Rates of Returning to Family Homeless Shelters by Exit Type (N=24,640)

Discharge to unknown arrangements
Discharge to own housing
Discharge to subsidized housing
Discharge to other destinations

Hazard rate

Number of days since leaving family shelter

Source: Wong, Culhane and Kuhn (1997)

which are the likelihoods, at a particular point in time, that families will experience a particular type of shelter exit. The figure suggests that, as families stay in a shelter longer, the hazard that they will exit a shelter "on their own" or to some makeshift arrangement decreases, while at the same time the likelihood of exiting to a subsidized housing placement initially increases and then stays roughly constant after about eight months; in other words, to get a subsidized housing placement requires families to wait. But, as shown in Figure 8.4, subsidized housing exits, taken together, also have the lowest hazard for shelter reentry out of any of the four exit types.[12] In contrast those families that leave "on their own" tend to leave quicker but also show a greater likelihood of experiencing a repeat shelter stay relatively quickly.

Closer examination of Wong, Culhane, and Kuhn's (1997) study further suggests that the quality of housing placement strongly influences the risk of a return shelter stay. Families discharged to *in rem* housing, the city program that places homeless families in renovated, city-owned housing, were, everything else being equal, 50 percent as likely to be readmitted as families leaving "on their own" (the comparison category). Families discharged through the EARP program were 31 percent as likely to get readmitted. And families discharged to New York City Housing Authority apartments, widely considered the most desirable housing placements, were 18 percent as likely as "on their own" exits to get readmitted. In another related finding, the likelihood of families being discharged to subsidized housing rose substantially for families entering in 1989 and was highest in 1990, but declines thereafter, hereby supporting assumptions made from the utilization trends reported earlier.

The issue of long-staying households and their disproportionate use of system resources is also worth noting with regard to families, but with less clear policy implications. If a long shelter stay is defined as 180 days, then 30 percent of families experiencing a first admission fit into that category, and these families will consume 75 percent of the days among families having their first stay in the system. But these long-staying families, as shown in Figure 8.3, are also those who are more likely to be "successful" by virtue of the greater likelihood of their exiting to subsidized housing placements. Making housing more available to sheltered families would reduce the need for families to spend long periods of time in family shelters (thereby saving shelter resources), but would also raise the plausible, though never substantiated concern that beset the Dinkins Administration—that opportunities for quicker exits to affordable housing will only increase demand for shelter from a seemingly endless population of inadequately housed but nonhomeless families. Instead, as the family shelter system currently functions, the prospect of a long wait in a series of shelters may deter greater demand for family shelter while simultaneously offering a viable yet unwieldy means for homeless families to obtain subsidized housing.

THE DIFFERENTIAL RISK FOR SHELTER ADMISSION BY NEIGHBORHOOD

So far this chapter has shown how the data collected by the New York City shelter system is useful in looking at patterns of shelter use and their possible implications for the city's homeless policy. This data can also shed some light on where homeless people come from, as it has records of the prior addresses of homeless families. While there is no detailed information collected regarding the nature of the prior residence, the address information nonetheless serves as a potentially critical indicator of the types of neighborhoods homeless families come from. For example, aggregation of these addresses by census tract has permitted Culhane, Lee, and Wachter (1996) to further characterize this distribution and the census variables that correspond to it. In so doing, such an analysis may be beneficial for understanding the structural processes that operate differentially by neighborhood to mediate the risk for homelessness, and how some broader housing issues may affect homelessness.

Culhane, Lee, and Wachter (1996) examine the proportionate distribution of homeless families' prior addresses, with results (Figure 8.5) showing that they are much more densely clustered than the poverty distribution. Nearly two-thirds (61 percent) of New York's homeless families come from three areas: Harlem (15 percent of total), the South Bronx (25 percent), and the Bedford-Stuyvesant/East New York neighborhoods (21 percent). Linking these neighborhoods with homelessness suggests that there is a disproportionate racial distribution among the shelter population, an assumption previously confirmed by Culhane et al. (1994), who show that from 1988 to 1992 the relative risk to African Americans of a shelter stay was over twice as high as for the general population and seventeen times the rate for whites.[13] African American families are also more likely than other families to stay in a shelter longer than other families and more likely to experience a repeat shelter stay (Wong, Culhane, and Kuhn 1997).

In the Culhane, Lee, and Wachter study, a regression analysis of census variables associated with the distribution of homeless families' prior addresses further confirms this racial imbalance among the sheltered homeless when it finds that African American race is the most im-

FIGURE 8.5
Census Tract Map of the Distribution of the Prior Addresses of the
Homeless (1987–1994) in New York

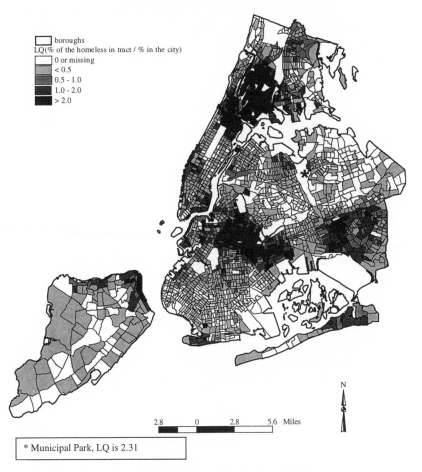

boroughs
LQ(% of the homeless in tract / % in the city)
☐ 0 or missing
< 0.5
0.5 - 1.0
1.0 - 2.0
> 2.0

N

2.8   0   2.8   5.6 Miles

* Municipal Park, LQ is 2.31

Source: Culhane, Lee and Wachter (1996)

portant predictor in the model. Among other demographic variables, the proportion of female-headed households with children under age six is also strongly associated with increased risk, even controlling for the ratio of female-headed households in a tract. The ratio of Hispanic households and low levels of educational attainment are also positively related to the risk of homelessness. Alternatively, these neighborhoods have fewer elderly, youth, and immigrant households.

As predicted, poverty is also strongly and positively associated with the distribution of shelter admissions, as is labor force nonparticipation. The areas from which the sheltered homeless originate also have a higher rate of housing crowding and persons living in subfamilies (that is, doubled-up arrangements). The housing is among the lowest-cost rental housing in the city but nevertheless is still relatively unaffordable to people who live there, as measured by the rent-to-income ratio. And despite being the lowest-cost housing, these areas have higher rates of vacancy. The fact that the housing market in these neighborhoods is highly distressed is further indicated by the comparatively high rate of abandonment.

These findings provide empirical support for linking housing distress, segregation, and other neighborhood effects with the generation of homelessness. In doing so, this study's findings are consistent with other works that document the effects of economic and residential isolation on the inner-city black poor (see, for example, Wilson 1987; Massey and Denton 1993), but, more practically, it also suggests starting points for homeless prevention efforts. While crowding is a precondition for homelessness among many households, it acts as an alternative to shelter admission among immigrant groups, which have both a lower rate of homelessness and an increased rate of crowding. Further study is needed to better understand how the rate of housing emergencies varies by race and ethnicity, and how various demographic groups mediate these emergencies, both through formal and informal mechanisms of support. Such research could help to inform homelessness prevention efforts if it is able to identify potential means by which housing emergencies can be more effectively resolved in the community, without involving the shelter system. This study also narrows down three geographic areas as foci for prospective prevention efforts, but alternately broadens the discussion of prevention issues to include segregation, housing, and family issues. Such a neighborhood study suggests that the concentration of these economic, housing, and social issues in particular neighborhoods will continue to generate families seeking shelter—regardless of and a priori to any changes that are made to the shelter system.

EMERGING POLICY ISSUES

Many significant policy changes have been proposed recently at the federal and state level that raise serious concerns regarding the future trends in homelessness and the provision of public shelter in New

York City. While the details of many of these policy changes are still unclear, the likely direction of change is distressingly clear. In this concluding section, we consider some of the policies that have been
proposed, and their potential implications.

With regard to housing policy, perhaps the most significant proposal at the federal level is the reduction of the Section 8 rental subsidy
program. Continued increases in the number of Section 8 certificates
has likely played an important, though undocumented, role in preventing homelessness for the roughly 20 percent of eligible households
who receive them. As the number of Section 8 certificates remains stagnant or, as in some recent years, declines (Schwartz and Vidal, chapter
9 in this volume), the number of poor households paying unaffordable
rents will grow, thereby increasing the number of people at risk for
homelessness. Moreover, given that Section 8 certificates play a critical
role in providing operating revenues for new housing developments,
many of which are targeted specifically for homeless persons with special needs, cutbacks in the program could halt many of the initiatives
that have relocated the chronically homeless to supported, permanent
housing.

Other housing policy changes worth noting are the likely reductions in the allocation of federal HOME, Community Development
Block Grant (CDBG), and McKinney Homeless Assistance Act funding.
The HOME and CDBG programs have likely had an impact on reducing the risk for homelessness, to the extent that they have reduced the
level of housing distress in areas where they have financed housing rehabilitation and development. To that end, the neighborhoods identified as at greatest risk of shelter admission in our research have also
been areas that have received significant shares of rehabilitation funding, from federal, state, and city sources. As those resources decline, so
will their cumulative impact on improving or maintaining neighborhood stability or in creating access to affordable housing. This could increase the risk for shelter admission from these areas, as well as reduce
the supply of housing to which the shelter system can discharge homeless families.

Similar reductions in creating affordable housing for homeless
households can be seen on a local level. Public housing preferences,
mandating that homeless families be given priority when filling housing vacancies, had previously been reduced by the New York City
Housing Authority and now have been eliminated on the federal level.
By policy, the city, since 1993, has stopped taking title to properties with
serious tax arrearages, eliminating the housing stock used in the *in rem*
program that constituted a major source of exit opportunities from shel-

ters. Mayor Giuliani has stated that a reduction of housing placements would ease the demand on the family shelter system, as fewer families would enter a system made less attractive by the lack of housing opportunities. Yet our findings show that there have been several years of decline in placements from family shelter to housing with no corresponding decline in prevalence rates for the family shelter system until 1995, the most recent year studied, when the prevalence was finally reduced, as desired, but the census actually increased as fewer households exited the shelters.

With respect to proposed cuts in direct federal aid for homelessness programs through the McKinney Homeless Assistance Act, this will also likely have an effect on the shelter system and efforts to reduce homelessness. The proposed shift in the McKinney programs to a formula-driven block grant could have some potential benefits, in that the block grant process is likely to require localities to establish a local planning process for the expenditure of funds. However, there will undoubtedly be less enthusiasm and impact from this redefined program strategy as the overall funding declines. McKinney is the only program set aside specifically for homeless persons, thus the cuts will likely have a more direct effect on the shelter system than other cuts. But while McKinney funding is valuable to the New York region, New York City is much less dependent on it than other areas of the country, given the more significant role of the state and the city in funding homeless services.

Finally, the elimination of AFDC as a federal entitlement, and the accompanying measures that curtail AFDC eligibility, must also be considered for its potential impact on housing stability. Likewise cuts in federal food stamp benefit levels will likely increase hardship among the poor. On the state level, proposals to reduce AFDC and Home Relief for single adults failed to pass in 1996, but they face an uncertain future in a political environment where income assistance measures of all kinds that target the poor are under attack. The implications for the shelter system are obvious, as it is likely to replace income entitlement as the public's notion of what constitutes the "safety net" for poor households.

It is likely that the shelter system will respond in ways that will limit the potential impact of these changes on shelter utilization. The resources for emergency shelter are not limitless; communities have resisted new shelter development; and the city has threatened a renewed legal challenge to its obligation to provide shelter under the *Callahan* consent decree. Alternatively, the city may attempt to restrict growth in the shelter system through various programmatic responses. For example, the eligibility screening that has been put in place for families and the shelter diversion program that operates out of the Income Maintenance centers are two approaches the city has already implemented as ways of narrowing the "front door" of the system. The overcrowding at EAUs is another, though perhaps unintended, way of discouraging people from following through the admission process to completion. A possible unintended consequence of such a "front door" management approach is that, if it has any significant effect, it will likely be removing from the system the people who have the most resources to exit on their own, or who would have exited shortly after admission, without a housing placement. This would lead to a change in the "case mix," in hospital parlance, and increase the proportion of more needy and longer-staying households. This is one potential explanation for the rise, in 1995, of the average daily census while the corresponding prevalence rates decreased.

In addition to reducing admissions, the system is also likely to respond to increases in demand by reducing stays ("back door" management). This could occur through several possible mechanisms. While the possibility of increased subsidized housing opportunities is unlikely in the current policy context, one likely scenario calls for the city to structure reimbursements for shelters such that it encourages earlier discharges, with or without subsidized housing. For example, the city could move toward a "capitated" system of reimbursement, over the current per diem system, much as is done in the area of health care. Such a system would include the need for close monitoring to prevent arbitrary discharges, and would likely need to engage shelter providers in resettlement programming to prevent readmissions. Alternately, the city could impose an absolute time limit for stays, such as the ninety-day limit mentioned previously.

CONCLUSION

This chapter examines homelessness policy and shelter utilization in New York City since the *Callahan* consent decree in 1981. Data collected in the New York City shelter system have permitted evaluation of past policy and the corresponding dynamics of shelter utilization, and offer an empirical basis for making recommendations concerning shelter policy. Looking ahead, the city's shelter system is likely to maintain its monolithic status and to continue an adversarial relationship with homeless advocates, to continue receiving direction from the courts, and to continue confronting crises borne of high shelter demand

and scarce funding. On the other hand, the current atmosphere is heavy with anticipation of the effects that changes in both social programs and in how the city carries out its commitment to provide shelter will have on homelessness.

Among the findings presented here is that, for most households, the shelter system appears to function as intended—as a brief emergency respite. Current city homelessness policy has placed a diminished emphasis on permanent housing for homeless households, although housing placements take homeless households out of shelters and reduce the risk of repeat shelter stays. Increased housing placements may, however, have the latent effect of increasing shelter admissions, although this is far from certain. What is clear is that housing is not a blanket remedy for homelessness, but neither is increased services, which has received increased policy emphasis as programs to promote self-sufficiency have become necessary to maintain political support for homeless programs. Our findings suggest that a services approach is potentially most effective, in terms of cost and results, when it targets specific groups of sheltered households or, in the case of preventative measures, certain areas of the city. Finally, while these recommendations are specific to increasing shelter efficiency and effectiveness, utilization data also carry the reminder that homelessness involves factors that extend beyond shelters. And while shelters are integral to New York City homelessness policy, ultimately any reduction in homelessness must involve a range of other concerns.

NOTES

1. See Culhane et al. (1994) for a more complete description of the New York City shelter database.

2. Using such a longitudinal perspective, the Clinton Administration, in outlining its policy on homelessness, acknowledges that the extent of homelessness is far greater than what is suggested by point prevalent counts, and, that, based on longitudinal studies including Culhane et al. (1994), "the number of adults experiencing homelessness was between four and eight million at some point in the latter half of the 1980s" (Interagency Coalition on the Homeless 1994, 22).

3. As these numbers represent the average over the course of a year, they smooth out the day-to-day fluctuations in this statistic that was previously mentioned.

4. Based on the 1990 U.S. Census count of a total New York City population of 7,322,564.

5. The higher incidence rates in 1987 represent an artifact of the dataset, whose earliest records are from 1986. Thus many people and families recorded as new in 1987, the first year of complete stay records, may have actually stayed in years prior but were not recorded. This effect may continue, but at reduced levels, through subsequent years.

6. The correlation (r) between annual incidence and prevalence, from 1988 to 1995, is .322 with p = .44.

7. About 96 percent of the families who left shelters to their own housing following a 1990 stay received this housing through a subsidized housing program (Metraux 1996).

8. On a methodological note, a "stay" is considered to be a continuous span that precedes a thirty-day exit from a shelter. Both family and single-adult records typically include, in their records, many stays for each individual or family that are of short duration (one to three days) and show contiguous dates or dates that are separated by several days. This analysis collapses these short stays occurring within thirty days of each other into one spell of homelessness. While thirty days, like any exit length, is somewhat arbitrary, it does indicate an extended time period spent away from shelters and assumes that alternate living arrangements have supplanted, not just provided temporary relief from, shelter use. It is also noteworthy that such a thirty-day exit may not necessarily mean an exit from homelessness, as it may lead to living "on the streets" with whereabouts unaccounted for or some other makeshift living arrangement (see also Culhane and Kuhn 1998.

9. This analysis tracks households from their first shelter entry into a shelter following a span of two years of not having had a shelter episode.

10. These rates represent the proportions above each curve at the far right of the figure, with the proportions under the curves representing those households that, upon their initial exit, stayed out of the shelter for the two years following their initial exit.

11. Weitzman, Knickman, and Shinn (1990) cover some of this ground in a more detailed way with a smaller sample, comparing homeless and housed poor families over time.

12. Weitzman and Berry (1994) similarly found low rates of shelter reentry in following up on families who received placements from shelters to subsidized housing.

13. This can be compared to the measured poverty rate, which is approximately three times greater for blacks than for whites.

References

Allison, Paul D. 1995. *Survival Analysis Using the SAS System: A Practical Guide.* Cary, N.C.: SAS Institute.

Blau, Joel. 1992. *The Visible Poor: Homelessness in the United States.* New York: Oxford University Press.

Brosnahan, Mary. 1994. "Hope for the Homeless: The Mayor's Empty Words." *New York Times,* June 9, A25.

Burt, Martha R., and Barbara E. Cohen. 1989. *America's Homeless: Numbers, Characteristics, and Programs That Serve Them.* Washington, D.C.: Urban Institute.

Culhane, Dennis P. 1992. "The Quandaries of Shelter Reform: An Appraisal of Efforts to 'Manage' Homelessness." *Social Service Review* 66, 3:429–40.

Culhane, Dennis P., Edmund F. Dejowski, Julie Ibanez, Elizabeth Needham, and Irene Macchia. 1994. "Public Shelter Admission Rates in Philadelphia and New York City: The Implications of Turnover for Sheltered Population Counts." *Housing Policy Debate* 5, 2:107–40.

Culhane, Dennis P., and Randall S. Kuhn. 1998. "Patterns and Determinants of Public Shelter Utilization among Homeless Adults in New York City and Philadelphia." *Journal of Policy Analysis and Management* 17, 1:23–43.

Culhane, Dennis P., Chang-Moo Lee, and Susan Wachter. 1996. "Where the Homeless Come from: A Study of the Prior Address Distribution of Families Admitted to Public Shelters in New York City and Philadelphia." *Housing Policy Debate* 7, 2:327–60.

Demers, Susan. 1995. "The Failures of Litigation as a Tool for the Development of Social Welfare Policy." *Fordham Urban Law Journal* 22 (summer): 1009–51.

Dugger, Celia W. 1994. "Giuliani Easing Election Stance on the Homeless." *New York Times,* March 20, A1.

———. 1993a. "Dinkins Plans Shifts in Funds for Homeless." *New York Times,* January 8, B1.

———. 1993b. "Shelter Costs Keep Growing." *New York Times,* July 26, B2.

———. 1992. "Limits Sought on Shelters for Homeless." *New York Times,* September 19, A21.

———. 1991. "Benefits of System Luring More Families into Shelters." *New York Times,* September 4, A1.

Economist. 1996a. "Housing for the Poor: Room at the Top." (June 1): 24.

———. 1996b. "New York's Homeless: On the Edge." (July 6): 28.

Ellickson, Robert C. 1990. "The Homelessness Muddle." *Public Interest* 99 (spring): 45–60.

Filer, Randall K. 1990. "What Really Causes Family Homelessness?" *NY: The City Journal* (autumn): 31–40.

Finder, Alan. 1993. "To Reduce Number, Dinkins Offers Rules on Who's Homeless." *New York Times*, April 1, B3.

Goldberg, Carey. 1996. "Shuttling through the Night: The Overnighters' Odyssey." *New York Times*, January 24, B1.

Grunberg, Jeffrey, and Paula F. Eagle. 1990. "Shelterization: How the Homeless Adapt to Shelter Living." *Hospital and Community Psychiatry* 41, 5:521–25.

Hombs, Mary Ellen, and Mitch Snyder. 1982. *Homelessness in America: A Forced March to Nowhere*. Washington, D.C.: Community for Creative Non-Violence.

Hopper, Kim. 1990. "Public Shelter as a 'Hybrid Institution': Homeless Men in Historical Perspective." *Journal of Social Issues* 46, 4:13–29.

Hopper, Kim, and L. Stuart Cox. 1986. "Litigation in Advocacy for the Homeless: The Case of New York City." In *Housing the Homeless*, ed. Jon Erickson and Charles Wilhelm. New Brunswick, N.J.: Center for Urban Policy Research.

Interagency Coalition for the Homeless. 1994. *Priority: Home! The Federal Plan to Break the Cycle of Homelessness*. Washington, D.C.: U.S. Department of Housing and Urban Development.

Kennedy, Shawn G. 1995. "New Look for S.R.O.s: Decent Housing." *New York Times*, March 28, B1.

Kirchheimer, Donna W. 1990. "Sheltering the Homeless in New York City: Expansion in an Era of Government Contraction." *Political Science Quarterly* 104, 4:607–23.

Kozol, Jonathan. 1988. *Rachel and Her Children: Homeless Families in America*. New York: Fawcett Columbine.

Krauss, Clifford. 1994. "Special Unit Ushers Homeless from Subway." *New York Times*, September 4, A1.

Kuhn, Randall, and Dennis P. Culhane. 1998. "Applying Cluster Analysis to Test a Typology of Homelessness by Pattern of Shelter Utilization: Results from the Analysis of Administrative Data." *American Journal of Community Psychology* 26, 2.

Massey, Douglas S., and Nancy A. Denton. 1993. *American Apartheid: Segregation and the Making of the Underclass*. Cambridge: Harvard University Press.

Metraux, Stephen. 1996. "Assessing Hazards of Shelter Reentry Among a Group of Homeless Women: An Exercise in Event History Analysis." Paper in review. University of Pennsylvania, Sociology Department.

New York City Commission on the Homeless. 1992. *The Way Home: A New Direction in Social Policy.* New York: author.

Roberts, Sam. 1991. "Crackdown on Homeless and What Led to Shift." *New York Times,* October 28, B1.

Rossi, Peter H., James D. Wright, Gene A. Fisher, and Georgianna Willis. 1987. "The Urban Homeless: Estimating Composition and Size." *Science* 235 (March 13): 1336–41.

Weitzman, Beth C., and Carolyn Berry. 1994. *Formerly Homeless Families and the Transition to Permanent Housing: High-Risk Families and the Role of Intensive Case Management Services.* New York: Edna McConnell Clark Foundation.

Weitzman, Beth C., James R. Knickman, and Marybeth Shinn. 1990. "Pathways to Homelessness among New York City Families." *Journal of Social Issues* 46, 4:125–40.

Wilson, William J. 1987. *The Truly Disadvantaged: The Inner City, the Underclass, and Public Policy.* Chicago: University of Chicago Press.

Wong, Yin L. I., Dennis P. Culhane, and Randall S. Kuhn. 1997. "Predictors of Exit and Re-Entry among Family Shelter Users in New York City." *Social Services Review* 71, 3:441–62.

Wright, James D., and Joel A. Devine. 1992. "Counting the Homeless: The Census Bureau's 'S-Night' in Five U.S. Cities." *Evaluation Review* 16, 4:355–64.

CHAPTER 9

BETWEEN A ROCK AND A HARD PLACE: THE IMPACT OF FEDERAL AND STATE POLICY CHANGES ON HOUSING IN NEW YORK CITY

Alex F. Schwartz and Avis C. Vidal

The national political swing to the right, mirrored as it is in many states, has dramatically reconfigured the policy landscape. Program specifics will continue to evolve, but the direction of the impending changes is relatively clear. On the one hand, changes in federal housing policy and spending will make it progressively more difficult for cities to craft housing policies that assist low-income households, their landlords, and their neighborhoods. On the other hand, welfare reform promises further to erode the ability of the poor to pay rents that cover the cost of the units they inhabit. The long-term impacts on cities' housing policies and on the low-cost end of urban housing markets could be profound.

Lower-income households are at an increasing disadvantage in those low-cost markets. The real incomes of low-income households have been falling, while the cost of building and maintaining dwellings has risen. As a result, the stock of low-cost rental units has been declining for two decades, and home ownership has become less accessible. A growing number of the poor pay more than half of their income for housing or live in seriously inadequate housing, and homelessness has become a major national issue—but of particular seriousness in New York—for the first time since the Great Depression.

This chapter examines the potential impact of federal and state policy shifts on housing and housing policy in New York City. We begin with an overview of the major factors shaping developing policies in Washington and Albany that have important implications for housing in the city. We then outline the prospects for specific programs. Our emphasis is on housing programs, but we also highlight nonhousing issues that could have important housing impacts. The core of the chapter then explores the implications of these possible changes both for New York's housing programs and for the housing, residents, landlords, and neighborhoods they influence.

THE SHIFTING SANDS OF POLICY IN WASHINGTON AND ALBANY

The locus of public policy debate in the country has been shifting steadily to the right for a quarter of a century. Discussion of the front-page issues of the moment, tied as they are to the election cycle, commonly underscores their short-run volatility. But the ebb and flow of policy details overlay three persistent trends that will continue to shape housing policy for the foreseeable future.

First, over the past two decades, federal policy has moved away from direct subsidies for the construction of affordable housing (supply-side subsidies) toward assistance provided directly to tenants (demand-side subsidies) and toward privatization. The last major production program, Section 8 New Construction and Substantial Rehabilitation, was eliminated when Congress confronted the long-run budget implications of committing twenty years of subsidy dollars to each newly built unit. Tenant-based Section 8 subsidies, which carry budget authorization for only five or fewer years, face ongoing political challenges. For several years in the mid-1990s, no incremental certificates and vouchers (that is, net additions to the number of subsidized households), were authorized. Some type of restriction on the reuse of existing certificates remains a distinct possibility in future years, especially if the economy slows.

Second, the long-term shift from categorical programs to block grants, begun in the Nixon administration, has gained renewed energy. Although the pattern has been somewhat uneven over time and across programs, the net effect has generally been to give greater discretion to states and localities. As Kathryn Wylde discusses in chapter 3 and Frank P. Braconi details in chapter 4, New York has been especially aggressive in taking advantage of this discretion to customize housing policies to its often distinctive needs. However, block grants tend to be more vulnerable to budget cuts than their predecessor categorical programs had been. Housing advocates therefore responded with concern to HUD's proposal, outlined in its 1996 Reinvention Blueprint ("Blue

II"), to consolidate much of its programming into three block grants. The main component programs targeted for consolidation—particularly HOME, Community Development Block Grants (CDBG), and McKinney[1]—have strong supporters, so the proposal faded from view and the funding for these programs remained fairly stable. Given the pressures on the HUD budget (described in more detail below), however, they are likely to attract new challenges.

Finally, political pressure for balancing the federal budget will continue to squeeze funding for housing. Despite the transfer of much of the cost of dealing with expiring use properties to the Federal Housing Administration (FHA) Insurance Fund (see Victor Bach's discussion in chapter 6 in this volume), real cuts in major housing and community development programs are the most likely prospect.

WHAT FUTURE LIES IN STORE FOR MAJOR PROGRAMS?

Federal Housing and Community Development Programs
Face Continuous Pressure

HUD programs and funding have been subject to a steady stream of criticism for over a decade, fueled by a diverse group of factors (for example, the rapid rise in the cost of Section 8, public disenchantment with public housing, allegations of mismanagement, and opposition to publicly funded efforts to deconcentrate minority residents of public housing). Recent years have seen congressional challenges to almost every major federal housing program and policy. While HUD proposed its own "reinvention," Congress has considered (but not passed) legislation to eliminate or restructure several key housing programs, including the Low-income Housing Tax Credit (LIHTC), the Community Reinvestment Act (CRA), public housing, assisted housing, and tenant-based rental subsidies. A bill to abolish HUD altogether has even been proposed. Some of these programs appear more secure than others, but all are vulnerable to restructuring, reduction, or elimination if the broad trends discussed above persist.

The overall HUD budget has been on a long term downward trajectory since 1980, when the Department's budget authority exceeded $50 billion. The HUD budget came under severe pressure in the drive to balance the budget starting in the mid-1990s. HUD funding for FY95 originally authorized at $25.4 billion, was cut to $20.1 billion (a reduction of 25 percent). It fell to $19.1 billion in FY96 and to $16.0 billion in

FY97—a decline of 37 percent in just three years. Congress increased HUD's budget authority in FY98 and FY99 to $24.1 and $25.0 billion respectively, largely to fund Section 8 contract renewals. While funding for the CDBG and HOME programs held steady, support for other discretionary programs has declined over this period, especially funding for public housing, elderly and disabled housing, and the homeless.

In addition, a number of programmatic changes have been enacted.[2] These changes include the following:

- Suspension of one-for-one replacement of public housing that is demolished.
- Suspension of federal "preferences" for receipt of housing subsidies.[3]
- Imposition of minimum rents of $25 (or up to $50 at the discretion of public housing authorities) for public housing and Section 8 (with provision for a three-month waiver in cases of hardship).
- Imposition of maximum ("ceiling") rents from public housing and Section 8 tenants (to keep working households in their units as their incomes rise).
- Reduction of the Fair Market Rent (FMR) from the 45th to the 40th percentile of median family income.[4]

Both the CRA and the LIHTC have survived congressional attacks in recent years. However, both are likely to be challenged again: CRA is unpopular with important segments of the banking industry, and eliminating the LIHTC is for some an attractive way to reduce the deficit. Both, however, also have the advantage of not being "on budget," and both have strong advocates—particularly the LIHTC, which is popular among corporate purchasers of tax credits as well as housing advocates and which has bipartisan support from numerous governors and House members (Roberts interview).

As suggested by the above list of rule changes, public housing authorities will have more discretion in selecting tenants, setting rents, and using diminished federal subsidies. One effect of the recent legislation is a subtle undermining of the Brooke Amendment. Minimum rents would mean that rents would no longer be set as a fixed percentage of a family's income. The likely effects of changes to public housing in New York are discussed in detail in this volume in chapter 5 by Phillip Thompson.

A final—and very difficult—issue, described by Bach in chapter 6 in this volume, concerns the problems raised by the expiration of project-based federal housing subsidies. Congress authorized additional funding in FY98 and FY99 for renewal of expiring Section 8 contracts and established a "permanent" mark-to-market program to reduce the subsidies required to support housing projects built under the Section 8 New Construction program (for details, see Chapter 6 in this volume and Edson 1997). However, if this program succeeds, it will address the needs of only a portion of the federally-assisted housing stock. At most immediate risk are FHA-insured developments financed under earlier programs. There has been no federal funding for the preservation of these projects since FY98.

Diminished State Support for the Needy Bodes Ill for Housing

The policy changes affecting New York City do not spring from Washington alone. State spending and policy have long been critical to the well-being of the city, and the broad latitude granted to states under the recently enacted welfare reform legislation heightens the importance of policies set in Albany. Long-standing differences between the Republican-controlled State Senate and the Democrat-controlled Assembly will complicate decision making about reform, but proposals offered by the governor signal clearly the course he will try to chart. These proposals focus more on spending for public assistance and mental health services than on the state's housing programs, but would have immense repercussions for low-income housing in New York City.

Had it been enacted, New York Governor George Pataki's FY96 budget proposal would have fundamentally altered the state's provision of public assistance. Following the lead of federal welfare reform, it included a five-year lifetime limit on the receipt of public assistance (Temporary Assistance For Needy Families [TANF]). In addition, it would have (a) limited Home Relief for single individuals and childless couples to sixty days; (b) reduced the average welfare grant by about 25 percent (consistent with the fact that federal block grants for public assistance will constitute a reduction in federal funding for this purpose); and (c) eliminated New York's welfare shelter allowance by establishing "a single flat grant allowance in which recipients would get a single grant instead of separate grants for food, shelter, heating fuels and special needs" (Citizens Housing and Planning Council 1996).

On the positive side, the proposal would have allowed public assistance recipients to offset part of their benefit losses with wages or other income. It also would have revised state regulations that treat doubled-up families as single households eligible for only one set of welfare benefits. Finally, it would have offered a Basic Care for the

Needy program for households that are dropped from the welfare rolls. Designed to conform to New York's constitutional mandate to provide for the needy, the program would have provided "in-kind support for food, clothing, and assistance in finding a job."

The governor's budget for FY96 also proposed a 25 percent reduction in funding for the state's Office of Mental Health (OMH). The governor would have restructured most of the OMH's programs into block grants to be administered by cities and counties. The proposed budget cut included the abandonment of the Community Mental Health Reinvestment Act. Signed in 1993, the Act transfers $180 million in savings over five years from closing and downsizing state mental hospitals to community-based programs. It also earmarks $30 million specifically for the homeless mentally ill (Foderaro 1996). Many providers of transitional and permanent housing for the homeless receive OMH funding for mental health services, case management, and in some cases security. A budget reduction of anything approaching the proposed size would almost certainly have resulted in decreased services for the homeless.

The governor failed to persuade the legislature to pass these changes in welfare and mental health policy in the fiscal 1996 budget. He proposed similar measures for the following year's budget, which also failed to gain legislative approval. In 1997 Governor Pataki signed the Welfare Reform Act of 1997, New York State's response to the federal welfare reform legislation. The Act institutes life-time limits of five-years for TANF benefits and two years for Home Relief.

WHERE THE RUBBER MEETS THE ROAD: HOW NEW YORK CITY IS LIKELY TO FARE

The impacts of these federal and state fiscal and programmatic changes on localities will vary considerably, depending on local demographics, market conditions, and housing policies. As noted earlier, New York City has been active and imaginative in using federal housing and community development resources to develop a package of programs customized to the city's distinctive housing conditions and problems. This section highlights key elements of New York City's housing programs and strategies, including its unique use of Section 8 certificates and vouchers. It then considers the impact of likely federal and state changes on those programs and on low-cost housing and neighborhoods more generally.

The City's Multifaceted Housing Programs

The current rethinking of federal and state housing and welfare policy comes at a time of transition for New York City's housing policy. In 1986, the city launched a ten-year plan to build, renovate, and preserve more than 250,000 units of housing at a cost of $4.2 billion (Willis 1987). In the subsequent ten years New York City invested far more resources in affordable housing than any other locality. A 1989 study, for example, found that New York had committed more own-source revenue to housing than the fifty next largest cities combined (Berenyi 1989), and its housing commitments were still rising. From FY87 through FY96, the city committed $4.2 billion of capital budget funds for the construction and renovation of more than 150,000 housing units. Annual capital commitments increased sharply from $149 million in FY87 to $738 million in FY89, the peak year (Figure 9.1). As a proportion of the city's total capital fund expenditures, housing rose from 2 percent in 1986 to a high of 16 percent in 1991 and 1992 (New York City Office of the Comptroller). Then, faced with worsening budget deficits and competing demands for capital dollars, the city began scaling back. Capital commitments for housing in FY96, at $273 million, were about one-third the total for 1989. By FY95, New York's housing expenditures had fallen to 8 percent of the city's total capital budget (New York City Office of the Comptroller).

The city's ten-year plan embraced a wide range of programs for building and renovating housing. As a result of a sustained period of private landlord disinvestment in low-cost rental properties, the city had accumulated over 110,000 *in rem* (tax foreclosed) housing units by 1987; of these, 64,000 were vacant (Willis 1987, 17). As described by Braconi in chapter 4 in this volume, several city programs have been implemented to manage and dispose of this extensive inventory. The ten-year plan also included several programs for moderate rehabilitation of multifamily buildings at risk of abandonment and foreclosure, as well as programs to assist individual homeowners.

Vacant buildings underwent gut rehabilitation under a number of programs involving both nonprofit and for-profit sponsors. From FY87 through FY96 gut rehab accounted for 29 percent of the housing units constructed or renovated with assistance from the city's Department of Housing Preservation and Development (HPD) and 61 percent of HPD's capital expenditures (Figure 9.2). In some areas with large concentrations of vacant land and buildings, HPD supported new construction instead of gut rehab. Large tracts of land were cleared and redeveloped in the innovative private/public partnerships described

FIGURE 9.1
HPD Construction Starts and Capital Expenditures for Housing

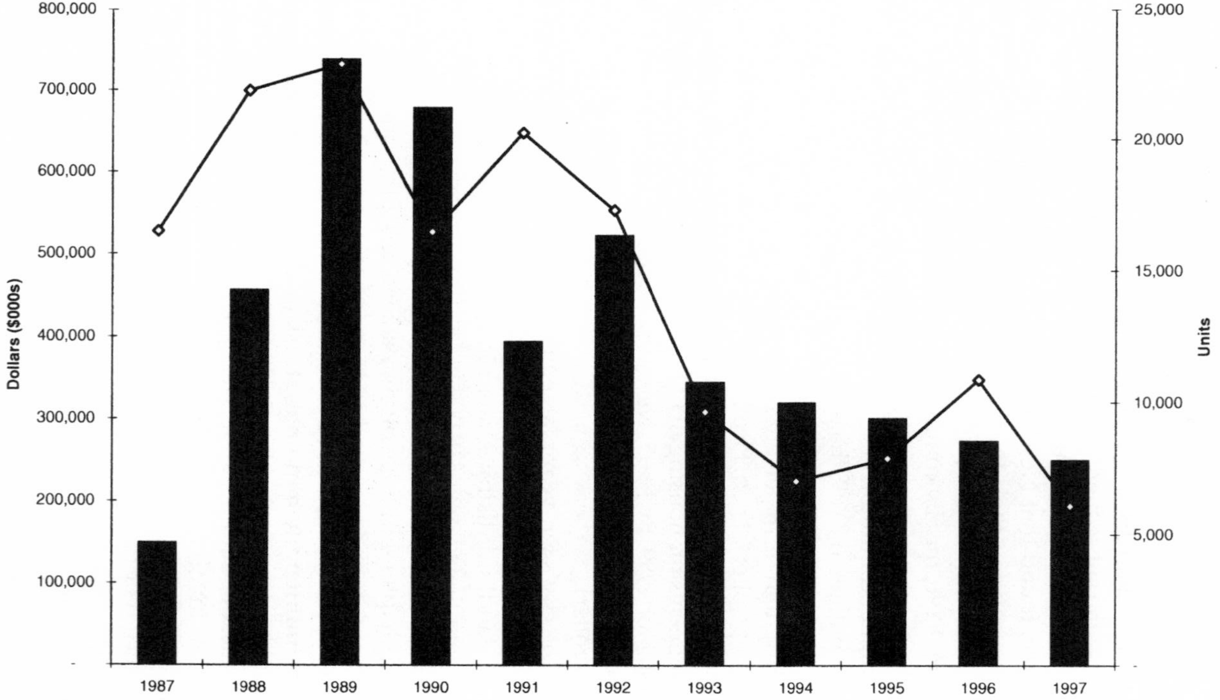

Source: New York City Department of Housing Preservation and Development.
Note: Bars refer to housing units and lines refer to capital expenditures.

FIGURE 9.2
Porportion of HPD-Funded Housing Developments by Type of
Construction, Fiscal 1987–1996

Percent of Total Units

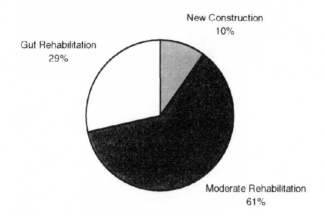

Percent of Total Expenditures

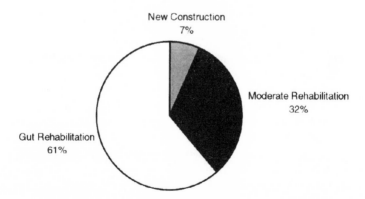

Source: New York City Department of Housing Preservation and Development.

by Wylde in chapter 3 that subsidized single-family and two- to three-family housing for moderate-income families. New construction represented 10 percent of all HPD-assisted starts from FY87 through FY96 and about 7 percent of total capital expenditures. By the early 1990s, much of the city's inventory of vacant buildings had been depleted, especially those buildings with twenty or more units (that is, those that were most cost effective to rehabilitate and manage).

The occupied *in rem* stock now falls under two broad categories. Buildings in the worst physical condition and of the smallest size are generally managed directly by HPD. Other occupied buildings, usually larger and in better condition, are overseen by HPD's Division of Alternative Management Programs (DAMP). DAMP oversees several programs, described in detail by Braconi in chapter 4 in this volume, in which nonprofit community-based organizations, tenant organizations, and, at times, private landlords and management companies, oversee moderate rehabilitation. When the renovation is completed the property is sold at a nominal price to the nonprofit community group or private landlord as a rental building or to the tenants as a limited-equity cooperative (Housing Development Fund Corporation, or HDFC).

Since the city's policy objective is to move the entire *in rem* stock from public ownership and management, HPD also seeks to head off foreclosures that would add to its inventory. Hence the agency has helped fund the moderate rehabilitation of privately owned buildings that are at risk of abandonment or tax delinquency. Under these programs the city provides low-interest loans, often in tandem with market-rate bank financing, for major capital improvements. Altogether, the moderate rehabilitation of occupied *in rem* housing and privately owned housing accounted for 61 percent of all HPD-assisted units from FY87 through FY96 and about 32 percent of total capital expenditures (Figure 9.2).

The *in rem* stock has decreased substantially in recent years as the city has transferred thousands of new and rehabilitated buildings to private and nonprofit owners and, more recently, stopped foreclosing on tax delinquent buildings. By 1998, only 27,412 occupied units and 7,563 units in vacant buildings remained in the *in rem* stock.

In 1995, New York revamped its approach toward the remaining *in rem* stock (see Braconi, chapter 4 in this volume). It decided to encourage the renovation and sale of the remaining *in rem* housing to private owners, including private entrepreneurs, nonprofit community groups, and building residents. Toward this end, HPD introduced the Building Blocks! program, under which the agency clusters nearby vacant and occupied buildings into single developments for simultaneous rehabilitation. After rehabilitation, vacant units are rented out at market rents to compensate for the low rents of occupied units (which cannot be increased). The Neighborhood Entrepreneurs Program (NEP) assigns clusters of vacant and occupied buildings to locally based for-profit property managers; the Neighborhood Redevelopment Program

(NRP) does the same with nonprofit community-based organizations. Forming the third element of Building Blocks! is the Tenant Interim Lease program (TIL), under which buildings undergo moderate rehabilitation and are converted into limited equity cooperatives. Unlike NEP and NRP, TIL is limited to individual occupied buildings and does not include vacant buildings.

The future of these programs, and the low-cost housing and neighborhoods they help support, is intimately tied to the fate of federal housing programs and policies—and is therefore tenuous. The most significant changes in federal policy for New York City's low-income housing include the reform of the public housing program, the slow growth of incremental tenant-based Section 8 subsidies, and welfare reform. In chapter 5 in this volume, Thompson discusses the impact of changes in the public housing program on the New York City Housing Authority and its tenants. The remaining sections of this chapter examine how cutbacks in Section 8 are likely to affect the production and preservation of low-income housing in New York City, and consider the ramifications of welfare reform (and possible cuts in funding for mental health services) on the city's low-income housing.

The Unique Role of Tenant-Based Section 8 in New York City

The Section 8 existing housing program has been critical to the provision of low-income housing in New York City. In 1996, approximately 87,000 households in New York City received tenant-based Section 8 subsidies. Almost 82 percent of these certificates and vouchers were issued by the New York City Housing Authority (NYCHA), which in addition to running the nation's largest public housing system also administers the largest tenant-based Section 8 program (Table 9.1). HPD has issued an additional 13,000 certificates and vouchers, mostly to residents of HPD-supported developments, and the New York State Department of Housing and Community Renewal (DHCR) has provided certificates and vouchers to about 3,500 households in New York City.

Tenant-based Section 8 certificates and vouchers do more than enable tens of thousands of low-income families to reside in decent, unsubsidized, privately owned housing without confronting an excessive cost burden. They are also central to the financial viability of thousands of low-income rental and cooperative housing developments built or renovated with the city's support. Most of New York City's housing programs rely on the presence of Section 8 voucher and certificate holders to generate necessary revenue. Section 8 is important for two key reasons. First, it stabilizes the rent roll by keeping the recipient's out-of-pocket

TABLE 9.1
New York City Households with Tenant-Based Section 8 Subsidies, 1996

Issuing Agency	Total Section 8 Certificates and Vouchers Issued	Approximate Number of Existing Certificates and Vouchers That Are "Recycled" Annually
New York City Housing Authority	71,000	4,000
New York City Department of Housing Preservation and Development	12,500	900
New York State Division of Housing and Community Renewal	3,500	300
Total	87,000	5,200

Sources: Sole interview, Geller interview, and Kedzierski interview.

rent expenses at 30 percent of income, regardless of how much this income may decrease. Second, and less widely appreciated, Section 8 certificates and vouchers generate additional revenue for the landlord. The Fair Market Rent for Section 8 certificates and vouchers greatly exceeds the rents that most low-income households can afford and what most other housing subsidy programs will allow.[5] For example, the 1996 FMR in New York City for a two-bedroom unit was $817 per month, substantially higher than the typical $475 per month rent for two-bedroom units in developments recently underwritten under the city's Local Initiatives Support Corporation (LISC)/Enterprise Foundation Tax Credit Program. Thus, the presence of Section 8 tenants increases a development's rent roll, enabling the owner to better maintain the property, to provide additional services, to build up reserves, and to tolerate somewhat higher operating costs and/or vacancy and arrearage losses.

Even though they are tenant-based subsidies, Section 8 certificates and vouchers are integral to many of the city's low-income housing programs. The LISC/Enterprise Tax Credit Program provides certificates and vouchers to 30 percent of a development's initial tenants, all of whom are formerly homeless. The underwriting assumes that these tenants will continue to receive Section 8 for five years; afterward, rents are assumed to decrease to the TANF shelter allowance. The additional revenue generated during this five-year period is used to build up the development's operating reserves. Similarly, the city's Special Initiatives Program (SIP) provides Section 8 certificates and vouchers to 60 percent of the tenants in the buildings it develops; all of these Section 8 recipients are formerly homeless. The rent revenue generated by the Section 8 certificates and vouchers enables the nonprofit sponsors of this housing to provide social services to the residents.

Tenant-based Section 8 has also been critical to programs involving for-profit property owners. Under the Participation Loan Program, for example, landlords obtain a package of bank and city loans to finance replacement of major building systems. Rents are adjusted to cover the costs of these improvements. To prevent displacement, the city issues Section 8 certificates and vouchers to tenants unable to afford these increased rents. Thus the 13,000 Section 8 certificates and vouchers issued by HPD to residents of HPD-financed housing keeps many additional units viable by contributing to their developments' bottom line.

For the first time since the program's inception, HUD did not issue any new (that is, incremental) Section 8 certificates or vouchers during the mid-1990s. Despite the reduction of Section 8 incremental subsidies, the city has a limited number of existing vouchers or certificates available for distribution each year. When Section 8 recipients die, move into nursing homes, move out of the city, or lose their eligibility, the certificate or voucher is returned to the issuing agency, which can then use the remaining period of the subsidy to assist another household. On average about 5,000 certificates and vouchers are recycled in this way every year, representing about 6 percent of the total number of certificates and vouchers in circulation. However, in recent years, the federal government ordered all issuing agencies to retain all returned certificates and vouchers for three months before issuing them to new families. In effect, this constituted a one-time reduction of 25 percent, forcing issuing agencies to recycle only 75 percent of the certificates and vouchers that were turned in. Although the Quality Housing and Work Responsibility Act of 1998 eliminated the three month holding period, the reductions have had an impact on city housing.

Although Congress appropriated funds for an additional 50,000 Section 8 vouchers in FY99, the rate of growth in incremental subsides lags the 1980s. In addition, most of the new vouchers will be earmarked for welfare-to-work initiatives and therefore not be freely available to municipalites such as New York. Federal cutbacks in Section 8, coupled with a more stringent capital budget for housing, are forcing New York to rethink its priorities, policies, and programs for producing new affordable housing and for preserving the existing stock. The city must devise new ways of funding housing production and preservation. The challenge is perhaps slightly less daunting on the production front, if only because new construction involves vacant buildings and empty lots, not occupied apartments. However, housing production is contingent on the continued availability of the LIHTC and on CDBG and HOME block grants. Without these programs, new development will be highly problematic if not impossible.

Section 8 and Housing Development

The city will undoubtedly fund less housing development in the future than it has in the past, and will revamp how it underwrites the housing it does develop. With a diminished supply of Section 8 subsidies, HPD must either target new production to higher-income households or find a way to fund significantly larger operating reserves. The city's current multifamily development programs mostly house very low-income households, at least 30 percent of whom are formerly homeless. Continuing to serve this target population will now require greatly increased operating reserves, which will almost certainly be tapped immediately to cover the inevitable shortfall between rents and operating costs. Indeed, HPD officials anticipate that the equity obtained from tax credits will be used exclusively to establish reserve funds; the city expects to use its own resources to cover construction costs.[6] In the case of supportive housing, the reserve funds would be used for both operating costs and social services.

The increased reliance on operating reserves to cover current expenses has also forced the city to reconsider the income mix of the tenants of new developments. If the city were to maximize the benefit of the LIHTC, the incomes of all tenants could not exceed 60 percent of New York's median family income. Even within this limitation, new developments could require less subsidy and lower operating reserves if they housed fewer homeless families and others with incomes far below the LIHTC's income threshold (for example, tenants with incomes at 50 percent of the area median income would be able to pay significantly higher rents than families at 30 percent or below). Should public assistance benefits be reduced, there is even more incentive to focus on higher-income families since they are likely to be headed by someone who is employed and not on public assistance.

If the city were willing to allocate its housing resources to developments that did not utilize the LIHTC, new production could focus on moderate- and middle-income households. Homeowner housing, whether single-family or two- or three-family housing, would then comprise a larger portion of the city's total housing development activity. Indeed, such structures now account for most of the city's remaining inventory of vacant buildings; almost all of the large multifamily buildings have already been renovated. Not only would an emphasis on homeowner housing reduce the need for operating subsidies, but, as Wylde indicates in chapter 3, it could save the city additional funds by permitting increased private financing.

Besides increasing income eligibility standards, the city could also decide to reduce the scope—and therefore the cost—of future developments. For example, instead of investing, say, $80,000 per unit, HPD could forgo certain improvements and spend perhaps $50,000 instead.

In some parts of the city, HPD may be able to continue to combine vacant and occupied buildings into a single development scheme so that the vacant units could be rented out at market rates, thereby cross-subsidizing the lower rents paid by current tenants. Indeed, this is the approach the city has adopted in two of its leading housing rehabilitation programs—the Neighborhood Entrepreneurs Program (NEP) for for-profit neighborhood-based landlords and the Neighborhood Redevelopment Program (NRP) for neighborhood-based nonprofit organizations (see chapter 4 by Braconi in this volume). However, this strategy may be of limited applicability due to the fact that the supply of vacant housing is very unevenly distributed and in some locations it may be very difficult to find families willing to pay market rents even in renovated buildings.

Section 8 and Homeless Housing

The reduction of incremental Section 8 subsidies also deprives New York of a critical resource in responding to its homelessness crisis. As noted above, most of HPD's Section 8 recipients are formerly homeless. So are an even greater number of households with NYCHA-issued Section 8 certificates and vouchers. As Culhane, Metraux, and Wachter observe in chapter 8 in this volume, many homeless families require assistance in paying their rents even though they may not need extensive social or community services. Without Section 8, housing these families would require extremely large operating reserves or other subsidies.

Section 8 and Preservation of Low-Income Housing

A longer term but perhaps more profound issue concerns the renewal of expiring Section 8 certificates and vouchers. Whereas the expiration of project-based subsidies has been widely discussed since the late 1980s (see Bach, chapter 6 in this volume), the renewal of tenant-based subsidies has received little attention since President Reagan reduced the term of certificates and vouchers from fifteen to five years.[7] In 1996, however, both HUD and President Clinton expressed some support for the idea of making Section 8 contracts renewable for only one year—a response to the rapidly mounting cost of renewing existing subsidies at a time of tight HUD budgets.[8] If these two budgetary trends continue, as seems likely, proposals to reduce the length of renewed Section 8 contracts, reduce Fair Market Rents, or otherwise decrease subsidy outlays will receive increasingly serious attention, because they are an obvious way to prevent Section 8 renewals from "squeezing out" discretionary spending on programs like HOME and CDBG.

A reduction in the length of Section 8 housing vouchers and certificates would create problems both for city government and Section 8 recipients. As the term of Section 8 vouchers declines, so too does their ability to guarantee a stream of rents, which in turn support the underwriting of new developments. This would undermine the city's ability to move city-owned units back into private or nonprofit ownership and management. NYCHA, HPD, and DHCR can draw on "unfunded Section 8 reserves" (that is, unspent budget authority) to extend subsidies for households in the event that the renewal of their vouchers is delayed (giving families and their landlords some added security). However, these reserves are limited and after a transitional period of perhaps two years would be depleted.

The possible expiration of tenant-based assistance also arouses concern for the residents of public housing and of HUD-assisted housing that might be "vouchered out" under several proposals currently being discussed in Washington (see Thompson's discussion in chapter 5 in this volume). Tenants whose project-based assistance would be converted to vouchers would be extremely vulnerable to the termination of their rent subsidies and therefore might be viewed by landlords as comparatively risky and less desirable tenants.

The expiration of Section 8 subsidies would be debilitating to both tenants and landlords. Cessation of rental assistance would make thousands of low-income renters unable to afford their homes. As Schill and Scafidi describe in chapter 1 in this volume, almost one-quarter of all tenants in New York City already pay over half their incomes for rent. Overall, the 71,000 recipients of NYCHA-issued Section 8 subsidies reside in buildings owned by 24,000 private landlords (Harold Sole interview). Many owners have a high concentration of Section 8 renters. For example, 15 to 20 percent of the tenants in privately owned buildings assisted by the Community Preservation Corporation have Section 8 subsidies. Similarly, one-fourth of the residents in the seventeen buildings that in 1996 were being converted into limited-equity coops under the city's Ownership Transfer Program held Section 8 certificates or vouchers and an additional quarter had pending Section 8 applications. Jointly administered by HPD, the Community Service Society, and the Chase Community Development Corporation, the Ownership Transfer Program takes multifamily buildings at risk of abandonment and works with residents to convert them into cooperatives and make the necessary capital improvements. Without Section 8, many residents could not afford the higher rents that are necessary to pay for these improvements.

When Section 8 is provided to the tenants of renovated buildings as a means to prevent displacement, the subsidy is limited to current tenants. If Section 8 tenants move out, the units they vacate can be rented out at market rates. Thus, if Section 8 subsidies expire, landlords could legally evict former voucher holders if they were unable to pay their increased rents. However, many observers question the likelihood of widespread evictions. Landlords will need to decide whether to evict tenants—many of whom they have known for years—or to accept lower rents and perhaps cut back on building services. Furthermore, Housing Court judges are likely to prolong if not thwart eviction proceedings for fear of increasing the homeless problem (see Galowitz, chapter 7 in this volume).

HOUSING AND NEIGHBORHOOD IMPACTS OF WELFARE REFORM

Welfare reform poses challenges to New York City's housing that are at least as profound as, if slightly less immediate than, the curtailment of Section 8. More than 500,000 New York City households, nearly one-fifth of the city's total, received TANF or Home Relief in 1996. At least half of these households did not receive any other housing subsidies or live in rent controlled apartments.[9] Benefit reductions, time limits, and eligibility restrictions—the hallmarks of the welfare reform legislation enacted in 1996—are likely to reduce the already low incomes of many households currently receiving public assistance.[10] To the extent that this occurs, welfare reform will impair the ability of recipient households to pay their rents, causing rent arrears to increase and making it increasingly difficult for building owners to maintain their buildings and pay their property taxes. Furthermore, over time, decreased rent collection can be expected to reduce the value of many rental properties.

These reductions in public assistance income, and their consequences, have the potential to produce strong neighborhood impacts. Neighborhoods with large concentrations of families on public assistance will be especially vulnerable to cutbacks. One-third of all households on public assistance reside in just nine neighborhoods, and half live in just fourteen neighborhoods (Table 9.2). In some neighborhoods

TABLE 9.2

Households on Public Assistance in 1992 Ranked by New York City
Neighborhood

Rank	Neighborhood	Total Households	Total Households on Public Assistance	Cumulative Percent of Households on Public Assistance
1	Mott Haven/Hunts Point	37,478	22,749	4.7
2	Morrisania/East Tremont	39,019	20,836	8.9
3	Washington Heights/Inwood	73,748	18,953	12.8
4	Highbridge/South Concourse	34,085	17,486	16.4
5	Soundview/Parkchester	57,124	17,194	20.0
6	East Harlem	42,098	17,176	23.5
7	Brownsville/Ocean Hill	35,838	16,485	26.9
8	Lower East Side/Chinatown	66,027	16,045	30.2
9	Central Harlem	40,512	16,002	33.5
10	Bushwick	35,263	15,904	36.7
11	University Heights/Fordham	36,403	15,726	39.9
12	Bedford Stuyvesant	39,047	14,447	42.9
13	East New York/Starrett City	41,292	13,668	45.7
14	Kingsbridge Heights/Mosholu	40,624	13,325	48.5
15	North Crown Heights/Prospect Heights	42,764	12,701	51.1
16	Coney Island	44,885	11,984	53.5
17	Williamsburg/Greenpoint	45,156	11,424	55.9
18	Morningside Heights/Hamilton Heights	42,946	11,338	58.2
19	South Crown Heights	39,055	11,053	60.5
20	Sunset Park	40,744	9,086	62.3
21	Sheepshead Bay/Gravesend	56,523	8,818	64.1
22	Bensonhurst	62,363	8,481	65.9
23	Astoria	69,385	8,396	67.6
24	Jamaica	62,177	8,394	69.3
25	Upper West Side	109,903	8,133	71.0
26	Brooklyn Heights/Fort Greene	44,068	8,020	72.6
27	Jackson Heights	47,268	7,894	74.3
28	Flatbush	53,996	7,613	75.8
29	Rockaways	34,495	6,796	77.2
30	Park Slope/Carroll Gardens	40,690	6,551	78.6
31	Riverdale/Kingsbridge	41,276	6,357	79.9
32	Pelham Parkway	43,043	5,768	81.1
33	North Shore	53,057	5,730	82.2
34	Elmhurst/Corona	39,856	5,699	83.4
35	Williamsbridge/Baychester	43,374	5,595	84.6
36	East Flatbush	44,707	5,365	85.7
37	Chelsea/Clinton/Midtown	65,601	5,051	86.7
38	Flushing/Whitestone	83,895	5,034	87.7
39	Borough Park	45,652	5,022	88.8
40	Kew Gardens/Woodhaven	38,875	4,626	89.7
41	Hillcrest/Fresh Meadows	52,084	4,583	90.6

TABLE 9.2 *(continued)*

Rank	Neighborhood	Total Households	Total Households on Public Assistance	Cumulative Percent of Households on Public Assistance
42	Forest Hills/Rego Park	53,717	4,566	91.6
43	Upper East Side	123,307	4,069	92.4
44	Flatlands/Canarsie	59,549	4,049	93.3
45	Bay Ridge	48,008	3,121	93.9
46	Sunnyside/Woodside	41,110	3,001	94.5
47	Middle Village/Ridgewood	55,102	2,976	95.1
48	Throgs Neck/Co-op City	38,510	2,965	95.7
49	Howard Beach/South Ozone Park	36,158	2,061	96.2
50	Stuyvesant Town/Turtle Bay	86,903	1,912	96.5
51	South Shore	43,847	1,754	96.9
52	Greenwich Village/Financial District	59,561	1,608	97.2
53	Mid-Island	39,564	1,543	97.6
54	Bayside/Little Neck	39,835	—	97.6
55	Bellerose/Rosedale	55,580	—	97.6
	New York City Total	2,783,150	487,051	

Source: Blackburn (1995).
Notes: Public Assistance includes AFDC, Home Relief, and SSI. Neighborhood totals do not add to 100 percent of city totals because of low representation of Public Assistance households in some neighborhoods samples.

welfare is the single largest source of income (Sexton 1996). Neighborhoods with concentrations of immigrant households will feel the ill effects first, since the federal welfare reform statute makes even some legal immigrants who are not citizens immediately ineligible for benefits. New York will be especially hard hit by this provision because of its disproportionately large immigrant population; over 30 percent of the city's residents are foreign born (Pear 1996).

While welfare reform will have national consequences for low-income housing, the impact in New York City is likely to be especially severe. Unlike most states, New York State partitions TANF and Home Relief benefits into three components: a shelter allowance, a grant for heating fuel, and a basic grant for other living expenses. State law requires the shelter allowance to bear a reasonable relationship to the actual cost of housing. In addition to benefit reductions, work requirements, and eligibility restrictions, welfare reform proposals in New York have also sought to consolidate these separate grants into a single lump sum. For example, in 1996 Governor Pataki unsuccessfully attempted not only to impose time limits for TANF and Home Relief but also to pool the three welfare components grants into a single grant so that total benefits would be reduced by about 25 percent (Citizens Housing and Planning Council 1996; Hernandez 1996).

Eliminating the shelter allowance would have major impacts on New York City. It would make moot a long-standing class-action law suit challenging the adequacy of the state's welfare shelter allowance. In 1996, the shelter allowance for New York City residents was $215 for one-person households, $312 for four-person households, and higher amounts for larger families. It has not been increased since 1988. The average New York City welfare recipient must therefore augment his or her shelter allowance with more than $140 from his or her "basic" welfare grant to pay the rent (Citizens Housing and Planning Council 1996).

The *Jiggetts v. Grinker* lawsuit was filed in 1987 in an effort to remedy this situation. During the pendency of this litigation, a state trial court ordered the State Department of Social Services to provide rental allowances above the statutory maximums. As a result of *Jiggetts*, supplemental rent payments of up to 210 percent of the maximum shelter allowance were made for TANF-eligible households at risk of eviction.[11] At the end of 1995 approximately 22,000 households received such relief (Crawford interview), with supplemental rent payments averaging $234 per month (Citizens Housing and Planning Council 1996). By eliminating the shelter allowance, and specifying specific welfare benefit levels in legislation, the Governor's 1996 welfare proposal would have undermined the *Jiggetts* litigation. Should the State Legislature eventually abolish the shelter allowance as part of welfare reform, the thousands of families currently benefiting from *Jiggetts* could see their supplemental rent payments come to an abrupt end.

The elimination of the shelter allowance would also call into question the state's current system for making restricted rent payments for welfare recipients. Without a separate shelter allowance, it is unclear whether the city's Human Resource Administration (HRA) and other social service agencies could continue to make rent payments to the welfare recipient's landlord through two-party checks or direct vendor payments. More than 150,000 households on public assistance in New York City are subject to restricted rent payments, including an estimated 40 percent of the tenants in HPD-owned buildings (Citizens Housing and Planning Council 1996). Without restricted rent payments, landlords would likely see increased rent delinquency, especially if overall benefit levels were decreased. Landlords might respond to this increased probability of nonpayment by discriminating against tenants who receive public assistance.

HOUSING AND MENTAL HEALTH FUNDING

Any discussion of the policy environment for low-income housing in New York City would not be complete without considering funding and programs for mental health services. Federal and especially state mental health programs have been central to homeless and special-needs housing. Mental health programs have helped fund the development of special-needs housing and the provision of case management, security, and other support services for this housing. For example, the state's Office of Mental Health (OMH), under the "New York, New York" agreement, financed the development of 1,913 units of assisted housing in New York City to accommodate the increased demand for such housing brought about by the closure of state psychiatric facilities. As of 1996, all but 2 percent of the OMH-funded units in New York City were completed. No additional housing development is planned even though the state continues to close large state mental hospitals.

Governor Pataki has proposed several changes in the state's mental health funding that would have sharply curtailed these services, including a 25 percent reduction in the OMH budget (Foderaro 1996, Hernandez 1996). Although the Legislature has, to date, thwarted his proposal, homeless and special-needs housing remains vulnerable to any future cutbacks in mental health funding.

COPING WITH THE FUTURE

Individually, most of the foreseeable policy and funding changes at the federal and state level could be dealt with by New York City in some way. Some would cause more pain than others, and most would move the city's housing policy in the direction of less production and more financially fragile rental properties. Ultimately, the magnitude of any impact on the city will depend on how many of the proposed changes materialize and on what timetable; if many take effect, or if several are enacted at about the same time, they could deal the city a significant blow—with unhappy ramifications for subsidized households, landlords in all three sectors, and inner-city neighborhoods.

Federal and state policy changes involving public assistance and rent subsidies will invariably cause rent rolls to decline in thousands of buildings housing low-income families. Building owners—both non-profit and for profit—will need to search out new ways of controlling their operating costs. The city will have to assist in this effort to avoid having rental properties deteriorate and fall into tax arrears. The most obvious types of relief involve water and sewer rates and tax assessments.

Water and sewer costs have escalated sharply since the late 1980s. The rising cost of water and sewer service is illustrated in the underwriting of rental housing funded under the city's LISC/Enterprise Tax Credit Program. Between 1988 and 1995, the budgeted cost of water skyrocketed from $90 per unit to $500, a 456 percent increase (Jahr interview). Low-income housing is especially vulnerable to increased water and sewer rates. Water consumption tends to be higher in predominantly low-income buildings as compared to other buildings because households are often larger and household members are at home more of the time than is the case in buildings with more affluent households (McCarthy interview). Moreover, the plumbing in buildings with predominantly low-income tenants is often less efficient. In 1994, the city imposed a two-year moratorium on water and sewer rate increases. It capped water and sewer charges at $500 and gave building owners the option of paying water and sewer charges based on building frontage (the system in place when most buildings were built) or metered water consumption (the newer system developed to promote water conservation). The city renewed this moratorium in 1996 and is likely to do so again. In the long term, however, the city must move beyond these stopgap measures and fundamentally restructure how water usage is billed so that affordable housing is not unduly burdened.

A second area for intervention concerns property taxes. The city should review its property tax assessments, especially in low-income communities. Real estate taxes have increased sharply in many of the city's poorest neighborhoods. According to a 1995 report by the Rent Guidelines Board of New York City, real estate taxes for rent stabilized buildings increased by 7 to 10 percent from FY94 to FY95 in such neighborhoods as Mott Haven/Hunts Point, Morrisania/Belmont, and Highbridge/South Concourse in the South Bronx and in the Brooklyn neighborhoods of Bushwick, Crown Heights, and Brownsville. In contrast, real taxes rose by only 0.5 percent for rent stabilized buildings in Manhattan (Rent Guidelines Board of New York 1995). Perversely, real estate tax increases are not affecting the low-income housing developed or renovated with city subsidies, most of which benefit from tax abatements. Instead, the increases have hit the private, unassisted stock. By improving neighborhood conditions, buildings renovated through the city's low-income housing programs seem to have stimulated higher tax assessments for surrounding properties. These buildings, which house very low-income families and are already pressed to cover their operating costs, now, themselves, require assistance.

NOTES

1. HOME is a block grant program that supports the development of homes affordable to low- and moderate-income home buyers. CDBG, itself the product of program consolidation undertaken in 1974, provides funds that enable communities to carry out a wide range of community development activities. The McKinney Act created a variety of programs, many operated by nonprofit organizations, to assist homeless households.

2. These changes were initially passed by the 104th Congress as temporary measures and made permanent in 1998.

3. The Federal government had required public housing authorities to give preference in allocating housing subsidies to very low-income households (below 50 percent of area median) that are either homeless, spending at least 50 percent of their income on housing, or are living in physically deficient housing.

4. One temporary measure that was not made permanent was the imposition of a three month delay in the reissuance of tenant-based Section 8 certificates and vouchers. Typically, when a Section 8 certificate voucher holder dies, moves into a nursing home, moves out of the metropolitan area, or becomes no longer eligible for a rental subsidy, the certificate or voucher is then turned over to NYCHA or HPD to be reissued to another eligible household.

5. While Section 8 certificates cover the difference between 30 percent of a tenant's income and Fair Market Rents, the rents provided by Section 8 vouchers are usually somewhat less. They are established by a "Payment Standard" set by local housing authorities as a percentage of the FMR. In New York City, the voucher Payment Standard is 80 percent of FMR.

6. For example, in August 1996 the city announced that nineteen large New York City companies had invested $147 million in Low-income Housing Tax Credits for the renovation of about 3,200 apartments. Most of this funding will be used as operating reserves to help subsidize the rents of low-income residents (Lueck 1996).

7. Technically, HUD does not renew individual certificates and vouchers. Public housing authorities and other agencies issue Section 8 certificates and vouchers to households. These certificates and vouchers are funded through Annual Contribution Contracts the issuing agency enters into with HUD. From the inception of the Section 8 program to 1983, these Annual Contribution Contracts had a budget authority of fifteen years. The Reagan Administration reduced the budget authority for Section 8 certificates to five years. When the budget authority of an Annual Contribution Contract expired, HUD always re-funded them so that the issuing agency could continue to assist the original certificate and voucher holders. While the sponsors of Section 8 New Construction and Substantial Rehabilitation projects entered into a subsidy contract directly with HUD and are therefore in-

formed of the duration of the subsidy period, recipients of tenant-based Section 8 do not have the same contractual relationship with HUD. Indeed, until recently, issuing agencies have not had to specify the duration of the subsidy period at all. However, in FY96 HUD informed all issuing agencies that they must use standard HUD forms when enrolling households into the Section 8 program. These forms stipulate that the duration of the subsidy is contingent on funding availability; the government, in effect, now reserves the right to terminate the subsidy at any time.

8. The cost of renewing Section 8 contracts has been rising exponentially—the same phenomenon that ultimately led to the end of the Section 8 New Construction Program. The cost of renewing all expiring tenant-based Section 8 certificates and vouchers rose from $0.5 billion in FY94 to $2.1 billion in FY95 and $4.3 billion in FY96. Contract renewals are expected to reach $10.4 billion in FY98, and to hit $16.1 billion by the year 2000 (GAO 1993; National Low-income Housing Coalition and National Congress for Community Economic Development 1996).

9. The 1993 Housing and Vacancy Survey shows that two-thirds of the 487,000 households on public assistance (AFDC, Home Relief, and SSI) in 1992 did not live in public housing, other subsidized housing, *in rem* housing, or rent controlled housing. The survey does not cover tenant-based housing subsidies, but if one were to make the highly unlikely assumption that all the 80,000 or so New York households then with Section 8 certificates or vouchers also received public assistance, there would still be about 234,000 households on public assistance without any housing subsidies, 48 percent of the total (Blackburn 1995).

10. Advocates of welfare reform have pointed to the success of some state reform efforts, most notably in Wisconsin, at moving TANF recipients into the workforce in an effort to argue that welfare reform will improve the well-being (and, by inference, the incomes) of TANF recipients. However, the ability of states and localities to replicate the Wisconsin experience hinges centrally on the ability of local economies to absorb significant numbers of new, typically low-skilled workers. The low likelihood that the city's economy is up to this challenge is signaled by the fact that enactment of federal welfare reform legislation spurred the city and the state to prepare for a major increase in the workfare program that permits public assistance recipients who cannot find private sector employment within the specified time limit to work for the public sector in exchange for their benefits (Firestone 1996). Unfortunately, the likelihood that the state and city could find the money to fund the program at its anticipated size is nil. Many of those who do find work, however, like other working-poor households, will benefit from the 1996 federal legislation increasing the minimum wage from $4.25 to $5.15 an hour.

11. For a description of the *Jiggetts* litigation, see Galowitz, chapter 7 in this volume.

References

Berenyi, Eileen. 1989. *Locally Funded Housing Programs in the United States: A Survey of the Fifty-one Most Populated Cities*. New York: Community Development Research Center, New School for Social Research.

Blackburn, Anthony J. 1995. *Housing New York City 1993*. New York: New York City Department of Housing Preservation and Development.

Citizens Housing and Planning Council. 1996. "Pataki Welfare Plan Rattles Housing." *Urban Prospect* 2, 1:1–4.

Edson, Charles L. 1998. "Congress Adopts Permanent Solution to Troubling Contract Renewal Mark-to-Market Issue." *Housing Development Reporter* (Dec. 1):470–72.

Firestone, David. 1996. "New York Girding for Surge in Workfare Jobs." *New York Times*, August 13, A1.

Foderaro, Lisa W. 1996. "Health Advocates Assail Pataki Spending Cuts." *New York Times*, March 6, B5.

Hernandez, Raymond. 1996. "After Standoff, Both Sides Take Credit for Victories." *New York Times*, July 12, B5.

Lueck, Thomas J. 1996. "$147 Million Pledged to Renovate Apartments." *New York Times*, August 9, B3.

National Low-Income Housing Coalition and National Congress for Community Economic Development. 1996. *Federal Policy in Transition: A National Briefing Book on Housing Economic and Community Development*. Washington, D.C.: Author.

New York City Housing Partnership. 1994. *Building in Partnership: A Blueprint for Urban Housing Programs*. New York: New York City Housing Partnership.

New York City Office of the Comptroller. Annual. *City of New York Comprehensive Annual Financial Report of the Comptroller*.

"Pataki Welfare Plan Rattles Housing." 1996. *Urban Prospect* 2, 1:1–4. Published by Citizens Housing and Planning Council.

Pear, Robert. 1996. "Mayor Opposes Some Revisions in Welfare Plan." *New York Times*, July 27, A1.

Rent Guidelines Board of New York. 1995. *Housing NYC: Rents, Markets and Trends '95*. New York: Rent Guidelines Board of New York.

Sexton, Joe. 1996. "The Trickle-Up Economy: Poor Areas Fear a Disaster if Welfare Is Cut." *New York Times*, February 8, B1, B9.

United States Department of Housing and Urban Development. 1996. *Renewing America's Communities from the Ground Up: Continuation of a Plan to Transform the Department of Housing and Urban Development*. Washington, D.C.: United States Department of Housing and Urban Development.

Willis, Mark A. 1987. "Housing: A City Perspective." *City Almanac* 19, 4:16–23.

INTERVIEWS

Jed Abrams, Director of Marketing and Leasing, New York State Office, U.S. Department of Housing and Urban Development. Telephone interview, January 29, 1996.

Eva Alligood, Assistant Program Director, Corporation for Supportive Housing. Telephone interview, February 20, 1996.

Allen Blitz, Director, Housing Development Assistance Program, Community Service Society. Telephone interview, February 23, 1996.

Amy Crawford, Paralegal, Legal Aid Society, Civil Appeals and Law Reform Unit. Telephone interview, January 5, 1996.

Matthew Diller, Fordham University Law School. Telephone interview, February 23, 1996.

Kathleen Dunn, Community Preservation Corporation. Telephone interview, February 14, 1996.

Barry Geller, New York City Department of Housing Preservation and Development (former Director of Rent Subsidies). Telephone interviews, February 15 and 20, 1996.

Steven Greenfield, Executive Director, Association for Community Living. Telephone interview, February 27, 1996.

Marc Jahr, New York City Program Director, Local Initiatives Support Corporation. Telephone interview, February 13 and March 1, 1996.

Linda Kedzierski, Director of New York City Section 8 Program, New York State Department of Housing and Community Renewal. Telephone interview, February 20, 1996.

Michael Lappin, President, Community Preservation Corporation. Telephone interview, February 23, 1996.

Steve Love, New York City Housing Authority. Telephone interview, February 19, 1996.

Laura Mascuch, Director, SRO Housing and New Development, New York City Department of Homeless Services.

John McCarthy, Executive Vice President, Community Preservation Corporation. Telephone interview, March 5, 1996.

Laurie Michelle Miller, Deputy Commissioner, New York City Department of Housing Preservation and Development. Interview, February 27, 1996.

Calvin Parker, Assistant Commissioner, New York City Department of Housing Preservation and Development. Telephone interview, February 14, 1996, and interview, February 27, 1996.

Carla Pedone, Principal Analyst, Congressional Budget Office, U.S. Congress. Telephone interview, February 29, 1996.

Andrew Reicher, Executive Director, Urban Homesteading Assistance Board. Telephone interview, March 5, 1996.

Benson Roberts, Vice President for Policy, Local Initiatives Support Corporation. Telephone interview, February 26, 1996.

Joseph Rosenberg, Assistant Commissioner of Intergovernmental Relations, New York City Department of Housing Preservation and Development. Telephone interview, February 19, 1996.

Jerry Salama, Deputy Commissioner, New York City Department of Housing Preservation and Development. Interview, February 27, 1996.

Harold Sole, Director of Leased Housing, New York City Housing Authority. Telephone interview, February 16, 1996.

Michael Sullivan, Director, Low-Income Housing Tax Credit Program, New York State Department of Housing and Community Renewal. Telephone interview, February 16, 1996.

About the Contributors

VICTOR BACH directs housing policy and research at the Community Service Society (CSS), a nonprofit organization addressing poverty in New York City. He is also Adjunct Professor of Urban Policy at the New School for Social Research. Prior to joining CSS in 1983, Bach served on the graduate faculty at the LBJ School of Public Affairs, and was a research associate at the Brookings Institution. Bach also participates in several Washington task forces dealing with federal housing preservation and provides local assistance to HUD tenants and to organizations assisting them. He holds a Ph.D. in Urban Studies and Planning from M.I.T.

FRANK P. BRACONI is Executive Director of the Citizens Housing and Planning Council of New York. He has written extensively on urban land use and housing issues. Braconi has particular expertise on the subject of *in rem* housing, having been research director with CHPC when it issued its 1992 report, "Preserving New York's Low Income Housing Stock." Braconi holds a master's degree in Economics from New York University and is currently completing his doctoral studies at the CUNY Graduate Center.

DENNIS P. CULHANE is Associate Professor of Social Work at the University of Pennsylvania and a Senior Fellow at the Leonard Davis Institute of Health Economics. His primary area of research is homelessness, with current projects including studies of the neighborhood origins of homelessness in Philadelphia and New York City. He is leading a team in the development of a homeless services management information system that tracks clients' use of services in the continuum of care, funded by HUD, HSS, and Fannie Mae. Culhane has been involved in homelessness and housing issues since working in a homeless shelter in 1982. He joined the University of Pennsylvania faculty in 1990.

PAULA GALOWITZ is Professor of Clinical Law at New York University School of Law. Her responsibilities include supervising students in a wide variety of public interest litigation, including lawsuits involving housing. Galowitz is former Chair of the Committee on Housing Court of the Association of the Bar of the City of New York. She has written articles on housing and women and on the professional norms and obligations of legal service attorneys. Prior to joining the NYU faculty in 1980, she was a staff attorney with the Legal Aid Society of New York.

STEPHEN METRAUX is a doctoral candidate in sociology at the University of Pennsylvania and holds a master's degree in Urban Studies from the University of Texas at Arlington. In addition to research on shelter utilization, he has written on issues of family homelessness, homeless enumeration techniques, and urban skid rows.

PETER D. SALINS is Provost and Vice-Chancellor for Academic Affairs of the State University of New York (SUNY). Prior to his appointment as provost, he was Professor of Urban Planning at Hunter College, Chairman of its Graduate Program in Urban Planning, and Director of its Urban Research Center. He is also a senior fellow of the Manhattan Institute's Center for Civic Innovation and has been editor of its quarterly publication *City Journal*. Salins has written and spoken extensively on policies of housing and development in New York and other American cities. His most recent work in this area includes his book *Scarcity by Design*, written with Gerard Mildner; his chapter "Zoning for Growth and Change" in *Planning and Zoning New York City*; and a number of related articles.

BENJAMIN P. SCAFIDI is Assistant Professor in the School of Policy Studies at Georgia State University. Prior to joining the faculty in 1998, Scafidi was a Research Analyst at the Center for Naval Analysis and a Research Fellow at the Center for Real Estate and Urban Policy at New York University School of Law. Scafidi received his Ph.D. in economics from the University of Virginia. He is presently engaged in research projects involving the role of school vouchers in education finance and the determinants of housing abandonment in New York City.

MICHAEL H. SCHILL is Professor of Law and Urban Planning at New York University School of Law, and Director of the Center for Real Estate and Urban Policy at NYU. Prior to joining the NYU faculty in 1995, he was a Professor of Law and Real Estate at the University of Pennsylvania. He has written a book and several articles on various aspects of housing policy, finance, and discrimination. His current research projects include analyses of the determinants of housing abandonment in New

York City, the impact of public housing on neighborhood poverty rates, the housing and neighborhood conditions of immigrants and a study of enforcement of laws prohibiting discrimination in the housing market. Schill received his A.B. from Princeton University and his J.D. from the Yale Law School.

ALEX F. SCHWARTZ is Associate Professor in the Department of Management and Urban Policy Analysis and Senior Research Associate at the Community Development Research Center at the New School for Social Research. He received his Ph.D. in urban planning from Rutgers University. Schwartz has recently completed studies on the accomplishments of nonprofit community-based organizations in New York State, the economic impact of New York City's housing programs, and the implementation of Community Reinvestment Act agreements. He is currently engaged in an eight-year evaluation of the Annie E. Casey Foundation's Jobs Initiative. His publications focus on housing, economic development, and community reinvestment.

PHILLIP THOMPSON is Assistant Professor of Politics at Barnard College. He also holds an appointment with Columbia School of Business. Prior to joining the faculty, Thompson held several positions in the Dinkins Administration, including a period as Acting General Manager of the New York City Housing Authority. His scholarly interests include housing policy, local politics, and community economic development.

AVIS C. VIDAL is a Principal Research Associate at The Urban Institute in Washington, D.C., where her research examines the role of community-based approaches in improving the well-being of residents of poor, disinvested neighborhoods. Her recent work includes *Community Organizing: Building Social Capital as a Development Strategy*; this book complements previous work, including *Rebuilding Communities*, a core reference on the characteristics and accomplishments of CDCs. Prior to joining the Institute, she served for ten years as Executive Director of the Community Development Research Center and Associate Professor of Urban Policy at the New School for Social Research; six years as Associate Professor at the John F. Kennedy School of Government at Harvard University; and two years as a Senior Analyst on the Legislative and Urban Policy Staff at HUD. Vidal received her B.A. from the University of Chicago, and her M.C.P. and Ph.D. in Urban Planning from Harvard.

SUSAN M. WACHTER is Professor of Real Estate and Finance at The Wharton School of the University of Pennsylvania and is Associate Director of the Wharton Real Estate Center. She has received the Lindback Award, the Anvil Award, and the Undergraduate Teaching Award and has written several volumes and many articles on U.S. real estate markets. Her research includes work on the determinants of housing abandonment in New York City. A former president of the American Real Estate and Urban Economics Association, Wachter currently serves on the Boards of Editors of several prestigious real estate journals. In addition, Wachter serves on Fannie Mae's Office of Housing Policy Research Advisory Board and on the National Association of Realtors Academic Council, and as Faculty Fellow of the Homer Hoyt Institute.

KATHRYN WYLDE is President and CEO of the New York City Investment Fund and previously held similar positions with the New York City Housing Partnership, a leading nonprofit producer of affordable housing. Since 1982, the Housing Partnership has been responsible for the construction and financing of more than 12,000 owner-occupied homes and apartments in New York City, with an estimated value in excess of $1.7 billion. Prior to joining the Partnership, Wylde led a nonprofit community development organization in Brooklyn and served as a senior executive in a community hospital and a local savings bank. She has also chaired Fannie Mae's National Advisory Board and HUD's Advisory Committee on Manufactured Housing. She is a member of the Board of Advisors of the NYU Center for Real Estate and Urban Policy. Wylde has written several articles and policy papers on issues of housing development, finance, and regulation.

INDEX